THE HISTORY PRINCIPLES AND PRACTICE

OF

SYMBOLISM IN CHRISTIAN ART.

THE HISTORY

PRINCIPLES AND PRACTICE

OF

Symbolism in Christian Art

BY

F. EDWARD HULME, F.L.S., F.S.A.

Author of
"*Familiar Wild Flowers*," "*Suggestions in Floral Design*," "*Wayside Sketches*,"
"*History Principles and Practice of Heraldry*," "*Myth-land*," "*Art Instruction in England*," "*Principles of Ornamental Art*," *etc., etc.*

Detroit
Gale Research Company · Book Tower
1969

This is a facsimile reprint of the original
edition of 1891 published in London by
Swan Sonnenschein & Co.

Library of Congress Catalog Card Number 68—18027

CONTENTS.

	PAGE
INTRODUCTORY CHAPTER	1
CHAPTER II.	9
CHAPTER III.	30
CHAPTER IV.	47
CHAPTER V.	73
CHAPTER VI.	101
CHAPTER VII.	121
CHAPTER VIII.	149
CHAPTER IX.	167
CHAPTER X.	184
CHAPTER XI.	203
APPENDIX	223

THE

HISTORY, PRINCIPLES, AND PRACTICE

OF

SYMBOLISM IN CHRISTIAN ART.

————— ◆◇◆ —————

INTRODUCTORY CHAPTER.

What a Symbol is—Definitions of Symbol, Allegory, and Type—Symbolism reveals or conceals—The Great Sources of Symbolism—Classes of Symbol—The same Form may mean two entirely different Things—Abuse of Symbolism—Parables—The Writings of Durandus—Extravagant Symbolism—Symbolic Rites of the Jews—World-wide Use of Symbolism—Arrangement of Subject in succeeding Chapters.

A SYMBOL is a form that in itself may be trivial, barbarous, or even repellent, but which nevertheless, from the association connected with it, is the sign of something higher than meets the outward eye. Symbolic forms can never again attain the importance they have done in the past. Their study is nevertheless deeply interesting; for, grotesque and quaint as they often are, we must remember that they were but the outer shell, and often beneath a rugged exterior bore a golden wealth of significance. To the artist and archæologist such study is indispensable. The field of inquiry is so vast, both in space and time, that it is evident that an exhaustive treatment is impossible; we purpose then in the present pages to do little more than deal with the subject in its association with Christianity and its illustration in art.

Though the terms symbol, allegory, and type appear to be ordinarily regarded as interchangeable, there is a difference

B

of meaning and application. Symbolism employs real objects, such as the lamb, the cross, the crown, to illustrate the truth. It is a picture language. Allegory uses fictitious things and imaginary personages. Symbolism appeals to the mind through the eye, is more or less artistic and pictorial; while allegory is more especially literary, and the picturesque treatment of such works as the "Pilgrim's Progress" or the "Holy War" affords us very excellent examples of its scope. A type is a something or somebody that prefigures some greater thing or person; thus the ark riding in safety amidst the waters of the deluge was a type of the Church of God. As the thing that originally prefigures also afterwards represents, many of these typical forms have been pressed into the service of symbolism.

The sculptured fonts or stained-glass windows in the churches of the Middle Ages were full of teaching to a congregation of whom the greater part could not read, to whom therefore one great avenue of knowledge was closed. The ignorant are especially impressed by pictorial teaching, and grasp its meaning far more readily than they can follow a written description or a spoken discourse.[1] Hence the clergy wisely supplemented their discourses with these appeals to the eye. But symbolism, though ordinarily a very effective way of imparting instruction, has at times been employed in an entirely opposite direction. Thus the priests of Egypt reserved to themselves an inner meaning to many of their rites; and thus too the early Christians employed symbols that, though full of significance to themselves, conveyed no meaning to the heathen around them. We too may at first see nothing but poverty of design and poorness of execution in these rude and strange imaginings; but when we recall how essential they once were as pledges and declarations of faith, they acquire a strong interest, and we see through and beyond the visible representation, and grasp something of the great ideas veiled in these simple and rude forms.

---

[1] Some few weeks before writing this we found ourselves in a large church in Brighton. What the text was, what the sermon was, and everything else concerning the service, we have utterly forgotten; but we vividly remember a fresco of the Last Supper, and poor, dishonoured Judas going forth into the outer darkness clutching at his bag. A whole course of sermons embodied in one touching figure.

Clement of Alexandria suggested to the Christians of his day that, in place of the heathen subjects cut on stones and rings by the Roman lapidaries and metal workers, they should have such devices as a dove, symbolic of the Holy Spirit of God within them, the palm branch of victory, the anchor, emblematic of their hope, and other devices of like import. The strong expressions of Tertullian in his treatise, " De Idololatria," are directed against the pagan rites, and in his zeal against error he objects to all representations whatsoever, and stigmatises the art of the painter as an unlawful thing; though he, in spite of his anxiety to prevent any tampering with arts that had been perverted to the service of heathendom, made exception in favour of the devices suggested by Clement. The influences of the life around them did in fact considerably affect early Christian art. Christ Himself, the Good Shepherd, we shall see, was often represented as Orpheus; while St. Paul finds in the Isthmian Games apt illustration of the Christian race. St. John Damascenus, writing in the eighth century, strongly defends the introduction of sculpture and painting as accessories to the teaching of the Church.

The great sources from whence our knowledge of Christian symbolism is derived are, from the third to the eighth centuries, the frescoes and sarcophagi in the catacombs, the mosaics in the Italian churches, and the vessels of glass or pottery found in tombs. Later on, for another three hundred years or so, we find a rich store of illustrations in the carved crosses or richly illuminated books of the Irish and Anglo-Saxon scribes; and, still later, the magnificent manuscripts of the Middle Ages, the profusion of sculpture, the glorious stained-glass windows,[1] the pavements of figured tiles afford us numberless other examples.

Symbolic forms may be readily divided into three distinct classes. The first of these comprises those that still survive, and convey their meaning to us as clearly as they have done to preceding generations. The dove is a good illustration of these, and it will ordinarily be found that such symbols are

---

[1] " In her oryall there shee was
Closyd wel with roial glas,
Fulfilled it was with ymagery
Every window by and bye."

based on some definite passage of the Bible. The second class comprises forms that for some reason or other have now wholly ceased to be employed, though their significance is still clearly understood. While a third and much smaller class includes forms that from their associations are clearly symbolic, but of which all clue to their meaning is lost. It is of course necessary to bring some little knowledge and experience to bear on the matter, as it does not certainly follow that a thing is meaningless because it is so to us. Many old legends and beliefs have now faded away; but no one to whom the legend of the phœnix is unknown, to whom the old belief in the pelican feeding its young with its own blood is unfamiliar, is in a position to express an opinion as to their introduction in old work. A knowledge of such superstitious beliefs, and with the various legends that are associated with the saints in the Church's calendar, is as needful to the due appreciation of early art or modern revivals of it as a knowledge of Greek and Roman mythology is to those who would desire to intelligently appreciate the paintings on classic vases or the masterpieces of Greek sculpture.

The student must moreover be warned that the points of resemblance between the symbol and the thing symbolised must not be pushed too far, nor too rigid a parallelism exacted. Often therefore but one face of a many-sided truth can be given. Thus our Saviour may be represented as the Good Shepherd, the guardian of the flock, and the symbol is a just and beautiful one; but such a symbol gives no suggestion of the fact that he was also the Lamb without spot or blemish, or that hereafter He will be the Judge in that dread tribunal that closes the drama of this world's history. A symbol too, we must remember, may mean two entirely different and opposing things. Thus the lion may symbolise the evil spirit walking about as a lion to devour his prey, or the all-conquering Christ, the Lion of the tribe of Judah. Our Lord too compared the kingdom of heaven in one of His parables to leaven; yet elsewhere He spoke in an entirely different sense of the leaven of the Scribes and Pharisees.

While symbolic teaching is of great service, and a most valuable means of imparting truth, it can, like most other things, be carried to a point where it becomes forced and almost ridiculous. Hence the abuse has been made an argument against the use. Our Lord's teaching, while clear and distinct, was clothed almost invariably in parabolic, figurative, descriptive, allegorical, and symbolic form. Our duty to our neighbour was not coldly set forth in a harsh, unbending formula, a rigid and frigid command, but brought home to us in the parable of the traveller who so sorely needed and so readily obtained compassion; and every discourse was lighted up and brightened by some picturesque allusion, the pearl of great price, the lost and wandering sheep, the working leaven, the house founded upon a rock, the sower and the seed, the labourers in the vineyard, the unjust judge, the beautiful story of the prodigal son.[1] The method of teaching thus inaugurated by the Founder of the Church may well be adopted by His followers.

At the same time, as we have already indicated, this symbolic teaching has suffered at the hands of its too zealous friends. There is perhaps no better illustration of this than the "Rationale Divinorum Officiorum" of Durandus, a book on the symbolism of churches and church ornaments. Durandus was chaplain to Pope Clement IV., afterwards captain of the Papal forces, and, finally, in the year 1286, became Bishop of Mende. The "Rationale" was the first book from the pen of an uninspired author ever printed. Though it passed through many editions, it is now of extreme rarity.

Durandus deals in his book with all the component parts and details of a church, and finds in each and all an inner meaning that, ingenious as it frequently is, is often sadly strained. We may give but one illustrative example of this, the bell, to most of us a useful but prosaic thing enough.

"Bells do signify preachers, who ought after the likeness of a bell to exhort the faithful; the which was typified in that the Lord commanded Moses to make a vestment for the high priest, having seventy-two bells, to sound when the high priest entered into the Holy of Holies. Also the cavity of the bell denoteth the mouth of the preacher, according to the saying of the apostle, 'I am become as sounding brass or a tinkling cymbal.' The hardness of the metal signifieth

---

[1] " If man had been incorporeal, God would have given him purely incorporeal gifts; but since his soul is joined to a body, things suprasensible are ministered to him by means of sensible things."—ST. JOHN CHRYSOSTOM.

fortitude in the mind of the preacher; whence saith the Lord,
'Behold, I have made thy face strong against their faces.'
The clapper or iron which, by striking on either side, maketh
the sound, doth denote the tongue of the teacher, the which
with the adornment of learning doth cause both testaments
to resound.   The striking of the bell denoteth that the
preacher ought first of all to strike at the vices in himself
for correction, and then advance to blame those of others.
The link by which the clapper is joined or bound unto the
bell is meditation.   The wood of the frame upon which the
bell hangeth doth signify the wood of our Lord's cross.   The
pegs by which the wooden frame is joined together are the
oracles of the prophets.   The iron cramps by which the bell
is joined with the frame denote charity, by which the
preacher being joined indissolubly unto the cross doth boast
and say, ' God forbid that I should glory, save in the cross
of our Lord Jesus Christ ! ' The hammer affixed to the frame
by which the bell is struck signifieth the right mind of the
preacher, by which he himself holding fast to the Divine
commands doth by frequent striking inculcate the same on
the ears of the faithful."

While pictorial and sculptured forms have their undoubted
value as exponents of truth, we must not forget that there
is a possibility of such use degenerating into mere picture
worship, as may be very evidently seen in the adoration paid
by the Russian peasantry to their sacred pictures.

The use of symbol may be as well seen in the earliest art
of which we have knowledge as in any later period, the
sacred writing of the priests of Egypt being essentially of
this nature.   Amongst the Jews again symbolism was one of
the most striking features; the Passover feast, the dismissal
into the wilderness of the scapegoat, the Feast of Tabernacles,
the sabbatic year, were all in the highest degree figurative,
while the Song of Solomon, and many others of the Jewish
writings are a mine of picturesque imagery.   Canon Westcott, in his " Christus Consummator," points out clearly how
the writer of the Epistle to the Hebrews " dwells with reve-
rent memory on the significance of the ritual which he had
known ; and then he shows how to the Christian every symbol had become a truth, every shadow a reality."   Writers
have noticed especially in the Epistle to the Hebrews, the
repeated employment of the word " true," showing over and

over again that in the fulfilment we have the reality of which in the Jewish dispensation there was but the shadow. The prohibition in the Jewish religion against the representation of the Deity or of any living thing to a great extent prevented the use of symbolic forms, a prohibition that we also find in full force amongst the followers of Muhammad. Where no such religious restriction is exercised, the love of symbolism has shown itself almost universally, from the cultured Greek, the learned priesthood of the valley of the Nile, or the followers of Hinduism, to the North American nomad Indians, or the dwellers in the mysterious cities of ancient Mexico and Peru. It is equally at home on a Japanese lacquer tray, in the carvings of a Celtic cross, the rich mosaic pavements of an old Roman villa, or in the wealth of sculpture of our grand cathedrals.

Having, we trust, demonstrated the importance of the study, we now indicate, in concluding our introductory remarks, the course we propose to pursue; for " whosoever shall address himself to write of Matters of Instruction, or of any other Argument of Importance, it behoveth that, before he enter therein, he should resolutely determine with himself in what Order he will handle the same, so shall he best accomplish that he hath undertaken, and inform the Understanding, and help the Memory of the Reader." [1] Symbolism may manifest itself in several ways; for though our thoughts naturally turn in the first place to symbolism of form, there may be, equally, symbolism of language, of action, of number, or of colour. Having briefly dwelt upon these points, we propose to deal more especially with symbolic forms as we meet with them in art, in the works of the painter or the sculptor, the embroiderer or the glass painter, burnt into flooring tiles, woven into hangings, stamped upon coins, or whatever other possibilities of production yet remain unspecified.

The symbols associated collectively and individually with the three Persons of the Trinity will first engage our attention, then the cross and passion symbols associated with the

---

[1] " A display of Heraldry manifesting a more easie access to the Knowledge thereof than hath hitherto been published by any, through the benefit of Method ; whereunto it is now reduced by the Study and Industry of John Guillim " (extract from the preface of the edition of 1679.)

earthly life and sacrifice of our Lord.   These in turn will
suggest a consideration of the ordinary emblems of mortality.
After this we may very naturally dwell for awhile on the
representation in art of the human soul and of angels, good
and bad, of heaven and hell, the apostles and saints of God,
the dragon and the serpent, symbols of evil.   We shall then
proceed to refer to the emblems of authority, such as the
crown, mitre, sceptre, orb, and staff.   The various forms
derived from the animal kingdom will be followed by those
based on flowers. Various symbolic forms again are founded
on the sun, the moon, and the starry host of heaven.   Geometrical forms must not be overlooked; and the sea too
will contribute its quota in such maritime forms as the
ship, the trident, the shell, and the fish.   Even stones have
their associations; while we shall require to deal also with
a large section of objects, such as instruments of martyrdom, the gridiron of St. Lawrence, or the wheel of St.
Catherine, that almost defy classification in any formal way.

CHAPTER II.

Symbolism of Language—Symbolism of Action—Of Number—The Number of Perfection—The great Councils of the Early Church—The Number of Probation—Symbolism of Colour—White—Pontifical of Bishop Clifford—Value of old Church Inventories—" Les Couleurs Liturgiques" of Malais—Heraldic Symbolism of Colours —Old Authors thereupon—Great divergence of Use in various Dioceses—Illustrations of this—Yellow—Colour used sometimes in Good, sometimes in Bad Sense—Golden Vestments—Red—Early Christian Art—The Colour-sense of the Ancients—Scarlet—Crimson—Green—Blue—Political Colours—Purple—Violet—Gray or Ash-coloured—Black.

SYMBOLISM may be of language. This imagery of diction is especially characteristic of savage and semi-civilized peoples, though by no means confined to them. The oratory of the New Zealanders or of the North American Indians owes much of its force and beauty to this symbolism of language, and it is a very marked feature in the literature and daily speech of many of the Eastern races. Thus, amidst the decoration of the Alhambra, we find entwined a great variety of laudatory inscriptions, such as the following : " Thou hast risen in the horizon of empire like the sun in the vault of heaven, mercifully to dissipate the shadows of injustice and oppression. Thou hast secured even the tender branches from harm and the breath of the summer gale." Biblical examples may also very readily be found: " As the apple tree among the trees of the wood, so is my beloved. I sat down under his shadow with great delight, and his fruit was sweet to my taste." We may instance also the blessing given to Jacob, "With corn and wine have I sustained him": corn, the source of the staff of life, and wine to make glad the heart of man, being selected as symbolising the general material and temporal prosperity which the expression was meant to convey. The proverbs that are found in the lite-

rature and speech of almost all races of men are a further
illustration of this delight in a picture-language.[1]

Symbolism may be of action. It may be seen in the smok-
ing of the pipe of peace and the burial of the war hatchet
amongst the Sioux, in the passing round of the loving cup
at the banquets of the city magnates. The rites of the
Levitical priesthood afford many examples.[2] The Arab
custom of tasting salt with one's guest is a binding symbol
of amity thereby established; and many other illustrations
will readily occur to our readers.

FIG. 1.

Symbolism may be of number. Examples of this section,
though frequently to be encountered, often escape notice, as
they do not so clearly and immediately reveal their meaning
as some other forms of symbolic treatment do. Threefold
arrangements, such as a three-light window, a trefoil, or
triangle, ordinarily symbolise the Trinity when found in
Christian art. Pythagoras calls three the number of completion, expressive of beginning, middle, and end. The
number was a favourite one in classic mythology, where we
meet with the three-headed Cerberus, the three Fates, the
three Furies, the three Graces, while the Muses are three
times three in number. The wise men, or kings, or Magi,
who followed the guiding star to Bethlehem were three in

[1] As for example :
   " Ill weeds grow apace."
   " The scalded dog fears cold water."
   " There is a silver lining to every cloud."
   " Birds of a feather flock together."
   " Where bees are, there is honey."
   " One sword keeps another in its scabbard."
[2] Other good Biblical examples will be found in Isa. xx. 2, 3, 4 ; in
Ezek. iv. 1 et seq., xii. 3 et seq., xxi. 6 et seq.; and in Amos vii. 7
et seq.

number, according to generally accepted tradition. In fig. 1, the reverse of an early medal, we have a representation of the visit of the Magi, three in number, to the infant Christ.

While we must be careful not to read meanings where they were never meant or intended, the number four will ordinarily in Christian art represent the evangelists; while

Fig. 2.

six stands for the attributes of Deity,—power, majesty, wisdom, love, mercy, justice.

Seven has by old writers been called the number of perfection, and it is curious to notice how often this idea seems to be involved in its use. Thus to quote some few representative examples out of many: Balaam, as an effectual test of the will of God, built seven altars and prepared seven

oxen and seven rams for sacrifice. Job, referring to the
effectual protection of Providence, says, " In seven troubles
there shall no evil touch thee " ; and again, " Wisdom hath
hewn her seven pillars." Jacob, as a sign of perfect submission, bowed himself seven times before his brother. The
sevenfold circuit of Jericho prior to its complete overthrow
is another example. Naaman was commanded to bathe
seven times in the Jordan as a prelude to his complete
restoration to health. Samson for full security was bound
with seven bands. The Jewish Church has seven great holy
days in each year. The Romish Church has seven sacraments. On the first appointment of deacons in the early
Christian Church seven men of honest report were to be
chosen. " How oft shall my brother sin against me, and I
forgive him ? " The question suggested seven times as the
limit of endurance of wrong. The golden candlestick of the
Jewish temple was seven-branched.[1] It is represented in
fig. 2, a portion of one of the sculptured panels on the
triumphal arch of Titus at Rome. The great apocalyptic
angels are seven in number; and Ephesus, Smyrna, Pergamos,
Thyatira, Sardis, Philadelphia, Laodocea were the seven
Churches of Asia. In the same book we read of seven candle-
sticks, seven stars, seven trumpets, the seven spirits before
the throne of God. Pharaoh in his dream saw seven oxen
and seven ears of corn. On the seventh day of the seventh
month a holy observance was ordained to the children of
Israel, who feasted seven days and remained seven days in
tents. The seventh year was to be observed as a Sabbath,
and at the end of the seven times seven came the great year
of Jubilee.

When we shall, later on, deal with the attributes of the
Trinity, mention must be made of the sevenfold gifts of the
Holy Spirit. At the creation of the world the seventh period
marked its completion. Psalms vi., xxxii., xxxviii., li., cii.,
cxxx., cxliii., are those known as the seven penitential psalms

---

[1] In the Talmud we read that over the throne of king Solomon hung a
chandelier of gold with seven branches, and on these the names of the
seven patriarchs, Adam, Noah, Shem, Abraham, Isaac, Jacob, and Job,
were engraven. On the second row of the branches were engraved the
names of the " seven pious ones of the world " : Levi, Kehath, Amram,
Moses, Aaron, Eldad, and Madad.

from their. especially contrite character. There are also seven deadly sins. The seven joys and the seven sorrows of the Virgin mother are frequently represented in the art of the Middle Ages. The first series comprises the Annunciation, the Visitation, the Nativity, the Adoration of the kings, the Presentation in the temple, the Finding of Christ among the doctors in the temple, the Assumption. The seven sorrows are the prophecy of Simeon, the flight into Egypt, Christ missed in the temple, the betrayal of her Son, the Crucifixion, the Deposition from the Cross, and the Ascension.

There were also seven great councils of the early Church;[1] while in the Roman Catholic service of consecration of a church, the altar is sprinked seven times in remembrance of the Lord's Passion and the seven outpourings of His sacred blood. " The first whereof was at circumcision; the second, in prayer in the garden; the third, at the scourging; the fourth, from the crown of thorns; the fifth, from the pierced hands; the sixth, when His feet were nailed to the cross; the seventh, when His side was wounded by the spear."

There are in addition the seven champions of Christendom; St. George of England, St. Andrew of Scotland, St. David of Wales, St. Patrick of Ireland, St. James of Spain, St. Denys of France, and St. Anthony of Italy.

We read too of the seven wonders of the ancient world. As a matter of fact there were eight, but in any list there is an " or," and not an " and," where they are enumerated.[2] This verbal difference may seem trifling; but while the use

---

[1] The first œcumenical synod at Nicæa, under Constantine the Great in the year 325, against the errors of Arius. The second at Constantinople, under Theodosius the Great in the year 381, against the heresy of Macedonius in denying the Divinity of the Holy Spirit. The third at Ephesus, under Theodosius in 431, against Nestorius. The fourth at Chalcedon, under Marcian in 451, against Eutyches and Dioscuros, who asserted that there was only one nature in Christ. The fifth at Constantinople, under Justinian in 553, against Origen. The sixth at Constantinople also, under Constantine Pogonatus in 680, against Honorius, Sergius, and Pyrrhus; and the seventh at Nicæa, under Constantine and Irene in the year 787, against the Iconoclasts.

[2] The pyramids of Egypt; the hanging gardens of Babylon; the tomb of Mausolus; the temple of Diana at Ephesus; the statue of Zeus by Phidias, the Colossus of Rhodes, the Pharos of Egypt or the temple of Cyrus.

of the latter word would make the total eight, the use of the former sacrifices one on the list to the desire to bring the total to the mystic number of perfection. We have also the seven wise men of Greece, while Shakespeare gives us the seven ages of man, from puling infancy to decrepit old age. The Hindus believe in seven mansions of all created spirits, the earth being the lowest of these, while the seventh and highest is the seat of Brahma. The Moslem pilgrimage is at last consummated when seven circuits have been made round the sacred stone at Mecca. The astronomers tell us of seven greater planets, the alchemists dealt with seven metals,[1] and we all of us recognise seven days in each week. With our forefathers the period of apprenticeship was seven years, and Jacob for the love he bore to Rachel was willing, in the old world story, to serve Laban for as long. The lease of a house is often for seven, fourteen, or twenty-one years ; and when we desire to give a rogue his deserts, he goes off to penal servitude for a like period. In the eyes of the law the stripling enters into manhood, with its contingent rights of sueing and being sued, paying his own debts, and serving on a jury, when three times seven years have gone over his head ; while the tenth seven marks the natural period and duration of human life.

Eight is the number of regeneration, hence by far the greater number of the old fonts and baptistries are octagonal. Twelve, the number of the apostles, has naturally been a somewhat favourite number in art symbolism, being applied not merely in this more limited sense, but also in a more extended meaning, as representative of the Church generally. As an example of the mystical meanings often attached to numbers we may quote the words of St. Augustine where, after referring to the passage in St. Paul, "What, know ye not that the saints shall judge the world?" and explaining that the twelve thrones represent the twelve apostles, he goes on to say : "The parts of the world are four: the east, the west, the north, and the south. From these four, saith

---

[1] "The bodies seven, eek, to hem heer anoon :
   Sol gold is, and Luna silver we threpe ;
   Mars yren, Mercurie quyksilver we clepe ;
   Saturnus leed, and Jubiter is tyn,
   And Venus coper, by my fader kyn."—CHAUCER.

the Lord in the gospel, shall the elect be gathered together.
Called, and how ? By the Trinity. Not called except by
baptism in the name of the Father, and of the Son, and of the
Holy Ghost; so four parts each called by the Three make
twelve."

Nine as a number scarcely appears in Christian art, though
Milton writes that the gates of Hell are thrice threefold,
three of brass, three of iron, three of adamantine rock, and
tells us that when the fallen angels were expelled from
heaven "nine days they fell." A sense of completion has
been associated with the number. There were nine Muses.
In the "Lays of Ancient Rome," it will be remembered that
Lars Porsenna swears by the nine gods ; while in our own
experience we still see leases granted for ninety-nine years.
We have been taught that it takes nine tailors to make a
man ; that a cat's tenacity of life is equal to nine times that
of other animals; that possession is nine points of the law;
that if we we want to make the flogging of our burglar
effectual and complete, the cat-o'-nine-tails must be brought
out; while we can pay the hero of the banquet no higher
compliment than to toast him with three times three. The
witches in "Macbeth" for the effectual working of the
charm sing around the caldron—

" Thrice to thine and thrice to mine
And thrice again, to make up nine."

The ten petals of the passion flower represent the apostles
in the mystical meanings that have been associated with the
flower, since among the twelve one betrayed and one denied
his Lord.

The number forty is expressive of a period of probation or
trial. The Israelites wandered forty years in the wilderness,
and forty years of bondage they also had to serve under the
hard yoke of the Philistines. Moses was forty days on the
mount of Sinai. Elijah was in hiding forty days. For forty
days the deluge fell, and for yet another forty days Noah
was shut within the ark. The men of Nineveh had a like
period of probation under the preaching of Jonah. The
fasting of our Lord in the wilderness again was for forty
days. Our readers will remember too that St. Swithin's
Day is still anxiously looked for by many who believe that

a very possible forty days of wet weather is in store for them; [1] while many old legal observances were based on this number, such as the privilege of sanctuary, the duration of quarantine, and so forth.

We pass now to a consideration of the influence of colour, and of the meanings that have been assigned to the various tints employed.

White has ever been accepted as symbolic of innocence of soul, of purity of thought, of holiness of life.[2] Hence the priests of the great divinity Osiris were robed in white, and thus too were the priests of Zeus. The ministers on the worship of Brahma, and the initiated in the Druidic rites, like the Vestal Virgins, wore robes of the same spotless hue. When the sins that are as scarlet shall have been made as the untrodden snow, that soul shall stand amidst the great army of the redeemed, clothed in stainless garb of white. Hence in the early ages of the Christian Church those admitted into its fellowship wore white garments. In 2 Chronicles v. 12 we read that the Levites at the dedication of Solomon's temple were "arrayed in white linen." At the transfiguration of Christ "His garment," St. Matthew tells us, "was white as the light," [3] while the angel at the tomb of the Saviour was clothed in "raiment

---

[1] " Now if on Swithun's day the welkin lours,
　　And every penthouse streams with hasty showers,
　　Twice twenty days shall clouds their fleeces drain,
　　And wash the pavement with incessant rain.
　　Let not such vulgar tales debase thy mind,
　　Nor Paul nor Swithun rule the clouds and wind."—GAY

The French have a very similar belief :

" S'il pleut le jour de Saint Medard,
　Il pleut quarante jours plus tard ;
　S'il pleut le jour de Saint Gervais et de Saint Protais
　Il pleut quarante jours après."

[2] Thus Cyprian during the Decian persecution wrote to the Church at Carthage : "Happy is our Church, illumined with so Divine a glory, and ennobled in our day by the blood of the martyrs. She was before white with the purity of her children, now she has found a robe of purple in their blood."

[3] "He was transfigured before them. And His raiment became shining, exceeding white as snow; so as no fuller on earth can white them " (St. Mark ix. 2, 3).

white as snow." The Apocalypse yields several illustrative texts of a like nature.

In the Pontifical of Bishop Clifford, Bishop of London from 1406 to 1426, we read, "Albus color inter omnes colores est prior purior, simplicior, et festivior." St. Jerome speaks of bishops, priests, and deacons being arrayed in white in his time, and the white surplice of the clergy is as marked a feature to the present day. It is used at all Feasts and at all seasons relating to the Lord that are not associated with suffering; such as the Annunciation, Presentation in the temple, Epiphany, and Easter. It is also associated with the blessed Virgin [1] and to those saints who were not also martyrs; used too at dedication and harvest festivals, at confirmations, and at weddings.[2]

In the Middle Ages white was the general Lenten colour; not from its association however with the idea of rejoicing or of purity. Its use probably arose from the custom of covering the altars, reredoses, etc., during Lent with white cloths, as signifying the absence or veiling of all colour; and thus regarded, its use during Lent is neither unseemly nor inconsistent. Later on the original meaning was not so

---

[1] At the coronation of Charles I. the royal robes were of white satin, The previous sovereigns had always been attired in purple ; but Charles being crowned on the Feast of the Purification, deliberately elected to be robed in white in honour of the feast day and " to declare the virgin purity with which he came to be espoused to his kingdom." This he did, notwithstanding a very threatening prophecy, popularly attributed to Merlin, of the disasters of all kinds that would attend the coming of a " White King " to the throne of England. Herbert records that at the king's funeral " the sky was serene and clear ; but presently it began to snow, and fell so fast, as by that time they came to the West end of the Royal Chapell the black velvet pall was all white (the colour of Innocency), being thick covered over with Snow. So went the White King to his grave."

[2] In a very good French work, " Les Couleurs Liturgiques," by the Abbé Malais, we find the following passages that bear upon, and further illustrate, our subject. " On voit tout de suite que le blanc caractérise la joie et la pureté ; la joie à Noël, à Pâques, par exemple, et la pureté aux fêtes des vierges." " Les Baptêmes, les Mariages, les Funérailles des petits enfants, la Dédicace des Eglises, l'Anniversaire de cette Dédicace, les Cérémonies d'actions de grâces comportent à peu près universellement la couleur blanche." "La fête de tous les Saints, à cause de la grande joie qu'elle respire, à la vue de tant de bienheureux, nos protecteurs et nos modèles, est assez génralment célébrée avec la couleur blanche."

C

strictly regarded, and instead of the plain linen covering, silk and other rich materials were introduced, and both vestment and altar covering became embroidered or painted with symbols of the Passion.

The old church inventories supply us with many excellent illustrations of this use. Thus, for example, at St. Cuthbert's, Wells, in the year 1393, we find in use " one white cloth for hanging in time of Lent." At St. Nicholas', Bristol, A.D. 1432, " viij clot⁵ of wyzht wᵗ crucyfyx for leynt." At St. Margaret's, Southwark, 1485, " iiij whyte frontelles with Red crosses for Lente seson "; and at Westminster Abbey in 1540, " a white clothe of sylk with a red crosse servyng for Lent." [1] The white hangings were exchanged for red during the last fortnight of Lent; while Good Friday varied from red, through purple and violet, to black.

Several portraits of Mary Queen of Scots are extant in which she is depicted as wearing white for mourning on account of the death of her first husband, Francis II. of France. The custom was by no means rare at that period. Elizabeth of England is recorded as wearing " Le Deuil blanc " for example, and several other instances could be cited. In China it is invariably the colour of mourning. At funerals the chief mourners wear robes of white, while friends don a sash of white in lieu of our crape trimming. The visiting cards used must be of white in place of the ordinary crimson. After a while salmon-coloured cards are substituted, then those of a deeper red, till ultimately the deep crimson cards are resumed. Any letter sent or received during this period of mourning must be upon white paper.

It has been held that the symbolic colours used in the Middle Ages in the services and adornment of the church were based on those used in the temple service in the vestments of the high priest and the hangings of the sanctuary under the Jewish dispensation, and that the liturgical colours of the mediæval Church would naturally be allied to the Levitical; but the facts are altogether against this theory. In the early Christian Church the rites were celebrated in a vesture that only differed from that of every-day life from

---

[1] The whole subject, together with very numerous references to these old inventories, will be found very ably and thoroughly worked out in W. St. John Hope's treatise " On the English Liturgical Colours."

its greater costliness and richness of quality. Even as early as the tenth century certain colours were associated with particular days, and were ascribed with liturgical authority and significance. In the Greek Church, according to the " Enchologion " of Goar, published at Paris in the year 1647, only two colours were in use, purple for the Lenten and other fasting days, and white for all other occasions. Amongst the Armenians there are no special colours in use; while in the Churches of the West where such symbolic vestments are in service there is a great diversity of custom. Had the colours been handed down from the temple observances we should have found all Christian Churches probably equally ready to employ them, and there would have been no divergence in the use from the old standard.

It has been fancifully and poetically pointed out that if every virtue has its own colour, white, the colour of light, being produced by the blending of all the tints in the spectrum, may with peculiar appropriateness be employed as a symbol of the union of every virtue. Whatever poetic idea however we may read into old observance, we must carefully distinguish between historic fact and ingenious afterthought; and there is no doubt that the grand discovery of Newton was not at the service of the mediæval ecclesiastics.

The old writers on heraldry often delighted to throw a glamour of symbolism over their science; hence we find Guillim, for example, writing, " The colour White is resembled to the Light, and the Dignity thereof reckoned more worthy by how much the more the Light and the Day is of more Esteem than Darkness and the Night." The subject, from the heraldic point of view, may be very well studied in " La vraye et parfaite Science des Armoires," published at Dijon in the year 1660. Other curious old authorities on the symbolism of colours are Krausen's " Dissertatio de Colore Sacro, speciatim Vestibus Sacerdotalis," published at Wittemberg in 1707, and the book of Innocent III., entitled " De Sacro Altaris Mysterio." This is the pope, it will be remembered, that king John was so unfortunate as to differ in opinion from, and his book is the earliest on the subject, dating from the year 1198.

It is somewhat curious, symbolism of colours being once recognised in the Western Churches, to find such a divergence of custom, as it might naturally be supposed that some definite and binding ordinance on the point, some precise code of rules, would have been forthcoming. Directly however we look into the matter and refer to the "uses" of the various dioceses, we are struck with the difference in practice. Thus while white is held to be the appropriate colour for Trinity Sunday in Rome, Milan, Troyes, Sens, Auxerre, Rouen, and Lyons, we find green in use at Rheims and Exeter, yellow at Poictiers, blue at Toledo, violet at Soissons, red at Laon, Coutance, Wells, and Cologne. All these colours have their legitimate and appropriate meaning, white, for instance, typifying the spotless dignity of the Godhead, while the violet, very sparingly found, characterizes the obscurity of the mystery of the Divine Trinity; [1] but the divergence from uniformity is striking.

Yellow is comparatively but seldom met with. It is a good example of the fact the student in colour symbolism must by no means overlook, that a colour may be employed either in a good or a bad sense, and it is therefore often necessary to judge from the surroundings before we are able to assign a definite meaning to any colour. In France, during the sixteenth century, the doors of felons and traitors were painted yellow; and in some countries the Jews were required to wear yellow, because they denied the Messiah. It is the colour of jealousy [2] and treason, and Judas is often represented in old glass painting in a yellow robe. Where

---

[1] " Quant à la fête du Saint-Sacrement beaucoup d'Eglises l'ont célébrée avec des ornements blancs, signe de joie et de pureté, comme Rouen, Bayeux, Coutances, Metz, et Beauvais; mais grand nombre d'autres diocèses ont fait usage de rouge, souvenir du sang et de la Passion du Seigneur, à savoir : Evreux, Paris, Chartres, Meaux, Versailles, Le Mans, Soissons, Amiens, Cambrai, Toul, et Laon. Pour Auxerre le missel ne désigne que les ornements les plus précieux, sans indiquer aucune couleur particulière."—MALAIS, " Les Couleurs Liturgiques."

[2] In " Much Ado about Nothing " the count is described as " civil as an orange, and something of that jealous complexion." In " Twelfth Night " we read of one who " pined in thought" and was afflicted with " green and yellow melancholy "; while in the " Merry Wives of Windsor " Nym declares that he will possess Ford " with yellowness." We are all familiar too with the disparaging and fault-finding nature that is involved in the idea of the " jaundiced eye."

" All seems infected that the infected spy,
    As all seems yellow to the jaundiced eye."
                                    —POPE, " Essay on Criticism."

however it is represented by gold, or is a substitute for
it, it signifies love, constancy, dignity, wisdom; thus one of
the early Fathers of the Church was called Chrysostom, the
golden mouth, from his eloquence and wisdom. " This
colour in Arms is blazed by the name of Or, which is as
much as to say Aurum, which is Gold. It doth lively represent that most excellent Metal, the possession whereof en-
chanteth the Heart of Fools, and the Colour whereof blindeth
the Eyes of the Wise. Such is the Worthiness of this Colour,
which doth resemble it, that none ought to bear the same in
arms but Emperors and Kings, and such as be of the Blood
Royal. And as this Metal exceedeth all others in Value,
Purity, and Fineness, so ought the Bearer (as much as in
him lies) to endeavour to surpass all other in Prowess and
Virtue."

We are told by Verrius that Tarquinius Priscus wore a
tunic of gold, and we read too that Agrippina, the wife of
the emperor Claudius, had a robe made entirely of woven
gold. When the tomb of the wife of the emperor Honorius
was opened in the year 1544 the golden tissue that had
enwrapped her was still intact, though she was interred in
the year 400; and when the foundations for St. Peter's at
Rome were being excavated, the workmen came upon the
marble sarcophagus of an illustrious Roman, Probus Anicius,
and his wife, each of whose bodies was encircled in a robe
woven of pure gold. Another regal association, and one
more familiar, will be found in the Field of the Cloth of
Gold. Biblical illustrations of its use as a symbol of royalty
and power are abundant, as for instance when king Belshazzar bestowed a chain of gold upon Daniel and made him
third ruler in his kingdom, and when the king of Hamath
sent an embassy to salute king David, and presented his
brother ruler with vessels of gold.

Red, as applied to spiritual virtues, signifies an ardent
love, a burning zeal for the faith; in mundane virtues,
energy and courage; in an evil sense, cruelty and blood-
guiltiness. It is used on the feasts of martyrs and at
Whitsuntide. In the former case it speaks of the blood
which was shed for Christ, and in the latter of the tongues
of fire which descended upon the apostles. Hence, in the
inventory of Westminster Abbey, of the year 1388, we find
" albæ rubeæ pro Commemoratione Apostolorum," and in that

drawn up about the year 1540 an "albe of sylk with parells of red nedyll work, etc., servyng for the chaunter at ye feast of Seynt Peter." In the pontifical of Bishop Clifford we find the various colours referred to, and the several occasions when they are to be used; and it is there stated, "Rubeus color igneus est et sanguineus : caritati Spiritus et effusioni sanguinis consimilis." [1]

The Good Friday colours we have seen have varied from red through purple or violet to black, but the majority of the old inventories give red or purple. Thus, in the list of vestments made in the year 1432 at St. Nicholas', Bristol, we find "j rede chysypull for gode fryday." We find also in the inventory of Peterborough Abbey, A.D. 1539, "red albes for passion week."

In the catacombs of Rome many of the paintings are evidently portraits of the persons buried there. Of these, several very interesting examples may be seen in the National Gallery. They are ordinarily accompanied by paintings of scriptural subjects or by symbols indicative of the faith of the deceased, who is usually attired in a flowing dress closely resembling surplice and stole. The surplice is either white, the symbol of the purified soul, or red, as washed in the blood of Christ; and the stole is the symbol of the yoke of Christ, borne over the shoulders.

According to Guillim, "heraldically red representeth fire, which is the chiefest, lightsomest, and clearest of the Elements. This colour inciteth courage and magnanimity in persons that do grapple together in single or publick fight." We read that those that "strengthened their battels with Elephants, when they would provoke them to fight, produced before them resemblances of this martial colour, as the blood of Grapes and of Mulberries," [2]—an analagous proceeding

---

[1] Malais again refers to its use in the following passage: " L'usage de la couleur rouge à la veille et à la fête de la Pentecôte, jour solennel auquel le Saint Esprit descendit sur les apôtres en forme de langues enflammées. Tous les offices dirigés spécialment vers le culte de l'Esprit divin, comme le Sacrement de Confirmation, veulent cette couleur vive et éclatante."

[2] This idea is clearly based on the thirty-fourth verse in the sixth chapter of the first book of Maccabees: " And to the end that they might provoke the elephants to fight, they showed them the blood of grapes and mulberries."

apparently to waving a red flag at a bull. The colour has a curiously exciting effect on various animals. It is a sure provocative of the grotesque ire of the turkey-cock, and we remember an old man in the country who supplied adders' fat as a rustic remedy, who used to angle successfully for his game amongst the heath and furze with rod and line, having a piece of scarlet cloth attached.

Whatever the ceremonial colour of the day may be, the Pope when he hears mass is vested in red, and at his death he is clothed in the same colour; while we need scarcely remind our readers that it is also the colour of the cardinal's robes and hat. Our familiar phrase, "a red letter day," a day of good fortune and happiness, refers to the old custom of printing the saints' days in red ink. On the other hand, the red flag is the symbol of insurrection and terrorism.

In China five symbolical colours are employed. " Red is appointed to fire, and corresponds with the south; black belongs to water, and corresponds with the north; green belongs to wood, and signifies the east; white to metal, and refers to the mist," says the commentator Li-ki. Yellow is apportioned to the earth. What led to this division of colours seems scarcely clear in some of the cases; but it is known to have been in force over a thousand years before the Christian era, so that it has at least antiquity in its favour. Red holds a conspicuous place in the Chinese marriage ceremony.

The term red is after all somewhat vague, and includes two colours so far distinct as scarlet and crimson. It is often difficult to determine what the ancient colours were, partly from our inability to decide what such terms as *purpureus, hyacinthus,* and *coccineus* conveyed to those who used them, and partly on account of the changeful effect of time on paintings, embroideries, and the like. It has been suggested that the ancients had either a very limited colour vocabulary or were absolutely less gifted with a sense of colour, or else we should scarcely find, as we do, one word, *purpureus,* doing duty as descriptive of the colour of the sea, of the sunrise, of the poppy flower, of the fruit of the fig, of the human hair, of blood, and many other things. It is also shown by Dr. Wickham Legg in his excellent work on "The History of the Liturgical Colours," that the same ignorance prevails as to the value of the mediæval words *rubeus, blodius,* and others. It will be noted that St. Matthew says that the soldiers in mockery placed on Christ a scarlet robe, while St. John calls it purple.

Scarlet is ordinarily found in the Bible as a symbol and sign of honour and prosperity. It entered largely into the adornment of the tabernacle. The daughters of Israel are mentioned in 2 Samuel i. 24 as " clothed in scarlet, with other delights." The ideally good wife of the last chapter of Proverbs has her household " clothed with scarlet," and the merchandise of the great city mentioned in Revelation xviii. 12 included " gold and silver and precious stones, pearls, fine linen, purple, and silk, and scarlet." [1]

In ecclesiastical and other decorative work we ordinarily meet with crimson as the red employed, rather than scarlet, the latter being too crude and garish. Thus to give but one example out of many, we find in the inventories of Westminster " a cope, a chezabull,[2] etc., of crymsyn serving for Palme Sonday."

Green, the characteristic colour of the Springtime, when all Nature appears to revive again, and in the bursting buds and blossoms gives rich promise of future fruitfulness, is naturally associated with hope. Hence, while the Easter ecclesiastical colour is almost everywhere white, as for example, at Salisbury, Paris, Toledo, Cologne, and Milan, at Soissons Cathedral we find it replaced by green. " The Latins call it viridis," saith an old author, " in regard of the strength, freshness, and liveliness thereof; and therefore it best resembleth youth, in that most vegetables so long

---

[1] There is considerable question amongst commentators as to what the biblical colours were, and we must not necessarily conclude that the scarlet of the Bible is the same thing as the scarlet of a Life Guard's tunic. The word rendered scarlet is in the original *tola*, a word signifying a worm. Besides the dyes produced from the murex, a crimson or scarlet was in ancient times derived from an insect allied to the cochineal, and called by the Arabs the *kermes* (hence our modern word carmine); and it is highly probable that this would be the source of the " worm-dye." Our modern word vermilion carries the same significance, a colour derived from a worm, though the facts of the manufacture do not in this case bear out the name of the pigment.

[2] In " the good old times," before school boards and Civil Service examiners, spelling gave our ancestors but little anxiety. We find this word in the different inventories and documents of the Middle Ages appearing not only as above, but as chysypull, chesebyll, chesebull. chesable, chyssypull, etc., etc.

as they flourish are beautiful with verdure. It is a colour most wholesome and pleasant to the eye."[1] In the pontifical of Bishop Clifford, written in the fifteenth century, we read, "Viridis color vividus est et visu jocundus atque comfortaturus."

Amongst the ancient Britons a strict rule limited the colour of the official dress assigned to each of the ranks of the bardic order, spotless white, as we have seen, for the druid or priest; sky-blue for the bard or poet; and green, the verdant decking of wood and downland, for the teacher of the virtues of herbs and the mysteries of leech-craft.

Durandus associates with green the idea of contemplation, an interpretation that it may well bear, since the lover of nature is ever thoughtful; hence Wordsworth exclaims,—

> "To me the meanest flower that blows can give
> Thoughts that do often lie too deep for tears."

Young affirms "the course of nature is the art of God." Chaucer calls Nature "the vicar of the Almightie Lord," while the Bible abounds in passages teaching the same truth. "All Thy works shall praise Thee, O God, and Thy saints shall bless Thee. Praise ye Him, sun and moon; praise Him, all ye stars of light, mountains and all hills, fruitful trees, and all cedars."

Green in mediæval days was ordinarily associated with the Feast of the Trinity.[2] Hence, in the instructions of Bishop Grandisson of Exeter, issued to his clergy about the year 1337, we find the direction, "On the feast of Trinity, if they have beautiful green vestments with copes, tunicles, and dalmatics in a sufficient number for such a feast, they must be used: otherwise let wholly white or light vestments be assumed."

Shakespeare, in "The Merchant of Venice," writes of "green-eyed jealousy," and again, in Othello:

> "O beware, my lord, of jealousy;
> It is the green-eyed monster."

[1] "A mead with lively verdure fresh."—DANTE.
[2] "Symbole d'espérance, couleur employée plus généralement au temps qui n'est point charactérisé par la joie, par le feu divin, par le sang, par la pénitence ou la tristesse. Cette couleur verte est donc appliquée au temps libre avant la Septuagésime, et surtout au temps qui s'écoule après la Pentecôte, jusqu'à l'Avent."—MALAIS.

In many ways green was regarded in mediæval folk-lore unfavourably, from its supposed association with the fairies, and from divers other superstitions that need not here be set forth, since our space can, we think, be better appropriated.

It is curious to find that in some of the Italian liturgical books green is given as an alternative for black in the office for the dead. It may be so found for example in the " Liber Sacerdotalis," printed at Venice in 1537, and in the " Liber Clericorum," A.D. 1550.

Blue, the colour of the clear sky, does not carry on its face so evident a meaning as the purity of spotless white, the burning ardour of glowing red ; hence it has somewhat arbitrarily been taken to represent eternity, faith, fidelity, loyalty, truth, spotless reputation. It was one of the Levitical colours, and many references to it will be found in Exodus, in the description of the tabernacle and of the priestly robes. In the book of Esther we read of Mordecai " in royal apparel of blue and white," but this probably should rather be rendered purple.

" Blew, which colour," says an old writer, " representeth the Aire amongst the elements, is of all the rest the greatest favourer of life, as the only nurse and maintainer of vitall spirits in any living creature. The cullor of blew is commonly taken from the cleere skye, which appeareth so after that the tempests be overblowne, a prosperous successe and good fortune to the wearer in all his affayres."

The Earl of Surrey, in his " Complaint of a Dying Lover," associates the idea of loyalty and devotion with blue in the lines,

" By him I made his tomb,
In token he was true,
And as to him belongèd well,
I covered it with blue."

Chaucer, again, in the " Court of Love," writes,

" Lo, yonder folke (quod she) that knele in blew,
They wear the colourage, and ever shal,
The signe they were, and ever will be true,
Withouten change."

" True blue " is now generally associated politically with the Conservative party.

Other political colours are the orange of the Ulsterman,

the green of the Irish Nationalist, the white of the Bourbon and the Stuart, the black of the House of Hanover, the red and white roses of Lancastrian and Yorkist, the violet of the Napoleons, and so forth.

Purple has always been associated with royal majesty, and accepted as the sign of imperial power. Thus in ancient Rome the toga of the emperor, or of conquerors on the day of their Triumph, was purple. The Babylonians and other Eastern heathen nations used to array their gods in purple robes. Homer intimates that garments of this colour were worn by princes alone, and a very early illustration of this royal use will be found in Judges viii. 26, where the kings of Midian, defeated by Gideon, are described as being clad in purple raiment. The pre-eminence still given to purple is no doubt a result of the old regal association. Probably the ancient preference arose when the relative superiority in beauty and brilliancy of purple to other colours was greater than at the present day, as the Tyrian dye prepared from shell-fish was highly esteemed, and the Phœnicians excelled all others in the manufacture of these pre-eminently beautiful garments.

Ecclesiastically purple and violet have borne an entirely different significance, being devoted, not to imperial pomp, but to penitence and fasting. "La couleur violette," says Malais, "représente l'obscurité, la tristesse, et la pénitence"; and amongst other items we find in the inventory, dated 1466, of a London church, "j purpyll chesebyll for gode fryday." Though white has ordinarily been used as the liturgical colour for Epiphany, violet has occasionally in some "uses" been substituted, in allusion to that text in Isaiah where the Gentiles are walking in darkness until the Epiphany manifestation has shone upon their path: "Populus qui ambulabat in tenebris vidit lucem magnam." Still more rarely green has been employed, the colour of hope, to symbolize the ingathering of the Gentiles that till then had been outside the fold.

Gray or ash-colour has sometimes been substituted for purple as the Lenten colour, and more especially on the Continent. Its use was of course suggested by the ashes distributed on the first day of Lent. Claude Villette in his book, "Les Raisons de l'Office et Ceremonies qui se font en l'Eglise," published in 1648, speaks of it as "couleur de terre, cendre, et pénitence." In the inventory of the church property of Exeter Cathedral, A.D. 1327, we meet with " una capa cinerei coloris pro Die Cinerium." Liturgically, gray, blue, and violet, and even white, are treated as alternative and secondary colours to black.

Black, suggestive of the material darkness and gloom that follows the withdrawal of the cheering light of day, is meet symbol of the spiritual darkness of the soul un-illumined by the Sun of righteousness. We see therefore how appropriately the title " Prince of Darkness " is applied to the arch-tempter, the great enemy of the souls of men. It is the colour of mourning, of shame, and of despair— "black despair, the shadow of a starless night,"[1] and of

> " all the grisly legions that troop
> Under the sooty flag of Acheron." [2]

In the apse of one of the Greek churches is a fresco of the Last Supper. All the apostles have the nimbus; but while those of all the other apostles are bright in colour, that of poor lost Judas is black as the gloomy path of Erebus, the valley of the shadow of death that led to Hades.

"Whatsoever Thing there is that hath in it either Light or Heat, or else a Life, either Animal or Vegetable, the Same being once extinct, the Thing itself becometh forthwith Black, which is said to be the colour of Horror and Destruction; for which respect mourning Garments are made of that Colour that doth most significantly represent the Horror of Death and Corruption."[3]

In Byzantium the emperor wore white on the death of a kinsman, as black garments were forbidden within the palace; and the same rule is, we are aware, rigidly enforced at the present day at the court of Morocco.

---

[1] Shelley.   [2] Milton.

[3] Thus far Guillim. Another old writer however, Ferne, willing to show that even black is not so black as it is painted, bestows upon it a somewhat less gloomy character. " The colour of blacke," he says, " is the most auncient of all colours, for in the beginning there was darkness over the face of the earth. And although that the colour of white was alwaies most praiseworthy for the brightness of the same, yet can we not omit the honours due to the colour of black; as first, it is the most perdurable of all colours, for it can hardly be altered into any other show or colour than the same which of nature it is, whereas of the contrarie part it doth easily extinguish and blot out any other colour."

On the conquest of Jerusalem in 1099, the crusaders installed a patriarch over the church of the Holy Sepulchre and attendant Augustinians, and in their liturgical formulæ we find the strange fact that all feasts of the Virgin were to be marked by black. " Omnes sollemnitates beate Marie cum pannis et vestibus nigris." In all other service books white is the invariable colour. It has been suggested that its use had reference to the passage in the Song of Solomon, " I am black, but comely "; but there seems no reason why on such a ground the church at Jerusalem should make so marked a departure from universal custom. Can it possibly have been from a feeling that Jerusalem was the scene of the betrayal and crucifixion of the Divine Son, and that whatever homage might elsewhere be meetly paid to the virgin purity of Mary must at the scene of her bitter sorrows give place to the sadder memorial of heart-breaking anguish ?

In the thirteenth century it was the custom on Christmas Eve to have a threefold vesting : first of black, to signify the time before the declaration of the law to Moses ; on the removal of this, white, to indicate the days of prophecy ; and then red, to symbolise the love and charity to mankind that the coming of the Christ brought into the world.

In an inventory of 1407 we find the item, "an hole vestiment of blac for masse of requiem " ; while in another, dating from about 1540, we come across "a pair of curtteynes black for dyrges."

Black was in the Middle Ages associated with witchcraft. It is naturally a type of darkness, and therefore the transition to moral darkness and dealing with familiar spirits is readily made ; hence such incantations and invocations of diabolic power were naturally known as the black art. Almost all allusions to the colour have a touch of the disquieting element in them. Thus a man who would fain get into a somewhat exclusive club fails to do so because he is blackballed ; he loses his cash through black-mail if he is so unfortunate and weak as to yield to the menaces of a blackleg ; while the knave himself, if he goes from bad to worse, may not impossibly see the judge put on the black cap when his sentence is pronounced.

CHAPTER III.

Representations of the Trinity—The "Trinità" in Art—Pictures in the National Gallery—Reasons for Avoidance by Early Christians of all Representations of the First Person—Policy—Reverence—The Gnostic Heresy—The Eye, Hand, and Arm of the Lord—Latin and Greek Forms of Benediction—The Head—The Whole Figure —Final Irreverence of Treatment—The Second Person of the Trinity—In Early Ages represented as almost a Youth—Change of Feeling—The Type adopted in the Latin Church—And in the Greek Church—The Incarnation—Christ as Orpheus—As the Good Shepherd—The Passion Plays of the Middle Ages—The Crucifix —The Holy Spirit in Human Form.

REPRESENTATIONS of the Trinity do not appear till somewhat late in the history of art. Figures or symbols of the Saviour may be met with at a very early period, as also the dove and other symbolic forms of the Holy Spirit; but for centuries no sculptor or painter ventured on any symbol of similitude of the first Person of the Trinity. Why this was the case we shall see later on, when we deal with the three Persons individually.

While we find amongst the Hindus a Trinity of Deities,— Brahma the great creator, who presides especially over the earth, Siva the destroyer, who reigns over fire, and Vishnu, whose empire is the water; and amongst the Greeks and Romans, Zeus or Jupiter reigning over earth and heaven, Poseidon or Neptune controlling the sea, and Aïdoneus or Pluto the governor of the shades of Hades;—the Triune God of Christendom is a Trinity of almighty Power, of boundless Love, of beneficent Wisdom.

Theophilus, bishop of Antioch, who flourished in the second century, was the first who used the word trinity to express the three sacred Persons in the Godhead, and the doctrine it expresses has been generally received amongst Christians. No reference will be found to it in the Old

Testament, but in the New it is very explicitly set forth in the directions as to the rite of baptism in Matthew xxviii. 19, and in other passages.

In the National Gallery will be found a picture by Garofalo entitled, " The Vision of St. Augustin." Augustinus, bishop of Hippo, and one of the Doctors[1] of the Church, relates that while engaged in a work on the Trinity, he had a vision in which he saw a child endeavouring with a ladle to empty the ocean into a hole which he had made in the sand; and upon the saint pointing out to him the uselessness of his toil, the child retorted by observing how infinitely more futile was the endeavour to explain what the Deity had left an inscrutable mystery.

Amongst later Italian painters the " Trinità," a conventional representation of the Godhead, was a favourite subject. A very good typical example may be seen in the National Gallery, by Pesellino, in which we see Christ extended upon the cross, while the Dove hovers above. The Father is seated, surrounded by cherubim and seraphim, and with outstretched hands beneath those of the Saviour sustains the weight of the cross. In other representations all three Persons are given in human form, the Father as an aged man, the Son and Spirit being younger looking; while in some few cases all three are as exactly alike, to carry out the idea of perfect equality, as the artist could make them. In such cases one extended cloak frequently enwraps all three figures, while one figure holds a globe, the emblem of dominion, the second the cross of sacrifice, while the third bears a roll or book, the attribute of wisdom. In the old church records we often find mention of representations of the Trinity, but unfortunately so briefly given, that we get no hint of the composition of the group. Thus in a parish book of St. Christopher's, London, dated 1488, we find " a chales with a patent of silver with a Trinite weyng xxi owncs," and "ij cloths stained white for thappostles altar, above with the Trinity and beneath with Our Lady," and yet again, " a Banner-Cloth with the Trynyte theryn." Illuminated manuscripts often supply illustrations, and in far

---

[1] These were Saints Athanasius, Basil, Gregory Nazianzen, and Chrysostom in the Greek Church; Saints Jerome, Augustin, and Gregory the Great in the Romish Church.

better condition than the sculptures on fonts and elsewhere,. that by stress of time and puritanical violence are so far disfigured as to make identification of subject often mere guesswork.

A picture of the Madonna and Holy Child by Domenico Veneziano, in the National Gallery, supplies us with another variation of treatment of the subject. In the "Trinità" we see the suffering Christ; in other examples, as in some we have referred to, He appears with the other two Persons in strict equality, co-ruler with them of heaven and of earth ; but in another class, of which this picture is a good example, Christ is the babe of Bethlehem standing on the Virgin mother's knee, or enfolded in her arms, while the Dove hovers over the group, and, above all, the Father bends down from heaven with arms outstretched in love and protection. While there is often in such representations a treatment that gives us a sense of shock and irreverence, we must nevertheless bear in mind that in all such cases intention is everything, and the intention undoubtedly, whatever we may now think of its expression, was beyond question reverential, and must be judged from that standpoint alone.

Three very different reasons influenced the artists of the early Christian period in their avoidance of any representation of the first Person in the Trinity—policy, reverence, and irreverence.

Jehovah, the eternal Father, "the Lord, strong and mighty, the Lord mighty in battle," He "who hath measured the waters in the hollow of His hand, and meted out heaven with the span," before whose almighty power Abraham and Job and all the sons of men are but as "dust and ashes," was in attributes too much like the Jupiter of the old religion to make it at all advisable to attempt a personification that would possibly remind the converts to the new faith of the great Olympic idol that they had so lately worshipped, while it was scarcely possible for even the most ignorant to confound the loving Redeemer, Christus Consolator, with any creation of pagan mythology. While the Word was made flesh and dwelt amongst the sons of men, the glory of God the Father has had no visible manifestation, for "no man hath seen God at any time." The glorified humanity of Christ was at least attemptable, but the ineffable majesty of "the King of Glory" was infinitely beyond all human imagination or the loftiest ideal: hence not policy alone, but a feeling of the deepest awe and reverence was a restraining influence. Later on, when the new religion had become more established, and a generation arose who had never bowed the knee before the shrine of Jove, the necessity for avoiding any representation that might suggest the old religion became needless. It may at first sight appear that it is a dishonour to Jehovah to suggest a comparison with Jupiter; but we must bear in mind that while the actual difference is infinite, such men as Phidias and other great artists had invested the images of the gods of Greece and Rome with the highest and noblest art that the world has ever seen, forms that it was impossible, no matter how immeasurably grander the new theme, for the art of man to surpass. Later on this noble reverence was almost wholly lost, and what the early ages in awe and a sense of its utter futility did not dare to attempt became at length so materialized that we find the great God who dwelleth "in the light which no man can approach unto, whom no man hath seen, nor can see," represented in the pontifical robes and tiara, or bearing the orb and sceptre and the royal crown of an earthly ruler.

Not policy nor reverence alone were restraining causes. In the first century of the Christian era there arose many strange heresies; and one of these, the Gnostic, held that Jehovah was a stern, unpitying tyrant, condemning all for the sin of one, and indifferent to the sorrows of the creatures He had made. Hence they turned with aversion from the Jehovah of the Old Testament to the loving and merciful Saviour of the New, and refused to acknowledge His claim on their allegiance.

For many centuries the eye, hand, or arm of God emerging from the clouds that veiled the brightness of the Divine Majesty were the only symbols employed. At a later date the head or entire figure was shown, but with not nearly so grand and impressive an effect as that produced on the mind by the more reverential treatments of the subject. The frequent allusions in the Old Testament to the hand and the arm of the Lord as the instrument of His sovereign power, such as, "His right hand, and His holy arm hath gotten Him the victory"; or of His might in creation, as "Thy hands have made me and fashioned me"; of His

D

goodness to the creatures dependent on His bounty, "Thou openest Thy hands, they are filled with good"; and of His justice, "the works of His hands are verity and judgment" —suffice to show how apposite such a symbol would be, and thus to clearly account for its frequent recurrence. Other texts, such as "His eyes are upon the ways of man, and He seeth all his goings," "The eyes of the Lord are upon the righteous," or, "The eyes of the Lord are in every place, beholding the evil and the good," justify and explain the use of the other early symbol of the God who is not only omnipotent, but omniscient.

The hand, as in fig. 3, at times sends down streams of light, and is often in the act of benediction.[1] Our illustration is from a Greek miniature of the tenth century. The inscriptions show that the figures introduced are the prophet Isaiah and representations of Night and Aurora, these latter being suggested by the passage in Isaiah: "I am the Lord, and there is none else. I form the light and create darkness." The writings of Isaiah dwell in a marked degree on the coming kingdom of Messiah, and in the illustration before us darkness passes away before the coming dawn, the advent of the Sun of righteousness. It is a curious blending of Christian and pagan ideas and symbols. In the earliest examples—those in the catacombs and in the mosaics of the early Italian churches—the hand is without the surrounding nimbus that we, later on, often find added. The earliest known representation is from a tomb in the catacombs, dated 359, where Moses is represented as receiving the tables of the law from the Divine hand issuing from a cloud. An interesting example to Englishmen will be seen in the Bayeux tapestry, where the hand of God is represented over the Church of St. Peter. It may be seen also on the coins of some of our Saxon kings, in one case accompanied by the Alpha and Omega. Constantine II. struck a beautiful gold

---

[1] In the Latin form of benediction the thumb and first two fingers are extended, and the last two bent down. It symbolises the Trinity. In the Greek form of benediction the forefinger is extended to resemble the letter I, while the middle finger is bent into a C-like form. The thumb and third finger are crossed to make an X, and the little finger is bent into a C again, so that we get IC XC, the initial and final letters of the Greek name for Jesus Christ—ΙησουϹ ΧριστουϹ.

medallion at Byzantium, representing Constantine I. with
his sons Constantine II. and Constans on either side, while
a hand from heaven crowns him with a wreath. This was

Fig. 3.

issued about the year 330. Eusebius speaks of the same
monarch as gaining the victory over all his enemies, and
enjoying the protection of the right hand of the King of
kings. In fig. 4, the Divine hand issues from the clouds, and

delivers the righteous that trust in God from the perils of
the world, for the souls of the righteous are in the hand
of God, and no evil shall befall them : " Into Thy hand I
commit my spirit." In a picture by Verrocchio of the
baptism of Christ in Jordan, the celestial Dove hovers over
His head, and above this again two outstretched hands are
seen issuing from the sky in a position suggestive of protection and blessing. In a bas-relief by Luca della Robbia of
the Virgin adoring the infant Christ, two arms issuing from
above are about to place a crown upon her head. These
are but illustrative examples of many others that might

Fig. 4.

readily be brought forward. Even in an Egyptian papyrus
in the British Museum, the god Horus, with widely outstretched arms, represents the vault of heaven extended in
protection over the figures shielded from harm beneath.
Many texts of the Bible refer to the arm of the Lord,[1] and
fully explain why such a symbol should so naturally and
frequently recur.

It was not until the twelfth century of the Christian era

---

[1] As for example Job xl. 9 ; Ps. xliv. 3 ; Isa. xl. 11, li. 9, lii. 10 ; Jer.
xxi. 5 ; Ezek. xx. 33 ; Luke i. 51 ; Acts xiii. 17.

Fig. 5.

that this reverential treatment gave place to the head, and then the half, and finally the whole figure. In a fresco by Paolo Uccello, in St. Maria Novella, of Noah's sacrifice, the patriarch and his family kneel around an altar, while overhead the rainbow spans the sky, and in the midst of it God, represented by a half figure, head downward, looks upon the little remnant of humanity, and gives the sign of benediction. A picture in the National Gallery, the Madonna in ecstasy, by Crevelli, shows the eternal Father bending over the Virgin; and in the famous and well known picture by Titian, at Venice, of the assumption of the Virgin, we get a very similar treatment, where the Father is floating in mid air, and surrounded by an attendant ring of cherubim.

On the walls of St. Francesco at Assisi, Giotto has painted various pictures illustrative of the life of St. Francis, and in one of these, again, the Father bends down, a half-length figure, from heaven, and blesses His followers; while, not to needlessly multiply examples, we may mention the Beatification of St. Ursula, by Vittore Carpaccio (fig. 5). In all such cases the eternal Father, God from everlasting to everlasting, "the Ancient of days," [1] is represented as a venerable, graybearded old man.

The celestial surroundings and the majesty of the figure in all these examples have rendered it impossible to doubt the Person intended, mistaken and lacking in reverence as we may deem the representation to be. But in some examples the figure is so wholly at one with ordinary humanity, that the last shred of Divine dignity and of grandeur of conception is lacking. Thus amid the sculptures of the cathedral of Orvieto we come on two figures, one prostrate and sleeping, the other leaning over the first and making a puncture in his side. As the whole façade is covered with the Bible history from the creation of man to his redemption, we recognise that the particular group in question is a representation of the creation of Eve, and that the two very similar figures are really the Creator and Adam. In the celebrated gates of Ghiberti at Florence, we find in one of the panels a dignified but essentially human

---

[1] "Or ever Thou hadst formed the earth and the world, even from everlasting to everlasting, Thou art God" (Ps. xc. 2). And thrice in Dan. vii., in vers. 9, 13, and 22, God is styled "the Ancient of days."

figure raising another from the ground—an incident that would not strike us as any way exceptional, that might, for instance, stand for the pitying Samaritan raising the robbed and wounded traveller, but which all the surroundings indicate is meant for the creation by the Father of Adam from the dust of earth.

To the second Person of the Trinity art has ever rendered, and continues to render, highest homage. He has been figured at every era, and under great variety of form and symbol. We purpose here to deal with representations of Him in the form of humanity, but we shall find elsewhere that the lamb, the pelican, the fish, the vine, are all equally symbols of the Redeemer, while many other forms, such as the Passion symbols, the cross, the sacred monogram, the chalice, owe their existence and their meaning to their association with Him.

During the early ages of Christianity the Saviour was almost always represented as a young man, little more indeed than a youth, no matter what the incident might be ; but about the twelfth century His age was represented as being in accordance with the period depicted. Thus we get the babe of Bethlehem, and the boy Christ in the midst of the doctors of the temple. During His public ministry we see Him in the prime of manhood, gravely gracious as He extends His hands in benediction, later on rising in glorious majesty from the tomb, and, finally, severe and unapproachable on the throne of judgment.

At the approach of the year 1000 of the Christian era, things political and social were greatly overcast, and it was a general belief that that date would mark the destruction of the world. Many charters about this time commence with the words, " As the world is now drawing to its close." The impression seems to have been founded on an expectation of the millennium. The earlier Christians had dwelt lovingly on the miraculous and benevolent actions and the gentle utterances of the Christ; but these now gave place to a gloomy theology that entirely banished that most favourite image of the former centuries, the Good Shepherd, and dwelt upon every painful episode of the Passion, which, till then, had never been introduced in art or assigned a prominent place in theology. Hence too scenes of the last Judgment were depicted, and with every accessory of morbid horror; while the ideal Christ of the earlier days disappears, and the Man of sorrows, wounded, bleeding, takes His place in art and in the thoughts of men.

Besides the youthful, beardless Christ, the ideal adolescent of eighteen years or thereabouts, and the later type that Western Europe is now familiar with, and of which we may see countless mediæval and modern examples in art, we get in the Greek Church, and in work done under the later Byzantine influence, yet a third type. The Latin Church has always held that, while Christ was Son of man, He was still Son of God, and that the sins He came to expiate, and all the sorrows and vices of humanity that He bore the burden of, were powerless to sully His glory and dignity; while the Greek Church, dwelling upon such a passage as that in the Epistle to the Philippians, where Christ was said to have made Himself of no reputation, and to have taken upon Himself the form of a servant, depicted Him as having, in the words of Isaiah, "no form nor comeliness, no beauty that we should desire Him." [1] Hence these representations depict the Saviour, crushed, impoverished, beaten down beneath the load of human wretchedness. This is however to represent the Conqueror of death and sin, the Redeemer of mankind, as well-nigh vanquished in the strife, and is surely, theologically and artistically, a mistaken view and treatment.

Christ is the author of Christianity, the fountain from whence all its blessings flow, and from Him, most naturally, the new religion derived its title. Hence to Him all the devout throughout the centuries have turned with profoundest gratitude and homage,[2] and to Him art, and all else, should ever render highest honour.

---

[1] "Despised and rejected of men; a Man of sorrows, and acquainted with grief: and we hid as it were our faces from Him; He was despised and we esteemed Him not. Surely He hath borne our griefs, and carried our sorrows: yet we did esteem Him stricken, smitten of God, and afflicted. . . . He was bruised for our iniquities; the chastisement of our peace was upon Him."

[2] "Millions of penitents find the peace and consecration of a new life in laying the burden of their sins upon One who has borne it. Millions of believers pass into the dark valley with a hope stronger than death, because they have cast themselves upon One whose death is their life. Christendom lives and dies upon one of His creative words, 'The Son

In the incarnation of Christ was met and satisfied the yearning of mankind for some visible manifestation of God. Man is crushed and awed by the idea of the infinite, and the impossibility of realizing the incomprehensible God.   Hence Job's cry was but the articulate utterance of the heart-ache of myriads: "Behold, I go forward, but He is not there; and backward, but I cannot perceive Him."   These yearnings

Fig. 6.

the noblest people of antiquity endeavoured to satisfy by statues of the gods that will ever remain incomparable in their beauty, while they were after all so unsatisfying that

---

of man came to minister, and to give His life a ransom for many.' He had but to breathe a few words into the air, and in unending succession martyrs spring forward to lead the 'forlorn hopes' of the army of the Cross : fearing but one thing, lest He may be ashamed of them ; hoping greatly but one thing, that the Captain's voice may make music in their hearts, and the Captain's smile fall with its sunshine upon their brows ' (" The Divinity of our Lord," by Dr. Alexander).

the final outcome was a statueless altar "to the unknown god." [1] By the same indwelling instinct, the savage of equatorial Africa carves the trunk of a tree, and decks it with opalescent shells, or adorns it with the gay plumage of rare birds; and it is to him an ideal of that higher Power which even he thus dimly recognises. Among the other and manifold benefits of the Incarnation is the satisfying of this craving. In this superhuman Humanity we recognise, not man alone, but the Divine.

In the earliest period of Christian art we not unfrequently, as in fig. 6, meet with representations of Christ as Orpheus. While evidently adopted from the heathen mythology, with which the early converts were so familiar, its application to Christianity was felt to be very legitimate. Orpheus seated with his lyre amongst the trees, and surrounded by the wild beasts that the sweetness of his music had tamed, might well be taken as an emblem of the attractive force of Christ. The symbol may be seen on early coinage and in the catacombs. In a chamber, for instance, in the catacombs of St. Calixtus, the central space immediately over the interment is taken up by a long, semi-circular painting of this subject; while on one side is the prophet Micah, on the other Moses striking the rock, and above it the Virgin mother and Holy Child.

The early Christians would be very familiar with the legend of Orpheus and the beasts, as it was a favourite subject of representation amongst the Romans. We need but refer, in illustration of this, to the mosaic pavements found at Horkstow and Winterton in Lincolnshire, and at Barton, near Cirencester.

In all these, the treatment of the subject is very similar. In the first of these, we have a series of ellipses, the centre one containing Orpheus; the next, rabbits, squirrels, weasels, and such like small creatures; the next, birds; and the outer and largest ring, the lion, elephant, bear, tiger, boar, etc. In the second we have Orpheus in a central octagon, and then eight outer spaces, with elephant, dog, fox, boar, stag, etc. In the third example, the inner circle has the figure of Orpheus;

---

[1] Or, as it is still more strikingly put in its vagueness in the Revised Version, "To an unknown God."

the next has figures of birds, such as the duck, robin, peacock, and several others; while the outer circle is occupied by the elephant, horse, boar, lion, and other quadrupeds.

Christ as the Good Shepherd holds a very conspicuous position in early art, and soon entirely supplanted the Orpheus symbol. This treatment may be met with freely in the catacombs, on the walls, on the lamps found in the tombs, and in the mosaics of the oldest churches. Figs. 7 and 8 are from gems dating about the year 300 A.D., and giving us a good illustration of the treatment of the subject in early Christian art. It is very strange that this most expressive symbol died out completely before the tenth century, and is never met with again until the sixteenth century, and even then very sparingly, while it was never

Fig. 7.   Fig. 8.

adopted in the Greek Church at all. The Saviour Himself most explicitly applied the title to Himself, " I am the Good Shepherd," and in the Epistle to the Hebrews (xiii. 20) He is again called " our Lord Jesus, that great Shepherd of the sheep." He is represented in art as tranquilly resting amongst the surrounding sheep, or as bearing one—the lost sheep of the parable—upon His shoulders. " The good shepherd layeth down his life for the sheep " : hence the symbol testifies, not of protection and direction alone, but of devotion carried to the extreme of willing sacrifice.

The dramatic representations in the Middle Ages, of which the Oberammergau play is a survival, were of great educational value, as the graphic and dramatic arts appealed most forcibly to those who were unable to read for them-

selves; while the living actors gave reality to the personages
painted in the cathedral windows, or sculptured round their
doorways, and thus quickened the sculptor's and the painter's
art. No doubt art gained much from the mysteries and
plays of the time, which were pressed into the service of the
Church; and the great truths of religion were offered on
every hand to the eyes and ears of the people by carver,
painter, musician, actor, and poet.

Gregory Nazianzen, desiring to banish profane plays from
the theatre at Constantinople, prepared several sacred
dramas to take their place; and Chrysostom wrote a tragedy
called "The Dying Christ," which was many times represented in the same city.

Christ as the infant was always, until the fourteenth century, depicted clothed, and it was only at the decadence of
Christian art that He was represented as nearly or quite
naked. Christ as the sufferer on the cross of shame is not
found at all until the fifth century. Though the cross itself
early appeared as a symbol of the crucifixion, it was nearly
five hundred years after the event commemorated ere it
became the crucifix. Until the eleventh century the body of
Christ upon the cross is always clothed, as we see in fig. 9,
wherein He is represented as the great High Priest. Afterwards, the breast is uncovered, and the drapery becomes an
apron descending from the waist to the knees, till in the
fifteenth century it becomes the simple band, as shown in fig.
10, where nevertheless He wears the kingly crown upon His
brow, and is shown with the rayed nimbus. The sun and
moon, typical of nature, often appear in early work on either
side of the cross. In the early centuries the serpent is
placed beneath the foot of the cross, as a symbol of sin
overthrown.

The Holy Spirit, the third Person of the Trinity, has from
about the sixth century down to the present day been constantly symbolized by the dove. On this we shall dwell
more at length later on, when considering the various animal
forms that have been pressed into the service of symbolism.
In the tenth century the custom arose of representing the
Holy Spirit in human form; but after being very freely in
use for nearly six hundred years, Pope Urban VIII (A.D.
1623) prohibited the practice as being contrary to the
traditions of the Church, and it was at once entirely aban-

Fig. 9.

Fig. 10.

doned, and the older symbol of the dove substituted in it;
place.   When represented in human form, the distinguishing
attribute of the Holy Spirit is the roll or book held in the
hand, the symbol of intelligence and wisdom

CHAPTER IV.

The Sacred Monogram—Its Appearance to Constantine—The Chrisma
—The Labarum—Construction and Meaning of the Monogram—
Examples from the Catacombs of Rome—On Coins, Charters,
etc.—The I·H·S·—The Nimbus—Its Pagan Origin—The Sun-god
—Modifications of Nimbus Treatment in Christian Art—The
Horned Moses—The Old Testament Saints Nimbed—Allegorical
Figures Nimbed—Hexagonal Nimbus—The two Uses of the Square
Nimbus—The Triangular Nimbus—Enrichment of Surface—
Name of Wearer within Nimbus—The Cruciferous Nimbus—Clus-
tering Rays of Light—Illuminant Power of the Nimbus—A Golden
Elliptical Line—The Aureole—A Glory of Flame-like Rays—When
applied to the Virgin Mary—Vesica Piscis—Divine Oval—Mystical
Almond—Mandola—Aureole of Cherubs.

We propose now to consider the various forms assumed by
the monogram and the nimbus: the first a symbol exclusively appertaining to Christ; the second a mark of holiness
or of power of far wider application.

The earliest form of monogram is the symbol which is
said to have appeared to Constantine, outshining the sun in
its splendour, while a voice was heard to exclaim, " By this
sign shalt thou conquer." Assigning any value we may to
this legend, the fact at least remains that Constantine did
receive some sudden shock to his old superstitions, and that,
joining the Christian Church, he henceforth removed the old
Roman eagle from the standards of the legions, placing in its
stead the sacred monogram. There is no reason to suppose
that this monogrammatic symbol was not in use amongst
the Christians previously. What the monarch saw or fancied
he saw was doubtless a form whose meaning he already
knew; it would, in fact, from its abbreviated character, have
been otherwise meaningless to him.[1] The monogram is

---

[1] One of the great difficulties in reading ancient inscriptions on tablets,
charters, coins, and so forth, arises from this very free use of abbrevia-

sometimes termed the *chrisma*, or, erroneously, the *labarum*.
The labarum is the standard marked with the sacred device,
and not the device itself. The labarum, see fig. 11, was
adopted by the Emperor Constantine after his victory over
Maxentius, duly described by Eusebius. The emperor also
caused the sacred symbol to be represented on the shields
of the soldiers.[1] Julian the Apostate removed it, but it was
again replaced by Jovian and his Christian successors, and
was continued in use by all the later Byzantine rulers.

FIG. 11.

The monogram is formed of the first two letters of the
Greek word for Christ, XPISTOS. X is equivalent to *ch*,
and the P is the Greek *R*. This is found on tombs of the
martyrs and others of the reigns of Adrian and of Antonine, in

tion. In mediæval Latin, for instance, the letters M and N are specially
liable to elimination, a straight line over the next vowel being ordinarily
the hint that they are missing, while terminations of words are often
omitted, and at times an apostrophe substituted. Thus on old brasses
the invariable formula, "Cujus anime propitietur Deus: Amen," is often
merely Cui' a̅i̅e̅ ppciet' de' a̅m̅e̅. The "D.g. Brit. reg. fid. def." on
our coinage in daily use would be equally meaningless to any one who
had not the key to their significance.

[1] In the mosaics of the sixth century in the church of St. Vitale, at
Ravenna, amongst the guards surrounding the Emperor Justinian a
very good example of this may be seen, the field of the elliptical shield,
some three feet by two, being entirely filled with the monogram.

the second century of the Christian era. After passing out of
use for some centuries, it has been in these latter days somewhat revived. The X is sometimes turned, so as to make
its arms come vertically and horizontally, instead of in the
sloping direction of the ordinary X: this arrangement
gives the added symbolism derived from its resemblance to
the cross. On the coins of Constantinus we get the Alpha
and Omega, one on either side, the acknowledgment of the
divinity of our Lord. " I am Alpha and Omega, the beginning and the ending, saith the Lord, which is, and which was,
and which is to come, the Almighty." As Alpha, God is the
beginning of all things at the creation in Genesis ; as Omega

Fig. 12.

in the apocalypse, He is the consummation of all things.
Or, to quote the words of the Venerable Bede : " Ego sum A
et Ω, initium et finis, dicit Dominus Deus. Initium, quem
nullus præcedit; finis, cui nullus in regno succedit. Qui
est, et qui erat, et qui venturus est, omnipotens." In fig.
12, a lamp of early Christian date and workmanship, we get
the cross-like disposition of the letters, together with the
Alpha and Omega; while fig. 13 is an instance of the more
typical form of monogram. More rarely the P is turned into
the Latin *R*, implying *rex*, the kingship of Christ. The
monogram is sometimes found inclosed in a circle, the
symbol of eternity, or standing upon a circle, symbol of the
conquering power of Christ over the world. At other times

E

we get the X alone or combined with the I, the initial letter
of Jesus, IHSOUS. When this latter arrangement, the X
and the I together, is placed within the circle, it resembles a
wheel with six spokes. Often in the catacombs the tombs
of martyrs have the monogram surrounded by a wreath, the
symbol of victory through Christ. Occasionally on lamps
or gems we see the dove, symbol of the Holy Spirit and of
heavenly peace, sitting upon it, or represented as descending upon it. Early inscriptions, charters, and other documents are often prefaced by the cross or the monogram;

FIG. 13.

one may see many excellent examples of the latter in the
British Museum, one for example on a deed of Edgar, A.D.
961, and another on a charter of Canute, dated 1031. The
familiar abbreviation of Xmas for Christmas, that possibly
some of our readers may have used without consideration,
is another illustration of the X being equivalent to Christ.

In Greek art representations of the cross are often accompanied, as we see in fig. 14, by the inscription " IC XC
NIKA," Jesus Christ the conqueror;[1] or in a still more abbreviated form XP and NI on either side. The chrisma was

---

It is also in the Orthodox Eastern Church impressed on the sacramental wafer.

in use during the whole of the Roman-Byzantine period, fell
into abeyance during the Dark Ages, and re-appeared in the
twelfth century.   On a coin of Constantius II., the emperor
in full armour is represented as standing in a galley steered
by Victory.   In his right hand he bears the phœnix standing
on a globe (for due significance of which see phœnix), and
in his left the labarum emblazoned with the sacred monogram.   On a coin of Gratian we see the emperor bearing
the same standard of victory, the idea of triumph over his
enemies being further enforced by the introduction of the

Fig. 14.

kneeling captive at his feet.   The sacred monogram was
placed by Louis VI. of France upon his coins, and was
maintained there by one sovereign after another until the
Renaissance scattered all the more ancient traditions and
revived classic forms.

    The more familiar monogram based on the I·H·S is ordi-
narily of later date than the XP, replacing it entirely from
the beginning of the twelfth century.   The earliest example
known is on a gold coin of Basilius I., A.D. 867.   This I·H·S
monogram is the abbreviated form of the word IHSOUS,
the omission of the other letters being marked by the dash
or bar, above the I·H·S.   This dash was afterwards pro-
longed through the upward stroke of the H, and thus formed

the cross. As the form of the Greek S differs from ours, being somewhat like a C, the monogram sometimes appears as I·H·C.[1] These letters are often read as signifying "Iesus Hominum Salvator," Christ the Saviour of men; and on their introduction into the Latin Church, this meaning was assigned to them. It is said that this reading was first suggested by Bernardine of Siena (1380–1441); but appropriate and beautiful as it certainly is, it is an after-thought. In the National Gallery may be seen a picture by Il Moretto [2] of a group of saints, St. Bernardine, St. Jerome, St. Joseph, St. Francis, and others. St. Bernardine is holding up in his right hand a circle containing the I·H·S, and in his left hand is an open book with the words, "Pater, manifestavi nomen tuum hominibus," Father, I have set forth Thy name unto men. Modern examples, stamped on Prayer-Book covers, painted on glass, embroidered on hangings, stamped on tiles, carved in the stonework, may be met with in profusion everywhere.[3]

We turn now our attention to the nimbus.

This form, which we naturally associate so entirely with the service of religion and of Christianity, is really pagan [4] in its origin, and was a symbol originally of power rather than of holiness. Its origin dates back to an antiquity too remote for identification. It has been conjectured that it may probably have been in the first place suggested by the

---

[1] Thus in an inventory of vestments and other church property of Westminster Abbey, A.D. 1388, a mitre is referred to, " cum ymaginibus habens in utraque parte hoc nomen insertum IHC XPC."

[2] Alessandro Bonvicino, commonly called Il Moretto de Brescia. His pictures range in date from 1524 to 1556.

[3] In the year 1643 an ordinance was passed for the utter demolition and removal of all monuments of superstitious idolatry. In the parish book of St. Bartholomew in the city of London we read the following minute : " Read an ordinance from a Committee of the House of Commons for the demolition of superstitious and idolatrous things, both within the church and without, where it was ordered that the three letters in the pulpit cloth I·H·S. should be put out." In the church-wardens' accounts for the year we meet with the entry, " p[d] to the imbroderer for taking I·H·S. out of the pulpit cloth, and imbrodered same again with other work, twenty shillings, besides five shillings he allowed me for the old stuff."

[4] " As to the whole company of Buddhist saints, with the golden glory encircling every head, they are scarcely to be distinguished from those of Christendom."—GORDON CUMMING, " Wanderings in China."

rays of the sun. In fig. 15, a coin of Rhodes, we see on the
obverse the rayed head of Helios the sun god, the reverse
being the rose, the device or badge of the city. Sun
worship has amongst pagan peoples been a very prominent

Fɪɢ. 15.

feature in almost all ages, and even when the time has
arrived that they have acknowledged a higher power, the
sun has often remained an emblem of the Divinity. Light
has therefore been one of the attributes of the gods; hence

Fɪɢ. 16.

Jupiter wields the lightning flash, Apollo is crowned with
the glowing sunbeams, as in fig. 16, while to Diana is given
the softer light and chastened beauty of the crescent moon.
The idols of China, of Burma, and of Hindustan are often

represented with a nimbus as characteristic as any seen in the carvings or stained glass of a Gothic cathedral. The face of Moses reflected with dazzling brightness the Divine glory on his descent from Sinai, and a similar manifestation is claimed for Muhammad after the cleansing visit of the angel Gabriel.

After the death of Constantine his sons struck medals in his honour, in which he may be seen crowned with the nimbus,—a symbol not necessarily bestowed upon him on account of his embracing Christianity (though no doubt this fact had its influence), as we may also find on some of the coins of the earlier emperors, as Claudius and Trajan, a similar feature.[1]   It was, as we have already indicated, a symbol of dignity and power.   So far was it from being at

Fig. 17.

first accepted as a mark of sanctity, that in some early Byzantine works even Satan is represented as wearing the nimbus. In a thirteenth century MS. the Magi and king Herod are alike nimbed, and in one of the cathedral windows at Strassburg are fifteen kings, benefactors to the cathedral, and all are assigned a nimbus; these date about the eleventh or twelfth centuries. One of them is Charlemagne, the nimbus having inscribed within the circumference the words Karolus Magnus Rex. The double-headed eagle in the arms of imperial Germany is, as we may see in fig. 17, represented as being nimbed. In one of the mosaics in the church of S[ta.] Sophia at Constantinople we see Christ sitting on a

---

[1] It was a custom with the emperor Commodus to sprinkle gold dust over his hair, so that, while walking in the sunlight, his head might appear to shine with supernatural splendour!

throne, and the emperor, richly attired, kneeling in submission and adoration at His feet. On either side of the throne are medallions of the Virgin and of the archangel Michael. Neither of these latter have the nimbus, while Christ, the King of kings, and Justinian, the earthly ruler, each have this symbol of sovereignty. On the other hand, Fra Angelico at a later period gives to the three Magi the crowns of earthly sovereignty, and reserves the heavenly glory for the holy maiden mother and the holy child.

Where a nimbus in Christian art is rayed, the rays spring from the centre of the circle, behind the head, and are generally very numerous; the individual rays, necessarily very narrow and linear, being just the opposite in this respect to the form seen on Greek and Roman coins. In these latter, the rays are few in number (often seven); and, while they, as a series, radiate from the head, they are individually broad at the base and running out to a sharp point. In the Christian form a circle is ordinarily shown as joining the extremities of the rays; while in classic examples it is more commonly shown as about half way up them. At other times, no less in Hindu than in Roman examples, the nimbus is composed of a series of pleats that give as a bounding edge a zigzag line or sawlike appearance. On the coins of Rhodes the head of the sun-god has, independently of it and of each other, a surrounding series of pear-like forms, fig. 15, which we may very naturally conclude to have been intended to represent flames.

The Christian nimbus is not met with on any monument prior to the sixth century, but during the next three centuries its use rapidly grew. Until the twelfth century the nimbus was luminous and transparent; but during the two following centuries it became an opaque disk. It then again became translucent, and was indicated only by the bounding circle, or by a series of fine rays without the circle at all. Still later on the circle is put into perspective and becomes an ellipse, more and more approaching, where the figures have their heads in profile, a straight line. All early nimbi were circular; the triangular form does not appear till the eleventh century; and the square nimbus, as characteristic of a living person, does not come into use until the ninth century. The first nimbus forms were assigned to God; later on the angels, His ministers, receive them; and only by slow degrees did the apostles, saints, and martyrs become thus adorned with the seal of holiness.

As the writers on heraldry in the mediæval period assigned arms to the earlier kings, to Edward the Confessor and others who had the misfortune to be dead and buried hundreds of years before the birth of "the noble science," and even devised coats of arms for Gideon and Joshua and other valiant heroes of the Old Testament records, so the religions painters of the Middle Ages gave to the pre-Christian saints like honour with their successors. This was more especially the case in the East.[1] Moses is always represented with a curious form of nimbus composed of two rays, or two groups of rays, only. In sculpture these become exceedingly like horns. An old theory, more or less satisfactory, held that God did not reveal Himself to him in all His glory, and that He only delivered to him such portion of the Divine law as was especially applicable to the Jews; and that as the advent of Christ, though foretold, was not accomplished, the nimbus of Moses only bears testimony to the other two Persons in the Godhead. This, we would venture to say, is a particularly lame theory, though we give it as one that has been gravely advanced, and we cannot supplant it by a better. In the fresco by Signorelli, the "History of Moses," in the Sistine Chapel, the great leader is twice introduced in the one picture, and each time with the characteristic nimbus, two groups of three rays each. The colossal statue of Moses by Michael Angelo on the monument of Julius II. has the curious horn-like forms to which we have referred. As a final example, out of many that might be adduced, of the bestowal of the nimbus on the saints of the old dispensation, we may refer to the wall paintings of Benozzo Gozzoli (1424-1455) in the Campo Santo at Pisa. They represent the stories of the Old Testament, beginning with Noah and ending with Joseph, and are full of patriarchal

---

[1] In the Greek Church the Jewish patriarchs and prophets are held in more visible esteem than in the West. Festivals are observed on the saints' days of Abel, Noah, Abraham, Moses, Samuel, David, and many other Old Testament worthies; and they speak as freely of St. Isaac and St. Jacob as we do of St. Matthew or St. Mark, and dedicate their finest churches to them. In a fresco representing the sacrifices of Cain and Abel, the latter has a golden nimbus.

simplicity, pastoral beauty, and incomparable *naïveté*. One of these is a vintage scene, wherein Noah figures twice in the composition as superintending the ingathering of the grapes; and in each case he is depicted with the nimbus.

Allegorical and ideal figures are also at times assigned a nimbus; such impersonations, for instance, as Faith, Hope, Charity, Prudence, Justice, and Fortitude. In the works of the Italian painters such abstractions often have a nimbus of hexagonal form, as in fig. 18, a head from the "St. Francis Wedded to Poverty" of Giotto. The picture is in the lower church of St. Franceso at Assissi. Poverty is no mere abstraction, but is represented by a comely female figure, though clothed in somewhat patched and torn apparel. Our illustration is the head of Poverty. The Saviour Himself celebrates the nuptial rite. Those imaginary personages to

Fig. 18.

whom the teaching of the Master has given semblance of life, such as the wise virgins of the parable, are also represented often in old pictures and carvings with this attribute of holiness. On the coins of Faustina, the peacock, symbol of the glorified soul, has its head encircled with the nimbus; and on the coins of the Antonines, the phœnix, the symbol of immortality, is also thus distinguished. The four evangelists when in human form are of course so honoured; but even when represented by their attributes, the angel, the lion, the ox, and the eagle, the heads of these creatures are almost invariably encircled by the nimbus.

Where the hand of God is seen proceeding from the clouds, it is ordinarily surrounded by the nimbus. This is often of three rays, indicative of the presence and sympathy of the Trinity in whatever the work may be that has drawn forth this symbol of the presence of God.

The idea of the nimbus as a symbol of saintliness being
once conceded, it might be thought that little or no practical
difficulty would arise in assigning it; yet in practice curious
deviations are found from what might be imagined a simple
procedure. For instance, in a picture of the Holy Family
by Andrea del Sarto in our National Gallery we notice that,
while the Virgin and Elizabeth each have a golden nimbus
of similar character, St. John and the infant Christ have
none at all. In a picture by Francia of the Virgin and the
dead Christ, the Saviour, the Virgin mother, and two attendant angels, we note that all have exactly similar nimbi;
while in another picture, the procession to Calvary, by
Ghirlandaio, Christ, the Virgin, St. Veronica, St. John, and
other saints, again all have nimbi of identical character.
We see the same thing again in a beautiful bas-relief by
Luca della Robbia of the Virgin mother in adoration of
the Divine Infant, where the Christ, the mother, and two
attendant cherubs form the group. The dignity and greater
technical difficulty of the sculptor's art doubtless go far
to justify this simplicity of treatment; but as the painter
could so readily enrich and vary his forms, it seems strange
that the greater or less dignity and importance of the persons
in such groups as we have indicated should not have been
noted and duly honoured by more or less enrichment of the
nimbus in each case assigned.

We occasionally find the square nimbus, though only in
Italian work. It is placed either with upright sides and
horizontal top edge, or else turned diamond-wise; and this
alternative in the method of its arrangement makes all the
difference in its application and meaning. The latter position
is exclusively bestowed on the first Person of the Trinity, and
it is ordinarily given concave sides. In the " Disputà " of
Raphael, the Divine nimbus has straight sides instead of concave; but it is placed, as is almost invariably the case, lozenge
or diamond-wise. Even here however we meet with an
exception or two; thus in the mosaic in the church of San
Giovanni in Laterano the square nimbus of God has upright
sides, but it is surrounded by a circle, emblem of eternity.
Much curious symbolism was associated by the Neo-plato-
nists and Pythagoreans and the Middle Age astrologers with
the square, though it would be foreign to our present purpose to dwell upon it here.

When the nimbus is a square having upright sides, it always implies that the person so marked was still living at the time. It may be freely found in Italian work, and a good early example may be noted in the South Kensington Museum in a portion of an eighth century mosaic from Ravenna. It may be seen too very well in the nimbus surrounding the head of Pope Leo III., and in that of the emperor Charles the Great in the mosaics of the Lateran church. A mosaic in the church of St. Cecilia in Rome is another good example, as it represents Pope Pascal similarly distinguished. He holds in his arms a model of this church, as it was erected through his instructions and assistance.

Fig. 19.

The mosaic dates from the year 820. The same pope, with similar nimbus, will be met with again in the churches of Sta Maria della Navicula and Sta Pressede. Both are in Rome, and the mosaics date respectively 815 and 818. Durandus says that "when any living prelate or saint is pourtrayed, the glory is not fashioned in the shape of a shield, but foursquare, that he may be shown to flourish in the four cardinal virtues."

Occasionally this rectangular nimbus, instead of being flat, is made with its two upright sides curling inwards, as though the man were emerging from within a big roll of paper. At other times we find a straight, upright back, and then the two sides thrown forward at a sharp angle, suggesting the idea of a small folding screen behind the head.

In the fifteenth century the nimbus in the form of an equilateral triangle appears. It is reserved for the first Person of the Trinity ordinarily, though we occasionally find the dove, the emblem of the Holy Spirit, with a similar nimbus. As emblematic of the Trinity, it would manifestly be equally properly applied to any one of the three Persons, though ordinarily the second Person has the circular nimbus, and a cross inscribed within it. In some cases beams of light radiate beyond the triangle, their extremities forming an exterior circle. In the sixteenth century, figures of the eternal Father no longer appear, but His name in Hebrew characters is sometimes placed within an equilateral triangle, and often the whole surrounded by a circular halo or radiation, as we may see in fig. 19.

The nimbus is often represented as a solid circular dish behind the head of the person so distinguished; so solid, in fact, that in many of the early pictures where many saints are represented the nimbi overlap almost like tiles on a roof, and allow only very small portions of the heads of those in the rear to be visible at all. In the beautiful picture of the Annunciation by Fra Angelico (fig. 20), the nimbus in each case, that of the Virgin Mary and of the angelic visitant, is of this solid type. "The righteous live for evermore; their reward is also with the Lord, and the care of them is with the Most High. Therefore shall they receive a glorious kingdom, and a beautiful crown from the Lord's hand: for with His right hand shall He cover them, and with His arm shall He protect them." [1] Durandus says that the crown of the righteous "is made in the fashion of a round shield," because the saints enjoy the Divine protection. Whence they sing with joy, "Lord, Thou hast crowned us with the shield of Thy favour." The solid nimbus is a necessity, of course, in sculpture, but in painting also it is often represented with most evident thickness and opacity. In a couple of heads of saints in the National Gallery by Domenico Veneziano the nimbi are of solid gold; but while the direction of the light in the pictures throws them mostly into shade, their margins are defined by a broad edge of brilliant light; while in a picture by Cossa, also in the National Gallery, of St. Vincentius Ferrer, the solid plate of gold has its thickness

---

[1] Wisdom of Solomon v. 15, 16.

FIG. 20.

emphasized by a broad line of vermilion. In a picture by
Zoppo, in the same gallery, of Christ being placed in the
tomb, Christ and two saints have all similar nimbi, that,
instead of being absolutely opaque, are like disks of glass
through which the sky can be seen, but having a very
definite and thick edge.

An added dignity was speedily given to these solid nimbi
by a very considerable enrichment of the surface, by painting, by puncturing patterns on the golden ground, by em-
bossing, or by the addition of jewels and pearls. In Fra
Angelico's picture of the Adoration of the Magi, Christ, the
Virgin, and St. Joseph all have similar red nimbi, thickly
covered with radiating and radiant golden lines. In a picture of the procession to Calvary by Ugolino de Siena in the
National Collection, both the nimbi and the background are
gold, so the former have to be brought out by means of in-
cised lines and punctures. These are arranged in quatrefoils
and other geometrical forms. Fra Filippo Lippi, in the
same gallery, affords several good illustrations of this method
of treatment; but the richest examples will be found in
Orcagna's grand picture of the Coronation of the Virgin,
where a wonderful variety of geometric and floral enrich-
ments will be found.

During the fourteenth century a custom arose of placing
the name of the wearer within the edge of the nimbus. This
lasted for some two hundred years, and may be seen alike in
Greek, Italian, and German art, except that in Greek examples, instead of the name they almost invariably give the
monogram of the person or some other abbreviation of the
full name, or even only its initial letter. Some very good
examples of these inscribed nimbi may be seen in the National
Collection. Thus in the Marriage of St. Catherine, by San
Severino, in the nimbus of Christ are the words " Sum
Lux "; in that of the Virgin, " Ave, gratia plena Domi ";
while in the golden glory of St. Catherine is the inscription,
"Santa Ktrina de Sena."[1] While it may be objected by the
hypercritical that the first two of these examples are not

---

[1] Two Catherines figure in art and legend: the St. Catherine of Alexandria, whose symbol, the spiked wheel of martyrdom, makes her always
readily recognised in the numerous pictures where she appears ; and the
St. Catherine of Siena of the present picture.

names at all, they fairly come within the scope of our remarks, as they are fully equal to them as a means of identification of those to whom they refer.

In Benozzo Gozzoli's picture of the Virgin and Child, surrounded by angels and saints, the various nimbi are circular plates of gold, and in every case the name of the wearer is painted in black upon it.[1] In Ludovico da Parma's picture of St. Hugh, a Bishop of Grenoble in the twelfth century, the nimbus is inscribed S·VGO; while, to quote but one other example, the Ecce Homo of Niccolo Alunno, in the glory around the head of the Saviour are the letters YHS.XPS.NAZ., Jesus Christ of Nazareth, and beyond these the inscription, " In nomine Jeu omne genu flect celestium, terrestrium, et inferno." The text in the Vulgate runs as follows : " In nomine Jesu omne genu flectatur, cælestium, terrestrium, et infernorum," At the name of Jesus every knee should bow, of things in heaven, and things in earth, and things under the earth.

We may frequently find the cross within the nimbus, and it is generally supposed that the Person so distinguished is necessarily the second Person of the Trinity. Thus Durandus writes : " But the crown of Christ is represented under the figure of a cross, and is thereby distinguished from that of the saints ; because by the Banner of His cross He gained for Himself the glorification of our Humanity, and for us freedom from our Captivity." The cruciform [2] nimbus is not however exclusively confined to Christ, though it is entirely devoted to Deity.[3] In the " Biblia Sacra " we see, for instance, an illustration of the creation of Adam. All three Persons of the Trinity are present, and all have cruciferous nimbi. In a " Coronation of the Virgin " by Borgognone the diadem is placed upon her head by her Divine Son, the Holy

---

[1] St. John the Baptist, St. Zenobius, St. Peter, St. Dominic, St. Jerome, and St. Francis.

[2] In all references to this subject we find the expression " cruciform nimbus." It is not a particularly happy idea, as it suggests the notion that the nimbus itself is in the form of a cross, instead of containing the cross. Cruciferous would be preferable.

[3] Nevertheless in the picture of the Virgin, St. Jerome, and St. Dominick, by Filippino Lippi, in the National Gallery, the nimbus of St. Jerome is distinctly cruciferous. It is the one exception, so far as we know, to the otherwise invariable rule.

Spirit in the form of the dove hovers over them, while standing behind with extended arms is the eternal Father. In this picture it is the first Person of the Trinity that has a cruciferous nimbus, while Christ has a plain one. In fig. 56 all three Persons of the Trinity are seen with the crossed nimbus. In the Greek Church, on the three visible arms of the cross we find the Omicron, the Omega, and the Nu respectively, signifying I AM; while in the Latin Church we occasionally find the letters R·E·X in token of the sovereignty of God.[1]

Fig. 21.

It is nevertheless true that the cruciferous nimbus is especially devoted to Christ; examples where He is without it, or where others are with it, being comparatively few and far between. Hundreds of examples are so readily to be found in mediæval and modern work, that it is almost needless to give illustrations of a fact so patent.

In fig. 21 the Master is at once distinguished from the disciples by its presence. The illustration is from a MS. of the ninth century. It is interesting too from its adherence

---

[1] " I AM THAT I AM " (Exod. iii. 14). " The Lord is King for ever and ever " (Ps. x. 16).

to the archaic principle, so distinctly seen in much early
work, of making the more important figures larger than the
others. Thus the Christ is the largest of all, the disciples
somewhat smaller, the churlish Pharisee much more insig-
nificant, and least of all the repentant outcast. The whole
story, see Luke vii. 36 *et seq.*, is admirably rendered. Fig.
22 is of much earlier date; it is the obverse of the medal of
which we have seen the reverse in fig. 1. It will be noted
that the legend " Emmanuel " is in characters partly Greek
and partly Latin.

The artists of olden time were quite capable of drawing
an equilateral triangle in a circle, or of dividing a disk into
three equal parts by divergent rays from its centre. A
theory has nevertheless been advanced that oftentimes the
mediæval painters did not in their apparently cruciferous

F<small>IG</small>. 22.

nimbi intend to refer to the cross at all, but that the three
rays that are ordinarily visible were symbolic of the Trinity.
In most cases the head or beard would prevent the fourth
ray of the cross being seen, even if it were there; but undoubtedly in some cases, where the position of the head would
render it visible, it is nevertheless omitted. While we cannot
dismiss the matter by assuming that the artist carelessly
overlooked the necessity in such cases of indicating the much
or little of the fourth arm that became visible, it certainly
seems curious that, if a suggestion of the Trinity were intended, the three arms should not be placed at the divergent angles that geometrical construction calls for in the
equal division of a circle into three parts. Theologically and
symbolically the idea of perfect equality is not adequately
expressed by a construction that divides a circle into two
quarters and one half.

Sometimes rays of equal dimensions spread equally, so that

the bounding line would be a circle; but at other times the
rays from the crown of the head and from the temples are
more pronounced, while the intermediate rays fall gradually
away. In this case the bounding line used would be a lozenge
with concave sides. At other times the circle is entirely
absent, and we get only these three clusters of rays; [1] or
the circle is present, and while the majority of the rays
stop at its circumference, these three groups stretch beyond
it. These clustering rays from their position naturally
suggest the cross form again, and are no doubt often distinctly intended to do so.

In Fra Angelico's interesting picture of "Christ surrounded by Angels," some of the figures, instead of nimbi,
have rays of light of varying length, a very early example
of the absence of the bounding circle. In later work, instead of the nimbus, we get a halo of light; as for example
in the " Christus Consolator " of Ary Scheffer, or the faint
gleam around the head of Christ in the " Flight into Egypt "
of Rubens. The illuminant power of the nimbus, an idea
full of poetry and admirably expressive of the " Light of the
world " is beautifully introduced in Correggio's " Adoration
of the Shepherds " at Dresden, and in the works of Raphael
and others, where the nimbus is an actual source of light in
the composition.

In late work the nimbus, if shown at all, becomes a mere
golden line, as in fig. 23, and instead of being a flat circular
form becomes amenable to the laws of perspective, and
more or less elliptical, as influenced by the position of the
head, until in the case of a directly side view of the head
it becomes almost or quite a straight line. The " Christian
Martyr " of Delaroche (fig. 24) affords us a good example
of this later treatment. In the " Holy Family " by Andrea
del Sarto in the National Gallery, the Virgin so nearly
faces us that the golden line of the glory is almost circular;
while Elizabeth, being almost in profile, shows in her nimbus the close approximation to the simple straight line.
In a picture in our National Collection by Cosimo Tura of
the " Madonna and Child Enthroned," Christ, the Virgin,
and two angels have nimbi that are just indicated by the

---

[1] A very good example of this may be seen in the " Vision of St.
Augustine " by Garofalo, in the National Gallery.

Fig. 23.

elliptical lines, while four other angels have nimbi as solid
as dinner plates.

In the sixteenth century the nimbus disappears, though
in these later days of art revival and study of ancient work
it is occasionally introduced, and especially in designs for
church glass.   In Holbein's beautiful picture of the Madonna
and Child, the Virgin stands in a niche that has its upper
portion fashioned in the form of a shell, that gives a radiation of line strongly suggestive, and no doubt intentionally
so, of the nimbus.

Fig. 24.

The nimbus adorns the head, while the aureole surrounds
the whole figure.   The aureole appears in art later than the
nimbus and disappears before it; and even when it was a
fully recognised feature, it was a much rarer form.   In the
fifteenth and sixteenth centuries the nimbus, as we have
noted, often lost the hard bounding line seen in earlier
work; and in like manner the aureole became a golden
halo at this period, a glory of simple or of flame-like rays,
or in some instances alternately one and the other.

The aureole is especially devoted to the Deity, though we

Fig. 25.

also find it associated with the Virgin mother when she carries the Holy Child in her arms; or at her assumption, when borne by angels to heaven; or at the last judgment, when she intercedes for the lost and fallen; or when represented as in the apocalyptic vision—" a woman clothed with the sun, and the moon under her feet, and upon her head a crown of twelve stars."

Abundant passages in the Scriptures suggest the idea of the radiance of the Divine glory. Thus at Sinai we read, " the sight of the glory of the Lord was like devouring fire." At the dedication of the Temple "the glory of the Lord filled the house." At the Transfiguration the face of Christ, St. Matthew tells us, " did shine as the sun, and His raiment was white as the light "; while St. Mark says that " His raiment became shining, exceeding white as snow, so as no fuller on earth can whiten them." St. John in his glorious vision saw the Christ with eyes as flame of fire, with feet as if in glowing furnace, with countenance as the sun shining in His strength.[1]

The aureole is often, when in the form of a pointed ellipse, called the " vesica piscis." We may see it in fig. 25, the screen of Hereford Cathedral, where the central figure is thus surrounded. It is also sometimes termed the "Divine oval," or the " mystical almond." The generic name aureole is however preferable, as it includes all the other forms.[2] Sometimes when the figure is represented as sitting, the aureole takes the form of a circle or a quatrefoil; or instead of being a geometric figure at all, it may be a mass of aërial vapour bounded by a waved and irregular line, or a glowing nebulous splendour fading imperceptibly away. In fig. 26, the Annunciation, by Fra Angelico, the Father and the Holy Spirit have both nimbus and aureole.

Very good examples of the ichthus or vesica piscis may

---

[1] When the worn and wearied exile saw the brightness of the glory, the vision of the splendour of God, he fell at His feet as dead, even as did St. Paul when the great light shone from heaven upon his path. It is hence most natural to express our sense of deep humility by some such symbolic action as prostration or kneeling. The Romans always covered their heads in the presence of their deities. The Jewish veiling during their devotions is another example.

[2] By Vasari and other Italian writers on art, the form is called the mandola or mandorla, from its similarity in shape to the almond.

be. seen in the picture of the Virgin and Child by Margari-
tone in the National Gallery, and in the picture by
Emmanuel, in the same collection, of St. Cosmas and
Damianus.   It was more especially in use in the Græco-
Byzantine school, to which the two painters just referred
to belonged; but we also find it in works of the later Italian

FIG. 26.

school, as in the "Sts. Anthony and George" of Pisano, or
the "Beato Ferretti" of Carlo Crivelli, both also in the
National Collection.   The Flemish painters, who comparatively rarely introduce the nimbus, equally seldom employ
the vesica, though it may occasionally be seen.
    We frequently, as in fig. 26, find both nimbus and aureole
employed; thus in the "Speculum Humanæ Salvationis,"
we may see a figure of Christ surrounded by the elliptical

aureole and the head crowned with the cruciferous nimbus. In the "Trinità" of Pesellino, in the National Gallery, the figure of the crucified Christ has again both nimbus and aureole. In the "Ascension" in the "Benedictionale" of Ethelwold, the risen Lord is crowned with cruciferous nimbus again, and enveloped in the radiant aureole. In the frescoes of Francesco da Volterra in the Campo Santa at Pisa, illustrating the history of Job, the eternal Father is more than once represented with both these accessories and symbols of power and glory. In the fresco of the last judgment at Pisa, Christ and the Virgin are side by side, and surrounded by equal and similar aureoles.

While in the work of the architect, sculptor, and metal worker the aureole, as in the screen at Hereford Cathedral, is necessarily bounded by definite lines, a characteristic also of the earlier paintings, it is often in later work an indefinite flood of golden glory, a luminous nebula. In a curious old mosaic at Rome, God interposes it as a solid shield to protect Moses and Aaron from the violence threatened by Korah and his company. In late art, as in fig. 5, adoring cherubs often form an encircling aureole. We may see a good example of this in a picture in the National Gallery of the Madonna and Child by an unknown painter of the Umbrian school. In the Madonna di Foligno of Raphael the seated Virgin and Child are placed within a circular aureole beyond the circumference of which are clustering cherubim; while in his Madonna di S. Sisto the stiffness of the line is wholly absent, and the glorious central group is surrounded by these radiant forms. In the "Assumption of the Virgin," one of Murillo's most celebrated works in the Louvre, a step further is reached; all suggestion of an aureole has vanished, though the Virgin has a glory of golden rays around her head, and the attendant cherubim float in happy freedom around the glorified Virgin. In the early legends and apocryphal gospels, such as the " Gospel of the Infancy," we find many suggestions that doubtless influenced the painters of a later age. Thus we read that the cave of the Nativity "was filled with light more beautiful than the glittering of lamps, brighter than the light of the sun. When the blessed Mary had entered it, it became all light with brightness." " Quando Christus natus est corpus ejus resplenduit ut sol quando oritur."

CHAPTER V.

The Cross—Morbid cross-worship—The Tau or anticipatory Cross—
Crux ansata—The blood on the Lintel—Special cognizance of St.
Anthony—Latin Cross—Greek Cross—Cruciform ground-plans—
Passion Cross—Cross of the Resurrection—Cross of Lorraine—
Triple Cross of the Popes—Deviation of line of Chancel from that of
Nave, the Reason—The multitudinous Variations of the Cross in
Heraldry—The prefatory Cross in Charters—Dedication or Conse-
cration Crosses—Legend tracing the Cross from the Tree of Life—
The wood of the Cross—The "Invention of the Cross"—The
Crucifix—Cross of St. Andrew—Celtic Crosses—Passion Symbols
—Destruction at the Reformation—The Chalice—Stigmata—The
Crown of Thorns—Symbols of Time and Death—The Scythe and
Hour-glass—The Skeleton.—The Dance of Death—God's Acre—
The broken Column—The Urn—Dust and Ashes.

THE cross, erewhile, like the gallows or the guillotine, the
symbol of the doom of the malefactor, has by the sacrifice
of Calvary become the symbol of sublime abnegation, of
Divine pity for the lost and sorrowing sons of men. Hence
for evermore it is no longer the badge of shame, but the
emblem of triumph and eternal hope; and what to the
Roman of old was a sign of infamy has by its association
with the Saviour of mankind become the symbol of victory.[1]

---

[1] By a natural tendency of the human mind, a certain morbid state of
feeling has from time to time arisen, and the honour due to the Saviour
has been largely transferred to the instrument of His sufferings. Thus
in a mediæval MS. of devotions we find the lines:

> " Sainte vraie Croix aouree,
> Qui du corps Dieu fus aournee
> Et de son saint sanc enluminee
> Par ta uertu, par ta puissance
> Deffent mon corps de meschance."

The French is somewhat difficult to follow. The lines would read, in
English: " True and holy Cross adored, adorned with the body of God,

It glitters on the crown of the monarch (fig. 27), while the crosses of St. George, St. Andrew, and St. Patrick form our national ensign. It crowns alike the loftiest spires of Christendom and the lowliest parish churches. It marks the resting-place of the departed who have died in faith in its efficacy; and it is the sign in baptism of their admission

Fig. 27.

to the kingdom of the Crucified. Hence the cross has become one of the most familiar of symbols throughout the whole range of Christian art.

Fig. 28.

The **T** or Tau cross (fig. 28) is sometimes termed the anticipatory or type cross, the cross of the Old Testament. It was the symbol of eternal life with the ancient Egyptians,

and brightened with His sacred blood, by thy virtue and thy power, defend me from evil."

In another book of prayers we find the same feeling still more strongly exhibited :

"O crux gloriosa. O crux admiranda. O lignum preciosum. O admirabile signum, per quod diabolus est victus, et mundus cristi sanguine redemptus, que sola fuisti mater cristi et redemptoris. O lignum dulces clauos dulce pondus sustinens que digna fuisti portare presium huius seculi. Crux domini sit mecum. Crux sicut vidi. Crux sit salus. Crux sicut ripa. Crux mihi prodest protector et adiutorium in presenti et in futuro et in secula seculorum."

and as such was borne by Thoth. On an Egyptian mummy
wrapping we have seen the dead man painted lying on a
couch, while above him a winged figure hovers, bearing in

FIG. 29.

one hand the hieroglyphic symbol for Breath, and in the
other the Tau, or *crux ansata*, as it is sometimes termed,
the hieroglyphic for Life. On a wall-painting may be seen
the monarch worshipping before Thoth, while the god pours

over him from a vessel in his hand what at first sight appears to be a thin line or stream of water, but which is seen on a closer investigation to be a series of these symbols, the gift, in answer to the prayers of the king, of eternal life. In fig. 29, also from an Egyptian source, we have a very similar rendering. The Greeks adopted it in a 'like sense, and the early Christians of Egypt at first used it instead of other forms of cross. In the early Christian sepulchres throughout Egypt and the great oasis numerous examples may yet be seen; and it has been urged, with at least great probability, that this symbol of life was the form made by the children of Israel in blood upon their door-posts when the angel of death passed through the land of Egypt to smite the first-born of the nation; and it was, maybe, the form of cross on which the brazen serpent in the wilderness was raised.[1] Many of the early basilicas were built on this as a ground-plan, and the symbol is found in the catacombs of Rome. Tertullian writes, " hæc est litera Græcorum T, nostra autem T, species crucis."

FIG. 30.

The Tau cross is the especial emblem of St. Anthony, and on the institution in 1352, by Albert II. of Bavaria, of the order of the Knights of St. Anthony, the members of the order wore a golden collar made in the form of a hermit's girdle, and suspended from it a stick cut like a crutch, the Tau cross of the saint.

Though St. Paul, Justin Martyr, Tertullian, Chrysostom, and other Fathers of the early Church made many trium-

---

[1] In Ezek. ix. 4–6, we read of a mark being set upon the foreheads of those that sigh for the abominations committed in the land, and of the instructions to the destroying angel: " Slay utterly old and young : . . . but come not near any man upon whom is the mark." In an enamel of the thirteenth century, where this is represented, the faithful are marked with the Tau. In a sermon by Bishop Andrews on this text we read, " This reward is for those whose foreheads are marked with Tau."

phant references to the cross, it was not till the fifth century that it began to appear in art, the monogram of Christ having till that time been exclusively used. The first occurrence is in a mosaic at Ravenna, and the date is about 440.

When the lower portion of the upright piece is longer than the rest, as in fig. 30, it is termed the Latin cross; when all four arms are equal, as in fig. 31, it is the Greek cross. At first both forms were used indiscrimatingly in each Church, and each form may be found in the catacombs. The church of the Holy Apostles at Constantinople was cruciform in ground-plan, the nave being somewhat longer than the upper part; for, as Procopius very explicitly states, "the western nave is longer than the choir by all the extent

Fig. 31.

necessary to constitute a cross of crucifixion or Latin cross." The Latin cross suggests the actual form, while the Greek cross is idealized; the Romans being an essentially matter of fact people, and the Greeks equally essentially an artistic and poetic race.

The Latin cross is also termed the cross of Calvary, or the Passion cross. The cross of the Resurrection is often placed in the hands of the risen Christ. It is ornate in character, and ordinarily bears a banner attached. The cross is sometimes represented as made of branches, in reference to such passage as that in the Acts of the Apostles, where Peter declares, "The God of our fathers raised up Jesus, whom ye slew and hanged on a tree"; and elsewhere, "Who His own self bare our sins in His own body on the tree." Sometimes instead of rugged branches the cross is idealized, and represented as bearing leaves and fruit.

On the cross of Calvary was nailed a scroll bearing an inscription, and, suggested by this, the Latin cross has occasionally, as in fig. 32, a double cross piece. This is the cross of Lorraine and of the Knights Hospitallers. It is a form constantly seen in Greek and Byzantine art, and dates from a very early period. The pope has borne before him a triple cross, cardinals and archbishops have the double form, and the single cross is devoted to the bishops.

FIG. 32.

In the " Descent from the Cross," by Quentin Matsys, the central cross is of the Latin form, while those on either side are of the Tau type. In the " Crucifixion," by Antonello da Messina, in the museum at Antwerp, Christ has a well-formed cross, while the malefactors on either side are bound on rough trees that are not at all cruciform in character.

When the basilica form was gradually abandoned, there was a general adoption of the Latin cross in the West, and of the Greek cross in the East, as the ground-plan. The Church of the Holy Sepulchre was made circular, a natural arrangement in that particular instance, as the traditional site of the actual sepulchre of our Lord thus became the central point; and all other circular churches in Europe were suggested by this, and had in themselves but little appropriateness of form. The Latin cross may be very well seen in the ground-plans of the cathedrals of Santiago di Compostella, in Spain; of Siena and Florence, in Italy; of Cologne, in Germany; of Elgin, in Scotland; of Lincoln, Rochester, Salisbury, and many other cathedrals and churches, both in the United Kingdom and abroad.

In the early churches a cross was frequently inlaid in the design of the pavement, part of it running into the chancel, the arms passing down the centre of each transept, and the rest along the middle of the nave; but a solemn anathema was pronounced at the second Œcumenical Council on those who should tread the sacred symbol under foot, and the custom of placing the cross where it could be thus trampled on at once ceased.

In many churches a slight deviation in the chancel from the line of direction of the nave may be found. It is very clearly marked in the cathedrals of York and Lichfield, and in many large parish churches. It symbolises the inclination

Fig. 33.

Fig. 34.

Fig. 35.

Fig. 36.

Fig. 37.

of the Saviour's head upon the cross. While generally to the south, it is not unfrequently toward the north, no rule of practice having been laid down in favour of either.

Not a few churches are dedicated to the cross. The cathedral of Orleans is that of the Sainte Croix, while at Florence we find the Santa Croce. Other instances are St. Cross at Winchester and the Scottish Holyrood.

Unless distinctly stated to the contrary, the various crosses of heraldry have arms of equal length. The shape of the shield would naturally render this the more convenient form, and as by far the greater number of these devices originated with the wars of the cross, the crusaders in their eastward wanderings would naturally come under Greek influence. Engrafted upon the original Greek cross, the heralds have produced great variation of detail.[1] Examples of ten of these are given in figs. 33–42. Dame Juliana Berners, at a time when blazonry was comparatively simple, declares in her "Boke of St. Albans" that "crossis innumerabull are borne dayli"; while Legh, another old writer,

FIG. 38.   FIG. 39.   FIG. 40.   FIG. 41.   FIG. 42.

affirms, "You bring in so many crosses, and of so sundry fashions, that you make me in a maner werye of them." Berry's "Encyclopædia Heraldica" enumerates and figures 385 varieties, but many of these are seldom employed.[2]

---

[1] Such as the cross pommée, where the ends terminate in circles, suggestive, as the name shows, of apples ; the cross fleurie, where the extremities end in forms like the fleur-de-lys ; the cross-crosslet, where each arm is itself crossed, as in figs. 41, 43, together with other forms, moline, recercelée, patonce, botonée, clechée, patée, and multitudinous other examples that may be found duly set forth in any good book on heraldry.

[2] Heraldry is largely symbolic ; but, interesting as the subject is, it would be impossible to deal with it adequately here. Our companion volume, "The History, Principles, and Practice of Heraldry," goes fully into the matter.

On early deeds and charters we often find the subject matter prefaced with a cross as a pledge that its contents are just and true, or in other cases having a dedicatory or invocatory meaning.[1]

Fig. 43.

[1] On the back of an ivory diptych, still preserved, the following inscription, dating A.D. 772, may be seen: " ✠ Let us stand well. ✠ Let us stand with reverence. ✠ Let us stand with fear. Let us attend upon the holy oblation, that in peace we may make the offering to God. The mercy, the peace, the sacrifice of praise, the love of God and of the Father and of our Saviour Jesus Christ be upon us, Amen. In the first year of Adrian, patriarch of the city. Remember, Lord, thy servant John, the least priest of the church of St. Agatha. Amen. ✠ Remember, Lord, thy servant Andrew Machera. Holy Mother of God ; holy Agatha. ✠ Remember, Lord, thy servant and our pastor Adrian the patriarch. ✠ Remember, Lord, thy servant, the sinner, John the priest."

We now turn to dedication or consecration crosses. Those who are at all interested in the subject will doubtless have observed crosses carved or painted on the walls of various old churches. These are known as dedication crosses, and they were placed at the various spots touched by the bishop while performing the ceremony of consecration. Very few dedicatory crosses of the Norman period are now extant, though they may be seen in the churches at Wiston, Ditteridge, Barfreston, and some few other places; but many crosses of later date and of varied and elegant design may be found.

In a consecration service of the eleventh century we find that an important part of the ceremony was the anointing of the walls with oil of chrism at various points in the building, and it was the custom to mark the places before-hand with the cross. A MS. of the sixteenth century in the British Museum shows us the bishop in the act of anointing one of these crosses. Injudicious restoration and wall-scraping have unfortunately destroyed many of these interest-ing relics of the past. Ordinarily three were placed on the north, south, east, and west walls respectively, both inside the building and out, thus making a total of twenty-four. The following extract from the old writer Durandus explains their significance and use. It will be seen that he refers to twelve instead of twenty-four, as his description clearly refers to the interior of the church alone. " Next when the Altar hath been anointed with chrism, the twelve crosses painted on the walls of the church are also anointed. The crosses themselves be painted, first, as a terror to evil spirits, that they, having been driven from thence, may be terrified when they see the Sign of the Cross, and may not presume to enter there again; secondly, as a mark of triumph, for crosses be the Banners of Christ, the Signs of His triumph. Crosses therefore are with reason painted there, that it may be made manifest that that place hath been subdued to the dominion of Christ. For even in the pomp of an earthly Sovereign it is customary when any city hath been yielded for the imperial Standard to be set up in it. The twelve lights placed before these crosses signify the twelve apostles who have illumined the whole world by the Faith of the Crucified, and whose teaching hath dispelled the darkness. Wherefore the crosses on the four walls of the Church are lighted up and anointed with chrism, because the apostles preaching the mystery of the Cross have by the Faith of Christ illumined the four quarters of the earth with knowledge, have lighted them up unto love, have anointed them unto purity of conscience, which is signified by the oil, and unto the Savour of a good reputation, which is signified by the balsam."

Old legends tell us that after the expulsion from Eden Adam begged for a seed of the tree of life. The request was granted, we are told, though this involves a direct contradiction of the Biblical narrative.[1] The tree that sprang from this seed was held in great honour, and its wood was preserved in Solomon's temple; but the queen of Sheba, apparently wiser for once than the great king, told him that He who should hereafter one day be slain upon that tree would by His death cause the destruction of Jerusalem. Solomon therefore, missing the obvious idea of having it burnt to ashes, had it removed and deeply buried in the earth. The Pool of Siloam sprang from it, and owed its healing virtues to it; but when the hour of the crucifixion drew nigh, the trunk floated to the surface, and as it seemed a useful piece of timber, it was drawn out of the water, and was presently used for the cross!

According to Sir John Maundeville, who travelled much over Europe and the Holy Land, and wrote his experiences in the year 1371, the cross of our Lord was made of four kinds of trees. The piece that went upright from the earth to the head was of cypress, and the cross-piece was of palm; the stock that stood in the ground, to which the upright was fastened, was of cedar, while the tablet bearing the inscription was of olive. The reason he gives is that the Jews were of so vindictive a mind that they determined that the victim of their hatred should hang upon the cross for ever, therefore they chose cedar for the foot, because of its lasting qualities; the cypress was selected from its pleasant

---

[1] "Behold, the man is become as one of Us, to know good and evil: and now, lest he put forth his hand, and take also of the tree of life, and eat. and live for ever : therefore the Lord God sent him forth from the garden of Eden. . . . And He placed at the east of the garden cherubims, and a flaming sword, . . . to keep the way of the tree of life" (Gen. iii. 22–24).

fragrance, as a corrective of the results of dissolution; the palm was chosen because it is an emblem of victory, in sign of their triumph; while the tablet was of olive, the emblem of peace, because they held that Christ had made discord and brought trouble to the nation, and that His death would restore to them political and religious concord.

If we are to credit tradition, Isaac, in carrying the wood for his sacrifice, held it in the form of a cross upon his shoulders, and therefore the angel was sent to rescue him from death; while the widow of Sarepta, in carrying home her two sticks, had them cross-wise, and thus received the blessing of the prophet, the restoration of her son to life,

Fig. 44.

and an inexhaustible supply of oil and meal: stories which, despite their morbid and extravagant character, and their wild impossibility, are at least a testimony to the honour and virtues ascribed to the cross.

According to the old writers, the cross was found, deeply buried in the ground, at Jerusalem, some three hundred years after the crucifixion, or, to be as absolutely precise as the legend, on May 3rd, A.D. 328. Hence this date was commemorated as the "Invention of the Cross." The word, of course, comes from the Latin *invenio*, to come upon or discover, though most of our readers doubtless will be fully prepared to accept the word in its more familiar sense, and regard the whole tale as very much indeed of an invention.

The discovery was made by St. Helena. All three crosses were found, but that of our Lord was at once discriminated from those of the thieves who were crucified with Him, because a woman who was grievously sick was immediately

Fig. 45.

restored to health on touching it, while a dead body laid upon it returned to life! The custom of crossing one's self was first practised by the Christians about A.D. 110, thereby to distinguish themselves from the pagans around, and as a sign of recognition amongst themselves.

The crucifix is the most materialized of the symbols of
the cross, and often develops into a mere representation of
acute physical suffering, that, whatever aid to faith it may
be to some who gaze upon it, is dishonouring to the Saviour
in its repulsive dwelling upon one side alone, and that the
least, of His great sacrifice. The agony of the cross was
not the smart of bodily pain, but the burden of the sins of
the whole race of mankind.

FIG. 46.   FIG. 47.

The cross of St. Andrew, as in fig. 44, the badge of the
Order of the Thistle, is shaped like the letter X, though it
was not till the fifteenth century that it was so represented.
One may just notice in passing the grotesque contrast between the suffering saint of God, the lowly follower of the
Prince of peace, and the aggressive and self-asserting motto
that surrounds the whole.

Early tradition affirms that St. Andrew was crucified on
a cross of the ordinary form, but with his body extended
horizontally. Like St. Peter, he deemed it far too great an

honour to be crucified as was his Lord; and he therefore gained from his persecutors the concession of being fixed sideways, while St. Peter was crucified head downwards. We may see this very well in fig. 45, "The Crucifixion of St. Peter," by Guido Reni, in the Vatican. Tradition has it that this form of cross appeared in the sky to Achaius, king of the Scots, the night before a great battle with Athelstane, and being victorious, he went barefoot to the church of St. Andrew, and vowed to adopt his cross as the national device. In Scottish heraldry St. Andrew's cross, as we may see in the Union Jack, is argent on a field azure.

Fig. 48.

The crucifixion of St. Peter has been a somewhat favourite subject with painters. A very good example may be seen in the church of the Carmine at Florence, by Filippino Lippi, and another by Guido Reni, in the Vatican.

Very early examples of the cross form, as in figs. 46, 47, may be seen in the sculptured Celtic crosses of Great Britain and Ireland. They are ordinarily found thickly covered with interlacing; but when figure subjects are introduced the scenes and incidents are generally those of the Bible. The cross at Clonmacnois, in Ireland, is called the Cross of the Scriptures, in an entry in the annals of Tigernach, dated 1060. The monuments themselves are more or less cruciform, and the cross also often enters as a detail into the ornament. Fig. 48 is the ancient Danish jewel known as the Dagmar Cross.

Besides the cross we meet also with other forms that are known as the Passion symbols. These are chiefly found in the wood-carving and stained glass of the fifteenth century, though even as early as the tenth century they may occasionally be seen. Such early examples are however distinctly exceptional. Like many other things, they were held, with more or less of reason, to be of superstitious tendency; and at the time of the Reformation, and again during the Commonwealth, a very clean sweep indeed was made of all such objects, so that only comparatively few examples now remain.[1]

Such symbols include the ladder, the dice, seamless robe, the cock, spear, sword, the thirty pieces of silver,[2] pincers, hammer, pillar, scourge, reed and sponge, the nails, and crown of thorns. Good examples may be seen at Bishop Lydiard church in Somersetshire, Swaffham church in Norfolk, Mildenhall in Wiltshire, Horsham church in

---

[1] The following document relating to the zeal of the Scottish Reformers is a good illustration of this :

"To our traist friendis, the Lairds of Arntilly and Kinvaid.

"Traist friends, after maist harty commendacion, we pray yow faill not to pass incontinent to the kyrk of Dunkeld, and tak down the haill images thereof, and bring furth to the kyrkzard, and burn thaym oppinly. And siclyk cast down the altaris, and purge the kyrk of all kynd of monuments of idolatrye. And this ye faill not to do, as ze will do us singular empleseur; and so committis yow to the protection of God. From Edinburgh, the xii of August, 1560.

"Faill not, bot ze tak guid heyd that neither the dasks, windocks, nor durris, be ony ways hurt or broken—either glassin wark or iron wark.

"Ar. Ergyll,
"James Stewart,
"Ruthven."

[2] "Titus, the son of Vespasian, laid siege about Jerusalem to overcome the Jews, because they put our Lord to death without the emperor's leave. And when he had won the city he burnt the temple, and beat it down and all the city, and took the Jews and put to death one million one hundred thousand of them ; and the others he put in prison, and sold them to slavery, thirty for a penny, because they said they bought Jesus for thirty pennies ; and he sold them cheaper, giving thirty for one penny."—Sir John Maundeville.

Sussex, and elsewhere. They are but rarely found on seals; but they occur on that of the Guild of Corpus Christi at Oxford, and on that of the Friars Minors at Cambridge. They are sometimes surrounded with the legend, " Vulnera quinque Dei sint medicina mihi."

Fig. 49.

On an Italian picture frame containing a representation of the scourging of our Lord we notice the introduction of the following symbols : two staves and the sword of St. Peter, torch and lantern, bag of money, faggots for making the fire at which St. Peter stood and warmed himself, the crowing cock, the pillar of scourging, two scourges, a chain for binding the hands to the pillar, the seamless coat, the purple robe, the reed-sceptre and thorny crown, the basin and ewer used by Pilate, the cross, the cup of wine mingled with myrrh, the dice, the three nails, hammer, pincers, ladder, sponge, lance, winding sheet, spices in a vase, the chalice, and rope and chain for the deposition of the body from the cross.

Pope Innocent VI. (1352–1362) affirmed in a decree that "the lance and nails and other instruments of the Passion are everywhere to be held in reverence of all Christ's faithful

Fig. 50.

people," and he instituted in their honour a religious festival, the Feast of the Lance and Nails.

The finest existing series in England is on the bosses of the vaulting in the choir of Winchester Cathedral, a roof erected by Bishop Fox in the early part of the sixteenth century; and a very good foreign example will be found on the bridge of St. Angelo at Rome, where the colossal statues of angels bear the various instruments of the Passion. These symbols were often introduced on the vestments and hangings; thus in one of the old church inventories that supply us with so much that is interesting and valuable, we find the item "ij steyned clothes for above and beneathe w^t the tokenis of the passyon in tyme of lent w^t ij curtyns accordyng to ye same"; and many other references of like nature might be added. In the picture of St. Dominic, by Zoppo, in the National Gallery, we may see Christ in glory surrounded by angels, each bearing one of the Passion symbols.

The chalice (fig. 49) and the crown of thorns (fig. 50) are frequently introduced to the exclusion of all the other Passion symbols, the latter especially being freely employed. In the picture by De Bles in the National Gallery, entitled "Mount Calvary," we see three angels receiving in chalices the sacred streams flowing from the wounded body of the Saviour.[1]

The crown of thorns, though essentially connected with the sufferings of our Lord, is also an attribute of St. Francis of Assisi, St. Catherine of Siena, and one or two other less well-known saints. It was a favourite subject for legend in mediæval times that certain men and women of peculiar holiness, desirous to share the sufferings of Christ, were so highly favoured of heaven as to be permitted to bear in their own bodies the *stigmata*, the signs of the sufferings of their crucified Lord, some bearing all the marks and others one or more of them. Thus several bore the scar of the spear wound in their sides, others the lacerations of the thorny crown, and others again the marks in the palms of their

---

[1] The necessary association of the chalice with the commemoration of the Lord's Supper gives it naturally a prominent place. Those who would care to see to what morbid lengths the human imagination may go may turn to a book written some two hundred years ago and entitled, "The School of the Eucharist, established upon the miraculous respects and acknowledgments, which beasts, birds, and insects have rendered to the Holy Sacrament of the Altar, whence Catholicks may increase in devotion towards this divine mystery, and hereticks find there their confusion." The following headings to a few of the stories will give an idea of the contents of this extraordinary volume: Bees adore the Host, and sing the Divine praises, dividing themselves into two quires—A lamb of St. Coleta kneeled at the elevation during the Masse—A Spider revenges an affront done to the Sacrament—Asses honour the Sacrament—Ducks are present at Masse—The admirable vigilancy and devoires of a dog in honour of the Sacrament—A pigeon brings to the Host to communicate one newly converted to the faith.

hands or on their feet of the nail prints.   The stigmatization
of St. Francis by the angel as he kneels in rapture on the
ground is a favourite subject with the older painters : such
marks, whoever may be the saint bearing them, are ordinarily surrounded by a halo of golden rays.

The *corona radiata* is a representation or suggestion of the
golden rays of Helios, a symbol of divine effulgence and of

Fig. 51.

the favour of the gods, that on the deification of the emperor
took the place in later Rome of the earlier laurel-wreath
of mundane glory.   An example of this latter may be seen
in fig. 51, the laureated head of Tiberius.   It has been
suggested that the crown of thorns was a mockery of the
radiate diadem assumed by the Roman emperors when they
arrogated to themselves both divine and human kingship.
While doubtless an instrument of physical suffering, it was
probably intended, like the purple robe, rather as an instru-

ment of moral suffering in scornful derision of the kingly claim, and brutal parody of the imperial insignia. The first representation, so far as is at present known, of Christ crowned with thorns will be found in the catacomb of Prætextatus in Rome, where the spiked and thorny wreath encircling the head of the Saviour has distinctly given to it the radiate character of the classic and imperial nimbus-like diadem.

In the frontispiece of the "Eikon Basilike," A.D. 1648, we see the king, Charles I., taking in his hand a crown of thorns, inscribed "Gratia." At his feet is the royal crown of England, marked "Vanitas," while in the air above is a starry crown marked "Gloria." Beyond we have a landscape, in which a palm tree bears a conspicuous position in the foreground, while several other emblems are introduced that we need not here dwell upon. Beneath is the "Explanation of the Embleme," in two columns, one being in Latin and the other in English. The portion that at present concerns us runs as follows:

> " That sp'endid but yet toilsom Crown
> Regardlessly I trample down.
> With joie I take this Crown of thorn,
> Though sharp, yet easy to be born.
> That heavenlie Crown already mine,
> I view with eies of Faith divine.
> I slight vain things and do embrace
> Glorie, the just reward of grace."

We now proceed to consider the various symbols of mortality.

At the Reformation a clean sweep was made of all pictures suggestive of the old creed. In the third year of the reign of Edward VI. an injunction was issued ordering all pictures in churches not hitherto disturbed to be either destroyed if movable or defaced if fixed; and it became penal, by fine or imprisonment, to possess, even privately, pictures of this forbidden nature. In 1558, after the accession of Elizabeth, the law was made still more stringent, and the various church officers were required to certify their obedience to the law; thus at Thorpe, in Lincolnshire, for instance, to give but one example out of many, we find the following entry: " Item, we had noe Roode nor other Imageis but that were painted on the wall, and thei we defaced and put oute."

The coats of whitewash being altogether too frigid-looking, and moreover presenting a tempting surface for renewed decoration, it became necessary to see what could be substituted for the obliterated work, that should have teaching value, without being illegal, and we find that figures of Time and Death were largely introduced.

The lapse of years, the damp that is often a conspicuous feature in old churches, and more especially " restoration," as it is termed, have played havoc with these ancient wall paintings; but in an old poem by Cowper, entitled " An Elegy wrote in a Country Church," we get many interesting details as to the furniture and arrangements of a village church. We quote three of the stanzas that bear on our subject.

> " Tho' Painting her Italian Pencil here
>   Has never dip'd, yet on that Western Wall
> Two formidable Powers allied appear,
>   Which shew Man's Rise, his Progress, and his Fall.
>
> To ev'ry Act of Duty to persuade,
>   On these two Forms the Preacher turns his Looks,
> Points to thy Scythe, O Time, or, Death, thy Spade,
>   And makes mere painted Stones affecting Books.
>
> When from God's Word he proves that Time shall cease,
>   And Death must to Eternity consign,
> He to the Hour-Glass points, and cries : ' Heaven's Peace
>   To gain, this Hour alone is truly thine ! ' "

Time is ordinarily represented as an old man, naked or but slightly clothed, and quite bald, with the exception of a single lock of hair on the forehead. In "King John" Shakespeare calls him "that bald sexton, Time" ; and we are all familiar with the occasional necessity of " taking Time by the forelock." In his hand he holds a scythe, or in one hand a scythe and in the other an hour-glass. In an engraving by Bernard, executed in 1560, Time has scythe and crutches, and in some few cases he is represented as winged.

> " Gather ye rosebuds while ye may,
>   Old Time is still a-flying."—HERRICK.

Though in later days Time and Death have been associated together, and the symbols they bear freely interchanged, in earlier days they were never represented as necessary companions. Time was associated with ideas of growth and life, rather than with destruction and decay. Time in the Greek Church was young and unbearded, while Death was a noble and angelic form, as in the Campo Santo at Pisa, and it was centuries before it changed to the ghastly skeleton that it afterwards became.

In the later figures of Death the skeleton forms are often horribly badly drawn, the bones incorrect in form, the articulations with no vestige of anatomical accuracy. So grotesquely horrible indeed are the forms, that it has even been

Fig. 52.

suggested that in many cases the bad drawing was not the result of ignorance, but of a deliberate intention to make the forms more repulsive.

In figs. 52, 53, 54, we have good illustrations of this mediæval treatment of the subject. Such drawings, illustrating the all-conquering power of Death, are very commonly to be met with. We give but three of these: the warrior with uplifted sword, himself succumbing to the fate that many others have suffered at his hands; the student poring over his books, mocked by the gift of the Elixir Vitæ

at the hands of Death ; and the wealthy dame, who awakens
suddenly to the fact that her life of ease and dignity is over,
and that her next step is to the edge of the grave.

The Dance of Death was a favourite mediæval subject.
Well-known examples may be seen at Basel, Lucerne, and
elsewhere.   In these we often see the scythe and hourglass
attributed to Death.   In Holbein's Dance of Death more than
half of the skeleton figures have one or other or both of these
emblems assigned to them ; and we may see the scythe again

Fig. 53.

in the work of Orcagna, in Titian's " Triumph of Death,"
and in many illustrations in the old MSS.   Figures of Death
as a skeleton are frequently introduced in the sepulchral
brasses of the sixteenth and seventeenth centuries ; and on
the older gravestones in many churchyards one finds a free
use made of skulls, cross-bones, and other such-like emblems
of mortality.   Much of the religious writing of that period
busied itself in representing the weakness, sinfulness, and
misery of man, and men were goaded heavenwards by fiery
denunciations and glowing descriptions of the torments of

the unregenerate.[1]   Even the gentle Jeremy Taylor made the key-note of his "Holy Dying," "He that would die well must always look for Death, every day knocking at the gates of the grave"; and the cross-bones on the tombstones are but one indication the more of the prevalent tone of mind.

On many of the rings and other personal adornment of this period these emblems of mortality are freely introduced. The watch of Mary Queen of Scots, for example, was in the form of a skull. On the forehead was a small figure of

FIG. 54.

Death standing between a palace and a cottage, and around it the passage from Horace, " Palida Mors æquo pulsat pede pauperum tabernas regumque turres."

---

[1] " All Adam's offspring through his sinne are made sinfull, not by imitation only, but by propagation, receiving the contagion of sin and uncleannesse before they behold the light of this life." " Man is now spoiled of freedome of will, and made subject to miserable bondage." " Out of the corrupt nature of man proceedeth nothing but what is damnable."—CALVIN.

H

On a mediæval trencher, with device of a skull, we find the lines:

> "Content y¹ felfe wth thyn eftat:
> And fende no poore wight from y¹ gatt:
> For why this councell I ye geue:
> To learne to die and die to lyue";

and in another example, with the same emblem of mortality, the inscription:

> "Truste not this worlde thou wooeful wighte:
> But lett thy ende be in thy fighte."

It was customary in the Middle Ages to provide richly decorated palls to be used at the burial of members of various guilds, and some of these still survive the ravages of Time. In one of these the general black surface is crossed by broad bands of white, and on these are embroidered skulls holding thigh bones in their mouths, scapulæ, ossa innominata, and other portions of the skeleton. Rings too were commonly, when of a memorial character, made in the form of a skeleton, or a skull was placed where we should ordinarily look for the stone or other adornment. Luther used to wear a gold ring with a small death's head in enamel, and the inscription "Mori sæpe cogita." This ring is still preserved at Dresden. It will be remembered too that in "Love's Labour Lost" Biron compares the face of Holofernes to "a Death's face in a ring."

We remember seeing in the "God's acre" at Basel a striking commentary on the truth of the stanza in the noble "Elegy" of Gray:

> "The boast of heraldry, the pomp of power,
> And all that beauty, all that wealth e'er gave,
> Await alike the inevitable hour:
> The paths of glory lead but to the grave."

On one of the tombstones the armorial bearings of the person interred were all duly set forth in their heraldic significance, but behind the shield was carved the figure of Death,[1] and his bony hands had seized the shield with all its testimony of earthly rank and dignity, and had torn it apart from top to bottom. "Sic transit gloria mundi."

---

[1] "An uncouth, hideous thing, nothing but bones."
"Flesh being turned to dust, and bones to sticks."—*George Herbert.*

The idea appeared to us a very striking one, as we came
suddenly upon it in the solitude of this home of the dead.
That the high-born relatives of the deceased should thus
admit the solemn truth for him and for them was perhaps
still more striking, as poor humanity ordinarily clings to
the last to all such distinctions, as we may so abundantly
see in

> " The marble tombs that rise on high,
> Whose dead in vaulted arches lie,
> Whose pillows swell with sculptured stones,
> Arms, angels, epitaphs, and bones :
> These, all the poor remains of state,
> Adorn the rich, or praise the great." [1]

Cowley, in a well-known passage, tells us how "beauty,
and strength, and wit, and wealth, and power," all flourish
and joy in their pre-eminence awhile, but the end is the
same after all ; for—

> " Alas ! Death mows down all with an impartial hand "—

as the reaper with his swinging scythe and steady, onward
step brings to one common fall the useless and noxious weeds,
the gay and brilliant blossoms, and the ripe heads of nodding
corn.

Other familiar symbols of death are the broken column,
and the urn.[2] Both were introduced at the period of the
Renaissance, when anything of classic association was welcomed ; the urn of course referred to the Roman custom of
preserving the ashes after cremation.

St. Jerome and Mary Magdalene are ordinarily represented
as having a skull in their hands or in close proximity to
them ; while St. Eutropius has his cleft with a sword.   St.
Francis of Sales and St. Catherine of Siena are often represented as bearing their hearts in their hands ; and we may
in like manner find SS. Winifred, Valeria, and Regula, Dionysius, Proculus, and Piat carrying their heads about with
them.   The famous healing spring or holy well in Wales is
said to mark the spot where St. Winifred's head fell on her
decapitation.

---

[1] PARNELL : " Night Piece on Death."
[2] " Can storied urn or animated bust
    Back to its mansion call the fleeting breath ? "—GRAY.

The dust and ashes of the penitent are equally symbols of death.

> " Can honour's voice provoke the silent dust,
>   Or flattery soothe the dull, cold ear of death ? "

The frequent Biblical use of the idea amply justifies the association. When man, made in the image of God, fell from his high estate, he learned the sad and solemn truth, " dust thou art, and unto dust shalt thou return." Job in his misery exclaims, " Thou hast made me as the clay: wilt Thou bring me into dust again ? " and elsewhere, " Now shall I sleep in the dust: and thou shalt seek me in the morning, but I shall not be " ; while the writer of Ecclesiastes, dwelling on the vanity of all earthly things, sums up, " then shall the dust return to the earth ": for, as he elsewhere writes, "All are of the dust, and all turn to dust again." The psalmist sings, " All that go down into the dust shall bow before Him," for death is but the threshold of immortality: " Mors janua vitæ." Therefore Isaiah writes, " Awake and sing, ye that dwell in the dust: for the earth shall yield her dead "—the glimmering light of the dawn that bursts into the full glory of the triumphant words of the New Testament: " Now is Christ risen from the dead, and become the firstfruits of them that slept. For since by man came death, by man came also the resurrection of the dead. . . . For this corruptible must put on incorruption, and this mortal must put on immortality." In this radiant vision of coming bliss the Master's gracious welcome is all in all; and in the light of that greeting skulls and cross-bones, scythes and urns, fade away for ever and ever.

CHAPTER VI.

The Soul of Man—as a Little Child—Naked or clothed—The Campo
Santo at Pisa—Soul as Serpent or Bird—Weighing of Souls in the
Balance—Butterfly Symbol—Elijah Depicted as a Type of the
Resurrection—The Torch of Life—Angels—Their Ministry to
God—and to the Saints—The Mystical Vision of Ezekiel—The
Orders of Angels—The Angel of the Mighty Will of God—The
Fallen Angels—The Tempter—The Mediæval Conception of Hell—
The Renaissance Hell—Satan as the Dragon—Dragons and Dragon-
Slayers—Satan as the Serpent—The Serpent as a Talisman—The
Deaf Adder—Serpent as Emblem of Immortality—of Eternity—
Serpent Worship—The Ophites—The Serpents of Goodness and of
Evil—Gnostic Gems—The Krishna of Hindu Mythology.

THE soul of man is usually symbolically depicted as a little
child coming out of the mouth of the dying person, and good
and bad angels are generally present to receive it, and to
contest its possession. It is sometimes naked, at other times
clothed and robed. Naked, for naked came man into the
world, and stripped of all must he return to Mother Earth;
"for when he dieth he shall carry nothing away." [1] When
the soul is clothed, it typifies the robe of Christ's righteousness. "Clothed upon," as St. Paul has it, "that mortality
might be swallowed up of life." Sometimes both soul and
body, the ascending spirit and the dying saint, are represented with the nimbus; while in other examples the soul
issues as a little black imp or fiend.

In the Campo Santo at Pisa will be found a wonderful
series of paintings, that up till the last few years have been
assigned to Orcagna, though it is possible that the ascription
is in fault. Whoever the artist may have been, he was a
man of great artistic power and of vivid imagination. In
the "Triumph of Death," gay and festive groups of ladies
and cavaliers sit beneath the orange trees and amuse them-

---

[1] Ps. xlix. 17; Eccles. v. 15; 1 Tim. vi. 7.

selves with songs and music, while Death approaches with
rapid flight and menacing scythe. At his feet are already
a great host of the departed, some wearing the kingly crown
or the coronet of the princess, some the robes and hat of the
cardinal, or the panoply of steel of the knight. The souls
of these, as they rise, fold their hands in prayer, or shrink
back in horror as they see the fiends awaiting them. On
the one hand, bright angels ascend to heaven with the souls
of some, while others are dragged to a fiery mountain crater,
and flung headlong into the raging flames. In another portion of the picture a crowd of beggars, the maimed, the
blind, and the halt, with outstretched arms call upon Death
to end their sorrows; but their appeal goes unheeded.

In another of these wonderful pictures, "The Last Judgment," the trumpet sounds, and the dead emerge from the
earth, clad in the appropriate dress of their former condition;
and on their rising the angels divide them into two great
companies, the redeemed and the lost.

We remember to have seen an example in Byzantine art
where the soul issues as a serpent from the mouth of the
dying man. It is sometimes also represented as a bird. In
one of the ancient Egyptian funeral tablets in the British
Museum, the spirit of a man is represented as a bird having
a human head; it is being fed with divine food by the
goddess Neith out of the sacred tree in which she stands.
Elsewhere on a mummy-wrapping we find the dead man
pictured, swathed for his burial, while above the lifeless
body hovers his soul in form of a bird (see fig. 55) having
human head and hands. It bears in one hand the hieroglyphic for breath,[1] and in the other the Tau, the hieroglyphic
for life. On another mummy case a man is depicted as
suddenly falling dead to the ground, while above him stands
another erect and with outstretched arms. The mortal man
is painted red; the spiritual man, his risen soul, is blue, the
colour of the sky. In this example, the two figures are the
same size, it is the same being, in spite of the change that
has come over him; but in Christian art examples of this

---

[1] The Egyptian symbol for breath is the sail of a vessel : a happy and
expressive idea, as the sail is inert and useless till quickened by the
breath of the wind, but springs beneath its influence into movement and
service.

identity of size are very rarely encountered, the bold figure of the Saviour in his discourse to Nicodemus, "ye must be born again," naturally suggesting the infant form.

The weighing of the souls in the balance by the archangel Michael is a favourite mediæval subject, and was often depicted on the walls of the churches as a sermon and a warning.[1] Very frequently evil spirits cling to the scale, and endeavour by their weight to depress it in their favour.[2]

FIG. 55.

The Egyptians entertained the belief that the actions of the departed were solemnly weighed before Osiris, and the final condition of the soul determined by the preponderance of the good or the evil. The Babylonians probably held a

---

[1] " On the point of separation of the soul from the body, the good and bad angels come, and the merits and demerits of the man are weighed. The good angel alleges and recites the man's good works, the bad angel calling to memory all the evil ones. And if indeed the bad preponderate, so that he departed in mortal sin, immediately the soul is delivered to the tormentors."—St. GREGORY, A.D. 604.

[2] " Let me be weighed in an even balance, that God may know mine integrity " (Job xxxi. 6).

similar belief, so that the mysterious writing on the wall
during the impious feast of Belshazzar would appear to
them the presage not only of national, but of eternal loss.
"God hath numbered thy kingdom, and finished it. Thou
art weighed in the balances, and found wanting."   With
that awful verdict against him, "in that night was Belshazzar the king slain," slain by his country's foes, while he
was yet under the ban of the Divine displeasure, and in all
that made for righteousness found wanting.

The souls of men are weighed too before Brama in Hindu
art, and by the Muhammadans the archangel Gabriel is
called the "soul-weigher."

The butterfly as a symbol of the soul is but rarely seen in
early work; for though the Greek word for the butterfly and
the spirit of life is the same—*psyche*—yet, owing to the
imperfect idea of all pre-Christian races as to the immortality of the soul, much of the force of the symbol was in
early days lost.   Even in later times, owing to the want of
study of the lower forms of nature, the analogy between
the spirit of life and the butterfly—first appearing as a
creeping, toiling caterpillar, and then, its span of existence
apparently over, burying itself in the earth a seemingly lifeless chrysalis, yet finally at the appointed season the perfect
creature soaring above its tomb into the sunlight,—was not
perceived.

> "Yet wert thou once a worm, a thing that crept
> On the bare earth, then wrought a tomb, and slept.
> And such is man! soon from his cell of clay
> To burst a seraph in the blaze of day."

In some few Greek examples the butterfly is represented
hovering over the dead, and in comparatively modern work
it may not uncommonly be found among us.   We have
already referred to the *Gottesaker* at Basel as supplying a
striking piece of symbolic teaching; and we remember to
have there seen also, sculptured on one of the gravestones,
the shrouded chrysalis and above it the soaring butterfly.

As a symbol of the ascension of Christ, Elijah borne to
heaven in the chariot of fire occurs often in early work.
Many examples may be seen on the tombs of the martyrs of
the early Christian Church.

The torch of life, though originally a pagan conception, is

occasionally introduced into Christian art, and, naturally, is
more especially found where the work is Renaissance in
treatment, and therefore influenced by the old classic ideas
and forms.

Angels, the ministers and messengers of God, are abundantly met with in ancient, mediæval, and modern art, either
in attendance upon the first Person of the Trinity, or the
Saviour, or ministering to the needs of the saints. Often
they are hymning the praises of God or playing on musical
instruments. In the National Gallery, for instance, in the
picture by Filippo Lippi of the "Madonna and Holy Child"[1]
attendant angels are playing on the lute and the violin; and
in old churches we often find paintings or carvings of the
heavenly host with various instruments of music, as though
taking part in the devotions of earth. In Fra Angelico's
beautiful picture in the National Gallery of the risen Lord
surrounded by angels and saints, the devotion of service of
the angels forms by far the greater portion of the picture.
As Dr. Alexander in his book, "The Divinity of our Lord,"
excellently observes: "Christianity is not a temporary influence, to be absorbed into pure theism. The religion of
heaven, like that of earth, is Christianity." A statement con-
firmed in the wondrous vision vouchsafed to the worn exile
of Patmos: "I heard the voice of many angels round about
the throne: and the number of them was ten thousand times
ten thousand, and thousands of thousands; saying with a
loud voice, Worthy is the Lamb that was slain to receive
power, and riches, and wisdom, and strength, and honour, and
glory, and blessing." And then the grand confirmatory cry
in unison of all creation, of "every creature which is in
heaven, and on the earth, and under the earth, and such as
are in the sea," bursts with one accord into the thrilling
anthem of devotion, "Blessing, and honour, and glory, and
power, be unto Him that sitteth upon the throne, and unto
the Lamb for ever and ever."

Of the ministry of angels to the saints we find abundant
examples in art and legend. Thus to quote but a few: by
angelic protection St. Hugh is defended from the lightning,
while an angel holds the plough for St. Isidore during his devotions; an angel makes clothing for St. Homobonus, while

---

[1] "Let all the angels of God worship Him" (Heb. i. 6).

another sings to St. Nicholas of Tolentinum, and yet another celestial visitor brings store of heavenly food to St. Congall.

We ordinarily associate the idea of white raiment with the angels; but the early painters did not by any means confine themselves to this,[1] as we may readily see in any collection of the works of the old masters. They are often represented as having a bright flame of fire, two or three inches high, rising from just above the forehead. This may be very well seen in a decorative panel in the National Gallery by Aretino, and in several other pictures in the collection. They are almost invariably winged, ordinarily with two wings, but sometimes with six: these are expressive of swiftness and alacrity of service. Sometimes they are standing upon flaming and winged wheels, forms suggested by the mystical vision of ·Ezekiel.[2] At times they are without bodies: incorporeal intelligences.

The orders of angels, as represented in art, would appear to have been suggested by a treatise, "De Hierarchia Cælesti." St. Thomas Aquinas gives them as follows: "Seraphim, Cherubim, Throni, Dominationes, Virtutes, Potestates, Principatus, Archangeli, Angeli."

> "But over the hye desse [3] in pryncypall place
> Where the sayd thre Kynges sat crowned all
> The best hallynge [4] hanged as reason was.
> Whereon were wrought the ix orders angellicall,
> Dyvyded in thre ierarchyses, not cessynge to call
> Sanctus, sanctus, sanctus, blessyd be the Trynite,
> Dominus Deus Sabaoth, thre persons in one Deyte."

In the Greek Church, St. John the Baptist, while clad in garment of camel hair, is winged, since that Church translates literally the text, "Behold, I will send My messenger (angel),

---

[1] "Les Saints Anges ont généralment partout la couleur blanche : cependant, le missal de Paris engageait à se servir, aux fêtes de ces esprits célestes, de la couleur jaune, ainsi qu'à l'église métropolitaine. Il en fut de même au diocèse de Lisieux. Serait-ce un symbole de l'éclat de leur gloire ? Mais pourquoi le rouge à Laon, à propos des Saints Anges : ce qui est difficile à justifier. Voudrait-on y voir le feu ardent de leur zèle pour la gloire de Dieu ?"—MALAIS.

[2] Ezek. i., also iii. 13 and the greater part of x.

[3] The high daïs.

[4] Tapestry hanging round the hall.

and he shall prepare the way before Me." [1]   He often has
two heads, one in the ordinary position, and a second, also
his own, borne in his hand in a basin !   Christ too, as the
bearer of reconciliation between God and man, is called in
the Greek Church " the Angel of the Mighty Will," result-
ing in a wonderful creation of Greek art, which in the
symbolism of the West has no parallel.

No subject perhaps has been more frequently painted than
the Annunciation. The celestial messenger is the great archangel Gabriel,[2] who stands in the immediate presence of
God. The only other archangel mentioned in the canonical
books of the Bible is Michael (Jude 9); but in the Book of
Enoch we read of the four great archangels, Michael, Uriel,
Raphael, and Gabriel, while in Tobit xii. 15 reference is
made to " the seven holy angels, which present the prayers
of the saints, and which go in and out before the glory of the
Holy One," the speaker being Raphael. Seven, as we have
already seen, has been accepted as the number symbolic of
perfection and completion; and thus both in artistic and
literary work, the great " angels of the presence " are ordinarily seven in number. To give but one illustration, when
Milton introduces, in " Paradise Lost," the archangel Uriel,
it is as

> " one of the seven
> Who in God's presence, nearest to His throne,
> Stand ready at command."

For the first four centuries we do not find in the catacombs
or elsewhere any representation of the devil, except as the
serpent, the tempter of Eve. Later on the fallen angels
and their leader have ordinarily been depicted with every
accessory of grotesque horror. The Satan of Milton is a
grand conception; but at the other end of the scale we may
place the Satan of the " Ingoldsby Legends," a Pan-like
creature with hoofs and horns and tail; and it is in some
such guise as the latter that he generally figures in the art
of the Middle Ages. In the illustration of a fourteenth
century missal before us, the mouth has great protruding
tusks that curl upward nearly to the eyes; the ears are long

[1] Mal. iii. 1; Matt. xi. 10; Mark i. 2; Luke vii. 27.
[2] Luke i. 19, 26; see also Dan. viii. 16 and ix. 21.

and pointed. At the shoulders and the thighs are other heads, from the mouths of which issue the arms and legs of the figure, the arms terminating in bears' claws, the legs in eagles' talons; the body, open at the waist, exposes a nest of serpents darting forth and hissing in fury, while the rest of the figure is covered with large scales. He is often represented also with wide-spreading draconic pinions.

The gurgoyles on old churches often represent evil spirits. They are supposed to be flying from the sacred building, and great faith was held in the church bells as a protection against evil. "The reason for consecrating and ringing bells," says a mediæval writer, "is this: that by their sound the faithful may be mutually cheered on towards their reward; that the devotion of faith may be increased in them; that their fruits of the field, their minds, and their bodies may be defended; that the hostile legions and all the snares of the enemy may be repulsed; that the rattling hail, the whirlwinds, and the violence of tempests and lightning may be restrained; the deadly thunders and blasts of wind held off; the Spirits of the storm, and the Powers of the air, overthrown."

The Tempter is represented as being driven away by the sign of the cross made by St. Hilarion; as chained by St. Norbert; as driven off by a large stone by St. Oswald; as seized with hot pincers by St. Dunstan; as trampled under foot by SS. Theodore, Cyriacus, and Euphrasia; as cast by SS. Zeno, Hermes, and Hidulphus out of one possessed. The histories of the saints, and the pictorial representations in old work of their lives, would yield numerous other illustrations of the assaults of Satan and his defeats.

While sometimes represented as of colossal proportions, the evil spirit is more commonly given the stature of a man, and occasionally is found much more diminutive. Thus in some old MSS. he is represented as tempting David and other good men in the form of a little black figure sitting upon their shoulders and whispering suggestions of evil in their ears; and often in representations of Christ casting out devils, the evil spirit issues in diminutive form from the mouth of the demoniac.

The Greek Hades, the Scandinavian Hella, originally the unseen world, has gradually become, in popular idea, the place of torment, the kingdom of Satan. As merely the

FIG. 56.

invisible state, it is referred to in Matthew xi. 23, xvi. 18;
Acts ii. 27, 31; Revelation i. 18; and several other passages.
As the place of punishment, it is referred to in Matthew v.
22, x. 28, xviii. 9; Mark ix. 43; Luke xii. 5; James iii. 6; and
elsewhere. In the original these two quite distinct meanings
are represented by two entirely different words.

Hell is generally, with the mediæval painters and sculptors,
the yawning mouth of a huge monster, breathing smoke and
flames (as in fig. 56), or a large caldron set on flames, into
either of which attendant spirits hurl their victims; and
often, with a grim touch of humour and bitterness of satire,
we find some of these with kingly crowns, or wearing the
cowl of the monk or the mitre of the bishop. It is curious
to note that when the Spaniards entered the City of Mexico,
they found that the doorway of the temple of the god of the
air was made like the mouth of a serpent or dragon, painted,
to quote one of their chronicles, "with foule and devilish
gestures, with great gums and teeth wrought, which was a
thing to feare those who should enter in thereat, and especially the Christians, unto whom it represented very hell,
with that ugly face and those monstrous teeth."

Representations of the kingdom of Satan are very numerous
in the Middle Ages, though in earlier work there is no suggestion either of hell or of evil spirits. These mediæval wall-
paintings in the churches probably suggested to Spenser the
lines —

> " He shewed him painted in a table plaine,
> The damnèd ghosts that doe in torments waile,
> And thousand feends that doe them endless paine
> With fire and brimstone, which for ever shall remaine."

It will be remembered how Dante's fellow citizens regarded him, such was the power of his poetry, with awe, as
the man who had " seen hell." [1]

The Renaissance idea of hell may be very well seen in

---

[1] " Vermes et tenebræ, flagellum, frigus et ignis, Demonis aspectus."
Thus in Dante's " Inferno " Charon says:

> " I come
> To take you to the other shore across,
> Into eternal darkness, there to dwell
> In fierce heat and in ice."

Milton in like manner in " Paradise Lost," writes of—

the "Last Judgment" of Michael Angelo, where Charon is landing the lost souls on the farther side of the Styx, near to the mouth of a dismal cavern, clearing his boat of its unwilling passengers by the vigorous swinging of his oar.

In the Rabbinical book, "Bab. Berachôth," we are told that, if we could but discern the evil hosts around us, no one could withstand the shock; for every man has ten thousand at his right hand, and one thousand at his left. Wier, in his book, "De Præstigiis Dæmonum," is content with a total altogether of lost spirits of 7,405,926.

Satan is most commonly symbolised as the dragon or as the serpent: the serpent representing the evil spirit as the wily tempter that first betrays to sin, the dragon as the devouring monster that remorselessly consumes those that have become its victims. "When lust hath conceived, it bringeth forth sin; and sin, when it is finished, bringeth forth death."[1]

The dragon and the dragon-slayer (fig. 57) appear in many creeds and form the subject of countless legends. While the story of the conflict varies with race and country, the legends of classic days, such as that of Perseus and Andromeda, the still older struggles carved on the slabs of Persepolis and Nineveh, the stories narrated around the camp fires to the awed rings of Eastern nomads, or listened to with glistening eyes or rapt attention in the nurseries of England, the great mass of legend that in the Middle Ages clustered around the names of God's faithful saints, the local traditions of every land, all point to the fatal presence of some evil principle, and record the ultimate triumph of good. Beneath the mass of everchanging fable we find at length the one foundation to all, the deadly strife between two great antagonistic principles.

The evil spirit is described in the Book of the Revelatior

"The bitter change
Of fierce extremes, extremes by change more fierce,
From beds of raging fire to starve in ice."

And Shakespeare, in "Measure for Measure," has a similar idea in the lines,—

"To bathe in fiery floods, or to reside
In thrilling regions of thick-ribbèd ice."

[1] James i. 15.

as "that great dragon." The conflict between St. Michael
and the dragon is a favourite subject in art. We may see
it, for instance, in Fra Carnovale's picture in the National
Gallery; while the combat of our own national saint with
the monster may be seen in the same collection in the works
of Memling, Tintoretto, Pisanello, and Domenichino, and in
old church carvings: as, for example, at Pitsford in North-
amptonshire, at Moreton Valence and at Ruarden, Gloucester-
shire, Brinsop, Herefordshire, and Fordington in Dorsetshire;
in a brass at Elsyng church, Norfolk,[1] and in considerable
profusion on tiles, stained glass, and so forth.

FIG. 57.

Besides the religious and artistic association of the dragon
with St. Michael and St. George, we find St. John of Rheims
and St. Cyriacus represented in art with a dragon held en-
chained. SS. Longinus and Servatius also have one at their
sides. St. Theodore is accompanied by a dragon having
three heads, while St. Germanus of Auxerre has one with
seven heads. St. Margaret is represented thrusting a staff

[1] In another of our books, "Mythland," we have gone at considerable
length into dragon lore and legend, and do not therefore repeat what
we have elsewhere written. We would also refer the reader interested
in St. George to an excellent paper in *Archæologia*, commencing at p. 243
in the second part of vol. xlix.

into the jaws of a dragon at her feet, while St. Romain has the monster bound with his girdle and captive at his feet. As we have not sufficient space, or possibly sufficient inclination, to give at full length the various legends, we are content to give but one as an illustration of all.

St. Romain was a bishop, and it is said that in his time a frightful winged dragon devastated the neighbourhood of Rouen, and indulged, after the approved fashion of such monsters, in sundry feasts on human beings, etc. St. Romain determined to rid the country of this scourge, and after many snares and traps had been set and laid in vain, he resolved to go in person to the forest-haunt of the monster, taking with him two companions to assist him in the chivalric deed. As they drew near the spot, one of his colleagues fled at the sight of the dragon; but the other, taking the girdle of the holy man, approached the monster. At the sight of the girdle it became " as gentle as a lamb," and submitted to be bound therewith, and was thus conducted to the prelate, who caused it to be taken into the market-place at Rouen and publicly burnt. Its ashes were then thrown into the river Seine. One cannot help feeling, on reading the story, that while the bishop gets most of the credit, his companion took most of the risk.

Another subject in which the dragon is represented is in connexion with St. John, in allusion to some poison which was once given to him to drink, but from which he took no hurt, as, on placing the cup to his lips, the poison rose out of the vessel in the visible form of a dragon.

The Biblical account of the temptation and fall of Eve naturally makes the serpent a peculiarly appropriate symbol of Satan. As early as the eighth century it was supposed that the serpent that beguiled Eve had the face and head of a woman,—

" A cherub's face, a reptile all the rest " ;

and we therefore often find it so represented in art. In a picture, for instance, by Ercole di Giulio Grandi, in the National Gallery, the tempter has a woman's head and bust, and long flowing hair,[1] though the form is otherwise serpentine ; the

---

[1] " Albertus saith that the hair of a woman, taken at some seasons and laid in the ground, will become venomous serpents. Which some have supposed to befall that Sex because of the ancient familiarity it had at first with that accursed Serpent."—GUILLIM.

head of the monster and of Eve are on a level, and face to face. We see this again in "the Fall" by Filippino Lippi, in the church of S. M. del Carmine at Florence; though here the human face is so small, and the writhing, serpentine convolutions so evident, that the woman's face, instead of being an attraction and a snare, is but an added horror. We see the human head again in the work of Pietro d'Orvieto in the Campo Santo at Pisa, and in many early illuminated MSS. Fig. 58, a sufficiently ghastly example, though the

Fig. 58.

ugliness is probably less intentional than indicative of want of artistic skill, is from the "Ortus Sanitatis," a Latin herbal printed first in the year 1491. From a praiseworthy desire to make his book as comprehensive as possible, the author starts from the Garden of Eden, and gives us this illustration, the *arbor vitæ*, the tree of life, with its golden fruit and beguiling tempter in the midst. The arms of the Fruiterers' Company are a tree having a serpent coiled round it and on either side Adam and Eve.

In one of these old MSS. we meet with the passage, "Quod-

dam ergo genus serpentis sibi dyabolus eligebat, qui cum
erectus gradiebatur et caput virgineum habebat." It is known
from very similar passages in the "Historia Scholastica" and
elsewhere, that this belief was held at least as early as the
eighth century: we have therefore both pictorial and literary
proof of the antiquity of the idea. Even Michael Angelo,
one of the later and greater men, an artist capable of the
grandest idealizations, still conforms to the old treatment in
his representation in the Sistine Chapel of the Fall of Man,
though his feeling for beauty and his art-power enabled
him to combine the human and the serpentine more plea-
singly than in the work of the earlier men. While the
betraying spirit is still beguiling Eve, the angel of the
drawn sword hovers above ready to drive out of the Garden
of Eden the guilty progenitors of our fallen race, a grand
and suggestive addition to the work, and emblematic of the
swift punishment that followed upon the fall.

On a medal struck in 1605 to commemorate the discovery
of the Gunpowder Plot, we see on the obverse a snake gliding
amongst lilies and roses, while on the reverse is the name of
Jehovah set amidst a glory of rays.

On a Greek vase in the British Museum we have the
daughters of Hesperus gathering the golden apples, while a
serpent coiled round the tree appears to be guarding them,
thus strikingly suggesting some far away echo amidst pagan
fancies of the Bible story. The serpent is often represented
as winged; but winged or wingless, footed or purely serpentine, with one head or a dozen, with false woman face or
stony ophidian glare, it coils round the tree of life full of
malignant subtlety and evil power, the sad symbol of enmity
to good and God.

> "Some flow'rets of Eden ye still inherit,
> But the trail of the serpent is over them all." [1]

The winged serpent was probably suggested by the passage in Isaiah that refers to the "fiery flying serpent," and
the additional attribute of swiftness would be accepted and
welcomed as one feature the more of terror, an added horror
bestowed on the loathsome crawling reptile, as a further

---

[1] Moore, "Paradise and the Peri."

means of compassing the destruction of its victims. The winged serpent is represented in the Egyptian wall-paintings many centuries before its appearance in Christian art.

In the Book of the Revelation Satan is "the dragon, that old serpent, called the Devil, which deceiveth the whole world." Various texts refer to the subtlety of the serpent, to its deadly poison, to its dangerous lurking in the dust; and only twice do we find anything commendatory : in the first instance, when the brazen serpent gave life to those who looked upon it, and was thus made the type of the great Saviour of mankind ; and, secondly, when the righteous were instructed to combine the wisdom of the serpent with the harmlessness of the dove. Even here the commendatory application is of the most oblique kind. The notion of the wisdom of the serpent probably sprang originally from the opening verse of the third chapter in Genesis: "Now the serpent was more subtle than any beast of the field which the Lord God had made." As the outcome of this was in the case of the serpent a malignant cunning, it can scarcely be made a legitimate basis for the higher idea we associate with wisdom.

As a talisman against evil and sickness we find the serpent the companion of the physician, the magician, the soothsayer. It may be seen at the foot of the tripod at Delphi, or twined round the staff of Esculapius; while Cassandra, licked behind the ear by the serpent, became gifted with prophecy and foresaw all the evil that should befall Troy. Blind Plutus, after a serpent had licked his sightless eyes, saw clearly all the past, the present, and the future; and strange powers of healing and of mysterious insight were ascribed to those who had come within the influence of the serpent's power and fascination.

In the Middle Ages men, for the possession of power, were held to have sold themselves to evil; and if a man were but a little wiser, a little sadder, a little more taciturn than his neighbours, he was held, like Dr. Faustus, to have invoked the enemy of mankind, and it was a moot point whether he should be viewed with awed respect as a magician, or burnt alive.

As the serpent refuses to hear the voice of the charmer, so the man of wisdom will imitate the prudence of the reptile, and refuse to listen to beguiling words that are full of future peril. Snakes are naturally attracted by sweet sounds, and the serpent charmers take advantage of the fact to capture them; a fact that was evidently well known in the days of the psalmist, who states that "the deaf adder stoppeth her ears, and will not heed the voice of the charmer, charm he never so wisely." The deafness, it will be noted, is no mere lack of the hearing faculty, but a deliberate turning away from peril. It was an old belief that when the asp heard the voice of the charmer it stopped its ears by burying one of them in the sand and coiling its folds over the other.[1]

Marguerite de France, the daughter of Francis I., who was styled by her subjects the mother of her people, bore as her device an olive branch entwined with serpents, and the motto, "Rerum sapientia custos," [2] signifying that all things should be guided and governed by wisdom.

The serpent has also been accepted as an emblem of regeneration or immortality from the annual casting of its skin. As a symbol of eternity, the serpent may often be seen having its tail in its mouth, thus forming a complete circle, the accepted emblem of everlasting life.

Amongst various early sects the serpent was regarded not only as the symbol of wisdom, but also of goodness, and its form was largely employed in charms and amulets. It appears from St. Augustine that the Manichæans used it as a direct type of Christ; but its employment was ordinarily antagonistic to Deity. Thus the Ophites, an offshoot of the Gnostics, and sharing with them their belief in the implacability of Jehovah, taught that God was jealous of man, and wished to prevent his acquiring more knowledge, but that the serpent came to teach man wisdom. The Ophites consequently adored the serpent,—a worship probably prompted and suggested by the reminiscences of the older faiths of Phœnicia and Egypt, where the serpent was revered as a beneficent being.

The Egyptian serpent of goodness, the cobra, is often

---

[1] " Pleasure and revenge have ears more deaf than adders
To the voice of any true decision."—*Troilus and Cressida.*

" He flies me now, nor more attends my pain
Than the deaf adder heeds the charmer's strain."
—*Orlando Furioso.*

[2] Wisdom the guardian of affairs.

represented with a human head. It stands erect upon its
folds, while the serpent of evil creeps along the ground. It
may be seen crowned with the diadem of the monarch, the
double crown formed of the distinctive head coverings implying lordship over Upper and over Lower Egypt. The
serpent of evil is very commonly met with in the Egyptian
sculptures and wall paintings. In one example the goddess
Isis is piercing it through the head;[1] in another we see
the advancing monster destroying mankind by the breath of
its mouth.[2]

Serpent worship is a widely spreading form of religion
that we find in many lands and throughout centuries of
time,[3] the idea in most cases probably being not a recognition
of beneficence, but rather a sense of the necessity of propi-
tiating a potent evil power. The subject is a most interesting
one, but its proper consideration would encroach upon our
pages more than would be justly its due.

In the Hindu mythology we read that there was once a
manifestation of the Deity who appeared on earth as coun-
sellor, warrior, and teacher. "They who trust in me," cried
Krishna, "know Brahma. I am the Victim, I am the Sacrifice, I am the Worship, I am the Road of the Good, the Creator,
the Witness, the Asylum, and the Friend." This same being
is the dragon-slayer of their creed, and none of the Indian
sculptures are of greater interest and beauty than those of
Krishna suffering, enveloped in the coils of a serpent that

---

[1] "I will put enmity between thee and the woman, and between thy
seed and her seed; it shall bruise thy head, and thou shalt bruise his
heel."

[2] On Gnostic gems and coins we naturally find many other illustrations. Thus on one we find the serpents of good and evil face to face,
rising from their coils for the coming conflict; while on another we have
a galloping horse and the serpent of evil upon its back—doubtless the
Gnostic treatment of the text, "I looked, and behold a pale horse: and
his name that sat on him was Death." The coins of the later Roman
emperors are rich with Gnostic and astrological devices.

[3] In Squier's "Serpent Worship in America," many legends are given
that admirably illustrate the feelings of the North American aborigines,
the Peruvians, Mexicans, and other dwellers on that continent with
regard to the great serpent that represents to them, as to so many
other races, the great evil power. Other books to refer to are Cooper's
"Serpent Myths of Ancient Egypt," Phené's work "On Prehistoric Con-
ditions and Customs in Connexion with Serpent Worship," or Deane's
"Worship of the Serpent Traced throughout the World."

fastens its fangs into his heel, and Krishna triumphant, trampling under foot the crushed head of the monster. In this myth before the eyes of the teeming millions of India of a terrible yet vanquished power of evil, of a wounded yet conquering saviour, who proclaims himself the sacrifice, the way, the truth, and the life, we find a wonderful parallel with the Christ of God ; while in fig. 59, a portion of a

Fig. 59.

Hindu picture, we see a strange similarity to the multitudinous pictures of the Virgin and the holy Child found in Christian art.

The serpent is not much associated in art with the saints. St. Didymus is represented as treading one under foot, and we also find it in association with SS. Paternus, Pirminius, Thecla, and Phocas. Unfamiliar as these names may be, and generally unknown the legends that make the introduction of the serpent appropriate, the same difficulty scarcely arises in the case of St. Patrick, the patron saint of Ireland, the benefactor who once and for ever banished snakes and all such noxious creatures from the Emerald Isle, and who therefore, very justly, in recognition of his deed, bears the serpent as an attribute.

CHAPTER VII.

The Church—as a Flock of Sheep—Figures in Mediæval Art of the
Jewish and Greek Churches—Old Testament Incidents treated
Symbolically—The "Biblia Pauperum," Illustration from—Apo-
cryphal Sources of Information of the Artists of the Middle Ages
—The Sibyls—Symbols of the Patriarchs—The Apostles—The
Evangelists—The Four Creatures in the Vision of Ezekiel—The
Mysterious Beasts of the Apocalypse—The Meaning of the Evangelistic Symbols according to St. Jerome, St. Ambrose, and Wyckliffe—The Iconoclasts—Saint-worship—Apparent Anachronisms in
Art—Art Traditions—Reckless Destruction of MSS. at the Reformation—St. Sebastian—St. Christopher—St. Cecilia—St. Laurence—
St. Catherine—St. Veronica—The Sudarium—St. Agatha—Attributes of Divers Saints—St. Luke, artist—The Kings in Heraldry
and Symbolism—Martyrdom—The Forces against the Early Christian Church.

WE proceed now to some brief consideration of the faithful,
the body of believers, the Church militant of God, and pass
in review the glorious company of the apostles, the goodly
fellowship of the prophets the noble army of martyrs.

FIG. 60.

The Church as a whole we shall find is often represented
either by a flock of sheep or of doves. The first symbol

121

naturally follows from the Saviour of the world speaking
of Himself as the Shepherd,[1] and from His solemn charge
to Peter, "Feed My sheep": while the dove, primarily an
emblem of the Holy Spirit, is secondarily applied to all
those upon whom He has breathed the breath of life eternal.
Hence in the catacombs we often find representations of
the Good Shepherd surrounded by His flock, and bearing
a sheep in His arms, as in figs. 60, 61, 62, or at other times
we see Christ as the Lamb of God, surrounded on either
side by the sheep of His pasture.[2] Fig. 63, an early Christian gem in the British Museum, shows us the soul resting

FIG. 61.

in peace on Christ, the believer being symbolised by the
dove with the olive branch, while the fish and the monogram

---

[1] "I am the good shepherd: the good shepherd giveth his life for
the sheep" (John x. 11). "Our Lord Jesus, that great Shepherd of the
sheep" (Heb. xiii, 20).

[2] In a lower sense the earthly monarch may

> "Act the shepherd in a noble sphere,
> And take his nation into royal care."

Hence on the coronation of Charles II. a medal was issued having on its
reverse the king as a shepherd tending his sheep ; while on a memorial
medal of Charles I., struck after the Restoration, on the reverse we see
a hand from heaven holding a celestial crown, and below a landscape
with sheep scattered without a shepherd.

are both emblems of the Saviour. The duplication seems at first needless; yet through it we get this double meaning, the sure rest for the wanderer on the Redeemer, and the steadfast gaze fixed on Christ. In fig. 64, a portion of one of the slabs in the catacombs of Rome, the single sheep with the palm branch aptly symbolises the victory over death of the member of the little flock thus commemorated.

In mediæval work we not uncommonly find sculptured two female figures as symbols of the Jewish and the Christian Churches; but these are ordinarily found more freely in the continental cathedrals and churches than in England.

Fig. 62.

The Church is represented as a woman, "the spouse of Christ,"[1] even in the earliest ages; but later on the second figure is added. The Jewish Church or synagogue is represented as blinded, a veil being over her eyes; in one hand she bears the tables of the law, in the other a drooping banner on a broken staff. The figure symbolizing the Christian Church wears the crown, holds in one hand the chalice, the pledge of communion with her Lord, and in the other the once despised cross, the symbol of her faith

---

[1] "As a bride adorned for her husband" (Rev. xxi. 2). "As the bridegroom rejoiceth over the bride, so shall thy God rejoice over thee" (Isa. lxii. 5).

and power.   Good examples of these figures may be seen
at Strassburg cathedral.   At Le Mans, in a painted window
of the twelfth century, the Church is depicted as crowned
by St. Peter, while the figure representing the synagogue
falls fainting into the arms of Aaron.

During the papacy of Leo the Great (A.D. 440–462) the
wonderful mosaics in the church of S. Paolo Fuori le Mura
in Rome were produced.   Here we see the enthroned Christ,
above Him the four winged creatures symbolic of the Evangelists, while on either side are the four and twenty elders,
those on the right being bareheaded, and those on the left
covered: the one group signifying the prophets of the Old
Testament, who only saw the truth veiled; the others, the
apostles of the New Testament, who beheld it face to face in
all its fulness and beauty.   Thus in one united ascription of

FIG. 63.

praise and adoration to the Christ the great teachers of the
olden time and the evangelists of the new dispensation join
in one grand outburst of joy and thanksgiving.

The Old Testament scenes are often represented, not only
from the historical, but from the symbolical standpoint, not
merely as depicting the actual incident, but utilizing it to
enforce other and greater truths such as the Incarnation,
the resurrection of the body, and the everlasting life of the
soul.   This kind of treatment is abundantly met with in
the catacombs of Rome.   The ark floating upon the stormy
waters of the deluge becomes a type of the Church riding
in safety amidst the strifes and turmoil of the world.
Abraham's sacrifice of his son reflects the sacrifice on
Calvary.   Moses striking the life-giving stream of water
from the rock in the arid desert, not obscurely points to
Christ, the great spiritual Rock and the source of living
water to the thirsty soul.   Daniel in the den of lions

suggests not merely God's protecting care over the faithful servant of God and the king, but becomes a type of victory over death. The ascent of Elijah prefigures the greater Ascension; and in the same way the prophet Jonah, the three faithful ones in the burning fiery furnace, the brazen serpent in the wilderness, and many other Old Testament histories and incidents, furnish the substratum upon which higher truths are built.

The following extracts from the "Biblia Pauperum" illustrate this teaching by type and symbol very clearly:

FIG. 64.

"It may be read in the book of Numbers that in one night the rod of Aaron brought forth buds and blossoms, whereby is figured the Virgin Mary, who miraculously brought forth the ever-blessed Jesus Christ. It may be read in the first book of Kings that the queen of Sheba heard of the fame of Solomon, and came into Jerusalem with great gifts in adoration for him; which queen was a Gentile, which will typify the Gentiles who came from afar to worship with gifts. We read in the book Genesis that when the Ishmaelites who had bought Joseph came into their own country, they sold him in Egypt; this boy Joseph is a type of Christ, who

was sold by the impious Judas. We read in the book of
Judges concerning Samson, that in the middle of the night
he arose, and of his own might cast down the brazen gates
of the city, and carried them away with him. Samson is a
type of Christ, who, rising from the grave in the middle of
the night, cast down the gates of the tomb, and left it in
freedom and power. We read in the first book of Kings
that when Bathsheba, the mother of Solomon, had entered

FIG. 65.

in unto him in his palace, king Solomon commanded a
throne to be placed for his mother next to his own throne.
Bathsheba signifies the glorious Virgin, whose throne is
placed next the throne of the true Solomon, that is Jesus
Christ."

As the old was made a type of the new, so the new was
occasionally a reflex of the old. Thus in representations of
the adoration of the Magi the travellers are almost always
depicted as kings, as in fig. 65, a picture by Fra Angelico,
though there is nothing in the Bible record of the visit to

justify the idea. It is based on that passage in the Psalms where we read, "The kings of Tarshish and of the isles shall bring presents: the kings of Sheba and Seba shall offer gifts: yea, all kings shall fall down before Him, all nations shall serve Him." Hence again in almost every representation of the Nativity the ox and the ass are introduced. This was not merely done from an idea that they formed very natural accessories in an event of which the scene was a stable,[1] but quite definitely in illustration of the words of Isaiah, "The ox knoweth his owner, and the ass his master's crib; but Israel doth not know, My people doth not consider."

Where we sometimes find a difficulty in comprehending a subject, we must bear in mind that, besides the canon of Scripture as now received, the ancient writers, sculptors, and painters drew their inspiration from various apocryphal sources; such as the "Evangelium de Nativitate Mariæ," the "Protevangelium Jacobi," the "Speculum Salvationis," the "Flos Sanctorum," the "Aurea Legenda," and many other writings of the kind.

During the Middle Ages, and especially where the Renaissance influence is paramount, we occasionally find the sibyls introduced. They were held to be next in dignity to the prophets: the function of the latter being to proclaim the Messiah to the chosen people, of the former to foretell His coming to the heathen world. References to the sibyls will be found amongst the writers of Greece and Rome, amongst the Jews, and in the writings of most of the Christian Fathers. Plato speaks of one, Pliny of three, Ælian of four, and Varro of ten. The Erythræan sibyl is said, by Livy, to have offered to Tarquin II. nine books containing the destinies of Rome, demanding for them three hundred pieces of gold. He declined the offer, whereupon the sibyl threw three of them into the fire, and asked the same price for the other six; this being still refused, she burned three more, and again demanded the same sum for those that remained, when Tarquin, conferring with the augurs, was advised to buy them. These books were destroyed at the burning of the Capitol, A.D. 670. In mediæval times the

---

[1] The scene of the Nativity is in the East always shown as a grotto or cave, while in Western Art it is depicted as a stable.

Fig. 66.

traditions of the Church had assigned to each of the sibyls her distinctive prophecy and proper emblem. Thus to the Libyan sibyl was assigned the statement, " The day shall come when men shall see the King of all living things," her emblem being a lighted torch. To the Persian sibyl was assigned the prophecy, " Satan shall be overcome by a true prophet," her attribute being a dragon. To the Delphic sibyl was imputed the prophecy, " The prophet born of virgin shall be crowned with thorns." These prophecies were manifestly merely monkish legend; but even so early as the second century certain writings were held in great honour amongst the pagans, and the pious fraud of interpolating passages bearing allusions to the Messiah was practised. These spurious predictions were held in veneration for centuries, and the sibyls were freely introduced into art, the best known examples being in the magnificent work of Michael Angelo in the Sistine Chapel at Rome. In Raphael's picture of the " Adoration of the Kings," [1] in the Berlin Museum two sibyls are placed in the upper portion of the work, and two saints in the corresponding lower portion.

In religious art the patriarchs and other Old Testament worthies are distinguished by their special symbols. Thus Aaron bears a censer or rod, and is clothed in the vestments of the priesthood, while Abraham has in his hand the knife of sacrifice; Daniel is accompanied by a lion; Amos has the crook of the shepherd; Moses carries the tables of the law, and is crowned with a radiant glory; Noah bears the dove and olive-branch, or a small figure of the ark, in his hand; David has the harp, or sometimes the stone and sling; Elias a scroll or chariot; Jonah a big fish or a ship.

The apostles, as the forerunners and symbols of the whole Christian Church, are in the earliest work represented as sheep, six on either side of the central figure of the Shepherd or of the Divine Lamb. Later on they are shown, as in fig. 66, in human form, and then the need was soon felt of giving them distinctive symbols to aid in their identification. They first appear wearing the nimbus in the mosaics [2] of the

---

[1] See Appendix A.
[2] The mosaics of the early churches supply us with most valuable materials. Had they been lost to us, there was nothing else that could have taken their place. The Christian mosaics date from the fourth

K

church of St. Maria, Ravenna, dating from the year 553. It
was the custom to bestow a certain personality upon each
of the Apostles : thus St. Peter always had a short, rounded
beard, while St. Andrew had a long, flowing one ; St. Philip
was of advanced age, St. John almost a youth. But it was
no doubt soon found that it was impossible by such means
to clearly distinguish from one another twelve or more distinct persons.[1] Attributes or symbols were therefore assigned
to them. St. Andrew bears the X shaped cross, the emblem
of his crucifixion. St. Bartholomew was flayed alive, and
therefore has in his hand a large knife. St. James the Elder

Fig. 67.

carries the scallop shell, water-bottle, and staff of the
pilgrim. St. James the Less has the fuller's pole, the instrument of his martyrdom. St. John bears in his hand a
cup with a winged serpent emerging from it, in reference
to the tradition that one of the priests of Diana challenged
the apostle to drink a draught of poison ; after St. John had

century. The early pictures are very simple in character, and deal with
the historical facts of the Old Testament, and such emblems as the
vine, Orpheus, or the Good Shepherd. Later on we see the gradual
development of various doctrines and the first indications of various
errors that had crept into Church government or Christian belief.

[1] The number varies, since sometimes Judas is not introduced, while
at others SS. Matthias, Barnabas, and Paul are included, though not in
the original band of twelve.

made the sign of the cross over the cup, Satan, in the form of a dragon or serpent, rose from it and flew away. Judas, the traitor, bears the bag, since he was the treasurer of the band. St. Jude bears a big knotted club, the instrument

Fig. 68.

of his death; and St. Matthew, for the same reason, a hatchet. St. Peter ordinarily carries a couple of keys, or at other times is accompanied by a cock; St. Simon a large saw, and St. Thomas a lance, in each case the instrument of martyrdom. St. Philip has a long staff or pillar, as he suffered death by being suspended from a lofty column; St. Matthias a battle-axe; St. Paul a sword, the instrument of his decapitation.

The Evangelists are abundantly introduced, and under very varying forms. Sometimes they are men with rolls or books in their hands, inscribed with their names; at other times we get the inscribed books or rolls alone. Most commonly the evangelistic symbols are the angel, the lion, the ox, and the eagle; and these also, as in fig. 67, are generally associated with the rolls. Sometimes the men are introduced with these four creatures by their sides, or at their feet, while in a few cases the forms are human, except that they have the heads of the angelic or animal type. In fig. 67, a piece of early carving from the church of Sta. Maria, Rome, instead of, as in fig. 48, having Christ surrounded by the evangelists, we have the hand in benediction, and around it the four evangelistic symbols, each bearing the roll in hand, paw, hoof, or claw. Fig. 68 is a much later piece of work, a portion of a picture by Van Eyck, representing St. Luke painting the portrait of the Virgin. Even though the treatment is purely pictorial and modern in character, we still see introduced in the background the symbolic ox bearing its scroll of writings. We may even occasionally find all four symbols combined into one, with the four distinctive heads, and supported on the foot of the angel, the paw of the lion, the hoof of the ox, and the claws of the eagle. In other examples again they are depicted as men holding urns, and pouring from them the living waters of the gospel, or at other times the four streams alone are seen issuing from Christ the rock.[1]

As some of our readers may find a certain difficulty in remembering the appropriate symbol of each evangelist, they will find the following mechanical aid to memory very serviceable: if the word ALOE be taken, it will be found to be composed of the initial letters of the four symbols, angel,

---

[1] " Paradisi hic fluenta
　　Nova fluunt sacramenta
　　Quæ descendunt cælitus:
　　His quadrigis deportatur
　　Mundo Deus, sublimatur
　　Istis arca vectibus."
　　　　　　　　　—ADAM DE ST. VICTORE.

lion, ox, eagle, and in their proper sequence for Matthew, Mark, Luke, and John. This key-word will at once give the symbol required.

These four figures, the man or angel, the lion, ox, and eagle, are in a marked degree common to almost all periods of art. Thus in Egypt we find the Sphinx human, eagle-headed, or leonine in character, while the ox is amply represented in the countless figures of the sacred Apis.[1] In the Assyrian remains we are confronted by bulls or lions with human heads, or by figures in human form, but having the wings and heads of eagles. The four creatures seen in the wonderful vision of the prophet Ezekiel were of this nature; for he expressly says in his description that they were similar to those he had seen while a captive by the river Chebar—a river of Assyria that runs into the Euphrates about two hundred miles north of Babylon—whither he and the great bulk of his nation were carried by the Assyrian king Shalmaneser, 721 years before the Christian era. The Assyrian sculptures therefore must have been familiar in appearance to him and to those to whom he was sent to prophesy.

The prophecy opens with the words, "Now it came to pass in the thirtieth year, in the fourth month, in the fifth day of the month, as I was among the captives by the river of Chebar, that the heavens were opened, and I saw visions of God." The whole of the first chapter is full of glowing imagery, and he reverts to it again in the tenth chapter; though we realize as we read it how utterly inadequate he must have felt all verbal description to be to express the glory of that vision of the opened heaven.[2]

---

[1] It is curious too to notice that the four Egyptian gods of the dead that stand before the Judge have four different natures, though in this case they have the heads of the dog or jackal, ape, man, and eagle. These four, as we may see in funeral tablets in the British Museum and elsewhere, always appear at the trial of the dead man, and mediate to Osiris on his behalf. When the body was embalmed, various parts of the internal organs were placed within jars having lids surmounted with these heads.

[2] "The Christian Church, looking at the origin of the four gospels, and the attributes which God has in rich measure been pleased to bestow upon them by His Holy Spirit, found a prophectic picture of them in the four living cherubim, named from heavenly knowledge, seen by the prophet Ezekiel at the river of Chebar. Like them the gospels are

In the apocalyptic vision of another captive exile, St. John of Patmos, the mysterious creatures adoring ceaselessly before the throne reappear to mortal eye. We read that the first creature was like a lion, and the second like a calf, and the third had a face as a man, and the fourth creature was like a flying eagle. Probably it was upon these passages in the Old and New Testaments that the evangelistic symbols were based.

St. Jerome and St. Ambrose assert in their writings that these four creatures represent, through the evangelists, our Lord under four aspects. Wyckliffe, in his translation of the Old Testament, published in the year 1380, refers to the beliefs of both these older writers. His English is almost too quaint for direct quotation, but the substance of it is that Matthew is represented as a man or angel, inasmuch as he dwells in his gospel chiefly upon the manhood of Christ; Mark is shown as the lion, as he treats most fully of His rising again; Luke is represented as the ox, writing as he does more especially concerning the sacrifice and the priesthood; while John is the eagle, since he passes in his writings over many of the little details given by the other evangelists, and dwells most lovingly on the sacrament and the higher mysteries. Another theory on which he touches differs slightly from this, as it sees in the life of our Saviour Himself four great incidents which the forms symbolize: the man, referring to His human birth; the sacrificial ox, to His death on the cross; the lion, to His resurrection; and the eagle, to His ascension into heaven.

Though art soon became an aid to faith, its previous association with heathenism made the early Christians shrink from its use, and the carvers of graven images were regarded as the servants of Satan, and forbidden the rite of baptism. This repudiation of art was however a matter of Church

---

four in number; like them they are the chariot of God who sitteth between the cherubim; like them they bear Him on a winged throne into all lands; like them they move wherever the Spirit guides them; like them they are marvellously joined together, intertwined with coincidences and differences: wing interwoven with wing, and wheel interwoven with wheel; like them they are full of eyes, and sparkle with heavenly light; like them they sweep from heaven to earth, and from earth to heaven, and fly with lightning speed and with the noise of many waters."
—BISHOP WORDSWORTH, " The Four Gospels."

policy, and was in practice for only a limited time, the prohibition being removed as soon as the contest between the
old beliefs and the new faith ended in the victory of the
latter. Later on we find Gregory II. writing : " The sacred
pictures elevate the feelings of men. Fathers and mothers
lift up their children to view them. Youths and foreigners
point with edification to the painted histories. All hearts
raise themselves to God." There was nevertheless, as one
may see at the present day in Russia, a tendency for this
appreciation of picture and image to presently develop into
worship and idolatry ; and in the year 726 the emperor Leo
III. published an edict condemnatory of the veneration and
use of religious paintings and images. Hence arose the sect
of the Iconoclasts or image-breakers, and this crusade was
in active operation for over a century, and doubtless an
enormous wealth of early art fell beneath the zeal of these
enthusiasts. Later on in our own country, in the sixteenth
and seventeenth centuries, inestimable treasures of mediæval
art were destroyed by men whose fanatical ardour was more
characterized by a burning zeal than a just discretion.

The reckless and ignorant destruction of the MSS. in the
monastic establishments at their dissolution is a conspicuous
illustration of this sadly misplaced energy. Bale, who was
himself an advocate for the dissolution of the religious
houses, cannot help exclaiming : " Never had we bene
offended for the losse of our lybrayes beyng so many in
nombre and in so desolate places for the moste parte, yf the
chief monuments and moste notable workes of our excellent
wryters had bene reserved, yf there had bene in every shyre
in Englande but one solemyne lybrary to the preservacyon
of those noble workes, and preferrements of good learnynges
in our posteryte it had bene yet somewhat. But to destroye
all without consyderacyon is and wyll be unto Englande for
ever a most horryble infamy amonge the grave senyours of
other nations. A grete nombre of them wych purchased of
those superstycyose mansyons reserved of those lybrarye
bokes, some to serve their jaks, some to scoure theyr candel-
styckes, and some to rubbe theyr bootes : some they solde to
the grossers and sope-sellers, and some they sent over see to
the bokebynders, not in small nombre but at times whole
shippes ful. I know a merchantman, whyche shall at thys
tyme be nameless, that boughte the contents of two noble

lybraryes for xl shyllyngs pryce, a shame it is to be spoken.
Thys stuffe hathe he occupied in the stide of greye paper
for the space of more than these ten years, and yet hathe
store ynough for as manye years to come. A prodygouse
example is this, and to be abhorred of all men who love
theyr natyon as they shoulde do."

Another good example of the destruction that went on all
over the land may be gathered from the following extracts
from the diary of William Dowsing, Parliamentary Visitor
for the county of Suffolk, recording the smashing and break-
ing of the "superstitious pictures and ornaments of
churches": "Sudbury, Suffolk, Peter's Parish, January
9th, 1643: We break down a picture of God the Father, two
crucifixes, and pictures of Christ—about an hundred in all;
and gave orders to take down a cross off the steeple, and
divers angels—twenty, at least—on the roof of the church."
" Clare, January 6th: We brake down one thousand pictures—superstitious. I brake down 200—three of God the
Father, and three of Christ and the Holy Lamb, and three
of the Holy Ghost, like a dove with wings ; and the twelve
Apostles were carved in wood on the top of the roof, which
we gave orders to take down, and twenty cherubim to be
taken down, and the sun and moon in the east window, by
the King's Arms, to be taken down." " Bramford, February
1st: A cross to be taken off the steeple ; we brake down 841
superstitious pictures."

The church of St. Agnes, originally founded by Constantine,
and rebuilt by Pope Honorius (A.D. 626–638), is an example of
how things were tending, since not the Saviour as heretofore,
but St. Agnes is made the central figure in the great mosaic;
and though the previous representation of various saints
as accessories to the Saviour could not suggest or provoke
creature-worship, the case was somewhat altered when the
one grand central figure that invited special attention was
that of a saint receiving such special honour, and this
feeling rapidly grew into invocation and adoration.

In many of the old pictures a certain anachronism would
appear to be involved ; but this is only apparently so, as the
groups of saints of various periods assembled together are not
intended to represent historic fact, but have symbolic reference to the communion of the faithful in one mystical body.
Thus in a picture in the National Gallery painted by Giro-

Fig. 69.

lamo da Treviso as an altar-piece for the Boccaferri Chapel
in Bologna, we have the Madonna and Child enthroned
under a canopy with SS. Joseph, James, and Paul, the
latter of whom is presenting the donor of the picture to
the infant Christ. In another picture in the same collection,
painted by Schiavone, of the same subject, the attendant
saints include SS. Bernard, John the Baptist, Anthony of
Padua, Catherine, Cecilia, and Sebastian, an assemblage
that certainly never met together in this world. Such
gatherings represent a heavenly rather than an earthly
assembly. The pictures were ordinarily altar-pieces, and each
church or religious body made its own selection of the saints
to be represented quite independently of all considera-
tions of geography or chronology. In Mantegna's "Madonna
of Victory," in the Louvre, the infant Saviour is surrounded
by two bishops, a cardinal, and a pope, all in gorgeous vestments; while in Van Eyck's "Adoration of the Lamb," three
popes, two of them amicably singing from the same book,
appear in the picture, a state of things that is materially,
though not spiritually, an impossibility and rank absurdity.
Fig. 69, the "San Sebastiano" of Titian, is another characteristic example of this.

Besides the essential knowledge of the symbols attributed
to each saint before identifiation is often possible, we require
to know something of the various art traditions. Thus, for
example, St. John is represented in Western art as the
young man that he was at the death of the Saviour; while
the Greek Church paints him as a venerable, gray-bearded
old man, writing the Apocalypse some sixty years after
the death of his Lord.

Amongst the noble army of martyrs there is no more
favourite and common subject in art than St. Sebastian. He
is always represented as divested of his clothing, tied to a
tree, and pierced by arrows. In the National Gallery we
have several examples: one by L'Ortolano, the figures life-
size, where he is accompanied by St. Rock and St. Deme-
trius; and another by Pollajuolo, where the saint is seen in
the middle of the picture, bound to a tree, and already pierced
with arrows. In the foreground are four of his executioners,
two of them in the act of discharging their weapons, and the
other two charging their cross-bows : here again the figures
are almost life size. A very beautiful example, the work

of Bazzi (Il Sodoma) in the Uffizi Gallery, Florence, shows the martyr bound and pierced, while an angel descends from heaven to crown the suffering saint with the diadem of victory. In the "Madonna and Saints" of Giovanni Bellini, in the Academy at Venice, St. Sebastian occupies a prominent position. When the subject may be considered as painted from the historical point of view, the treatment generally leaves nothing to be desired; but in a group of saints, including possibly a cardinal or other 'gorgeously robed ecclesiastic, the appearance of St. Sebastian, attired with a mere strip of cloth around the loins, and three-foot arrows sticking out all round him, is at first sight quaint. We may without breach of charity assume that doubtless one reason why this saint so often appears in art is that draughtsmen of the nude figure find in his sufferings an excellent opportunity of exhibiting their skill and anatomical knowledge.[1]

Another very popular saint in art is St. Christopher. He may be seen in the picture of Joachim de Patinir in the National Gallery, and he is also on one of the panels on the tomb of Henry VII., at Westminster Abbey. He may always be recognised from his bearing on his shoulders a little child, and he often also has the bough of a tree in his hand. The little child is the Saviour of the world; the saint's name signifies the Christ-bearer. It would be manifestly impossible to give at length the legends associated with the various saints, but that of St. Christopher is so interesting that we may place it at the end of our book, for reference. (See Appendix B.)

St. Cecilia, a Roman lady who suffered martyrdom in the third century, was said to have been the inventor of the organ. She may therefore be recognised in art from the organ or other musical instrument that is represented with her. She is the patroness of musicians. In the fine "St. Cecilia," by Raphael (a portion of which is given in the frontispiece), the saint gazes in rhapsody into the heavens, where an angelic choir is singing. She holds in her hands an organ, and at her feet are scattered various other musical instruments. In the picture by Domenichino in the Louvre,

---

[1] Amongst the specimens of majolica preserved in the South Kensington Museum is a figure of St. Sebastian by Maestro Giorgio.

she is depicted as playing the violoncello, an attendant angel standing by and aiding the performance by holding out the music-book.

St. Lawrence the Deacon was broiled to death A.D. 258, and is therefore recognisable by the great iron framework or

FIG. 70.

gridiron that he holds at his side.   He may be so seen in a Memling in the National Gallery.   In the basilica of Galla Placidia at Ravenna, we may see him in a mosaic, standing before the heated gridiron, holding a copy of the gospels in his hand, to symbolize his office of deacon, and a cross, the cross of martyrdom.   In the fourth bay of the north aisle in Henry the Seventh's Chapel, Westminster, St. Lawrence,

clothed in dalmatic as a deacon, is sculptured amongst the
many other interesting figures of saints that may there be
found. He reads from a book which is supported on a
gridiron.

SS. Catherine, Euphemia, and Quintin all have a wheel as
a symbol; but the first-named of these is by far the most
popular, and is almost always the one represented. She was
a virgin of royal birth at Alexandria, and publicly confessed
the Christian faith at a feast to the gods; for which con-
fession she was put to death. The sentence of the emperor
was that she was to be crushed and torn by toothed wheels;
but the apparatus was broken by angelic agency, if we may
credit the legend, and she was therefore beheaded. In a fine
picture by Raphael in the National Gallery she is looking
upward with an expression of resignation, and leaning with
her left arm on the spiked wheel, the intended instrument

Fig. 71.

of her death. Another good example in the same collection
is by Pinturicchio, where the saint stands erect, with the
crown of a princess upon her head, the nimbus of the saint
also, a sword erect in her right hand, and the wheel behind
her. Representations of her recur constantly in mediæval
work. Of these fig. 70 may be taken as a good illustration. In some examples, the wheel is much larger, and
more of the matter of fact character seen in fig. 71. The
wheel borne by the saint in fig. 70 is but a graceful symbol
of the actual instrument of martyrdom, while the sword is of
much more realistic type. The illustration is from a German
source.

Other favourite female saints are SS. Veronica and
Agatha. The legend of the former is given by John Damascenus, in "De Fide Orthodoxa." We are told that Berenice,
the woman who had an issue of blood for twelve years, and
who was healed of her plague by her faith in the great
Physician, encountered our Lord on His journey to Calvary,

and in loving pity gave him her kerchief to wipe His bleeding brows. When He gave it back to her it bore the impress of His features, and became the Vera Icon, the miraculous portrait, and she was ever afterwards called St. Veronica. In the National Gallery we may see, in a picture by William of Cologne, the saint holding before her the *sudarium* or white cloth containing the sacred portrait.[1]   St. Agatha is indicated in art by her symbol, the pincers, her breast having been lacerated by those instruments before she was put to death.   She may be seen accompanied by this symbol in Sebastian del Piombo's picture representing her; a picture called by Vasari "divine."   It is one of the works in the National Collection.

The pincers are also associated with SS. Apollonia, Macra, Lucy, Pelagius, and Dunstan.   With the first of these a tooth is always held in the pincers, as Apollonia, like the mediæval Jews and many other unfortunates, had to submit to a severe experience of involuntary dentistry as an inducement to abandon her way of viewing matters.   St. Lucy is the patron saint of the blind.   A heathen ruler praised the beauty of her eyes, and desired to marry her; so she tore them out with pincers and sent them to him, with the message, "Having these, let me now live to God."   Heaven, we are told, restored her sight; but the rejected wooer accused her to the authorities of holding the Christian faith, and she was put to death.   Her attributes in art are the palm branch of the martyr, and the more distinctive symbol of a platter having two eyes in it.   The pincers of St. Pelagius are always depicted as being red hot; but St. Dunstan, who also has them as an attribute, and in like manner represented as of a glowing red, was more fortunate in his association with them.   The former saint had them applied to

---

[1] This poetical fable is of great antiquity, and re-appears under many modifications.   This miraculous kerchief or veil was said to have healed Abgarus at the hands of St. Thaddeus, and it was also, we are told, carried to Rome for the healing of the emperor Tiberius.   According to other versions of the legend, Abgarus, in his zeal to know something of Christ, sent his own painter to Jerusalem to take the portrait of the Saviour; but the Divine face far outshone the feeble powers of the artist.   The Christ, ever kindly and full of consideration, pressed a handkerchief over His countenance, and sent it to Abgarus, stamped with the glorious image, the Vera Icon, of his Divine features.

himself, while the latter applied them to some one else, which makes, practically, a very considerable difference. The old legend tells us that while St. Dunstan, who was a great handicraftsman in metals, was working in his cell, the devil in disguise came to his window and chatted with him. The saint soon detected from the tone of the conversation the person he had to deal with, and picking up a pair of red-hot pincers seized the tempter by the nose, and only let go on faithful promise of no further molestation. His statue may be seen in Henry the Seventh's Chapel, and elsewhere, with the cope and crozier of the bishop, and in his left hand a formidable pair of tongs or pincers.

It is impossible to dwell on the legends that explain the attributes borne by the various saints. We must therefore perforce be content with little more, or in most cases nothing more, than just mentioning them. The prominent display of a cloak probably refers to an act of charity especially associated with St. Martin; but if spread out on the ground before the figure represented, that figure will be St. Alban. St. Hyacinth floats out to sea upon his, while St. Raymond uses his cloak as a sail.

A lamp in the hand will probably betoken St. Hiltrudis or St. Nilus, while in a general sense the lamp implies truth and righteousness, and the illumination of the Holy Spirit: " Let your light so shine before men, that they may see your good works, and glorify your Father which is in heaven." The lamps of the early Christians are found in abundance in the catacombs[1] and other cemeteries. They were accustomed to place them with the dead, and from the fourth century lamps were often kept burning before the tombs of the revered departed. They supply numerous and excellent examples of symbolic design. Christ as the good shepherd, the fish, lamb, monogram, cross, palm tree, ark, dove, and many other devices of like nature, are found upon them.

Where we find a saint carrying a lantern which a fiend is trying to extinguish, we are in the presence of St. Hugh. The torch is more especially a heathen symbol, and is often associated with Aurora, while the reversed torch signifies that the light of life has departed. It is seen in Christian art as a symbol of some few saints, and generally, as in the

[1] See Appendix C.

case of SS. Dorothy and Dioscurus, as an instrument of pain
and death.

We not unfrequently find statues and pictures of saints
represented as holding books in their hands : these are
divines and Fathers of the Church, whose writings have con-
tributed to the building up and defence of the faith. St.
Jerome, for example, is ordinarily thus represented.   At
other times we may find the individual carrying the small
model of a church in his hand, thus marking him as the
founder of the building, or in some other way betokening
his connexion with it.   In Orcagna's picture in the National
Gallery of the " Coronation of the Virgin," we find amongst
the various saints depicted a figure of St. Peter.   He is
supporting on his knees a model of the church of San Pietro
Maggiore in Florence, not, of course, because he founded
it, but because it is dedicated to him ; and it was for the
altarpiece of this church that the picture was originally
painted, and the ecclesiastical authorities naturally wished it
to be understood by all who saw the picture that the great
apostle had them under his especial care.   In the public
library at Boulogne is a MS. copy of the Psalter that contains
on its fly-leaf the symbolic description of a church.   Though
it soon runs into extravagance, and gives a forced meaning
to everything, the beginning struck us as being excellent :
" Fundamentum est Fides, Altitudo ejus est Spes, Latitudo
ejus est Caritas, Longitudo est Perseverantia."   In Crivelli's
picture in the National Gallery of the Annunciation, beside
the angel is kneeling St. Emidius, the patron-saint of Ascoli,
and in his hand he holds a model of that town.

St. Luke is claimed as the patron saint both of the artists
and of the physicians ; but it is naturally in the former rela-
tionship that he appears in art.   The doctors may be as
fully convinced of their claim ; but while their lack of artistic skill prevents their representing the saint as healing, the
practical art power of the painters enables them to represent
him as one of themselves.   Many old pictures still extant
have at one time or another been ascribed to St. Luke.
Metaphrastus mentions his skill as an artist, and John of
Damascus refers in his writings to his portrait of the
Virgin.   Hence besides his best known symbol of the
ox, the paraphernalia of the painter may often be found
bestowed upon him.

The bag of money that generally indicates Judas is also sometimes bestowed as a symbol on St. Matthew, in allusion to his occupation before he became one of the chosen band of apostles. St. Mary Magdalene bears the jar and box of ointment, as also do SS. Cosmas and Damian; while St. Wilgeforte, besides her flowing tresses of hair, has a long beard. She may be seen thus represented in Henry the Seventh's Chapel at Westminster, in the ninth bay on the south side, in company with SS. Dorothy, Barbara, and Mary Magdalene. Her beard was bestowed upon her, we are told, in answer to her prayers, in order that she might escape matrimony. As it might therefore reasonably be supposed that she would sympathise with others who were of like feeling, she was the patron saint of all ladies who desired to get rid of their lovers or husbands, and was popularly therefore called St. Uncumber [1] in England, Oncombre in Flanders, Kummernicht in Germany, and Liberata in France.

The great apostle St. Peter is sometimes represented with a single key, but more often with two, one of silver and the other of gold. The symbol is in obvious allusion to the text, "I will give unto thee the keys of the kingdom of heaven" (St. Matt. xvi. 19).[2] In Perugini's fresco in the Sistine Chapel of Christ's charge to Peter, the Saviour hands the apostle two large keys; and we see this again in Raphael's cartoon of the subject. They are naturally a favourite charge in ecclesiastical heraldry. They may be seen, for instance,

---

[1] In Sir Thomas More's "Dialogue concerning Heresies and matters of Religion," we find the following passage : " Sainct Apoline we make a toth drawer, and may speake to her of nothing but of bad teeth. Saint Roke we set to se to the great sykeness, bycause he had a sore. And with hym they joyne Saint Sebastian, bycause he was martiret with arowes. Some serve for the eye onely, and some for a sore brest. Saint Germayne onely for children, and yet wyll not ones loke at them, but if the mother bring with them a whyte lofe : and yet is he wiser than Saint Wylgeforte, for she, good soule, is as they say served and content with otys. Whereof I can not perceive the reason, but if it be bicause she should provide an horse for an evil housebonde to ryde to the Devyll upon : for that is the thyng she is sought for as they say. In so much that women have therefore changed her name, and instede of Saint Wylgeforte call her Saint Uncumber, bycause they reckon that for a pecke of otys she will not fayle to uncumber them of their housebondys."

[2] " Pannus aureus antiquus rubei coloris cum ymaginibus diversis Sancti Petri cum clavibus pendentibus ad zonam suam " (Inventory of St. Paul's Cathedral, A.D. 1402).

L

alone, or in conjunction with other charges, in the arms of
the dioceses of York, Ripon, Exeter (fig. 72), Gloucester,
Peterborough (fig. 73), and St. Asaph; in each case two keys
being introduced, and crossing each other like the strokes of
the letter **X.** At Winchester the two keys are both sloping

FIG. 72.

in the same direction, but are crossed by a sword, the symbol of St. Paul, in the opposite direction. In the arms of
Truro (fig. 74), we get key and sword again. The arms of
the cathedral church of St. Paul are very appropriately two

FIG. 73.   FIG. 74.   FIG. 75.

crossed swords, as we may see in fig. 75, and we get the
sword again at St. Alban's, but this time as the symbol of the
death of the great proto-martyr of Britain.

St. Adrian was put to death by having his limbs and head
chopped off on a smith's anvil; his attributes therefore are
an anvil and an axe or sword. St. Adalbert is pierced with

a lance. SS. Aurea, Christina, Callixtus, Quirinus have a millstone round their necks. A caldron of boiling oil is the attribute of SS. John and Felicitas; of boiling lead, of St. Fausta. Red-hot ploughshares are the symbol that marks St. Cunegundes. The rock from which he was pushed into the sea is associated with St. Pantaleon; while others bear red-hot stones, are covered with burning charcoal, are pierced with the sword, are tormented in every conceivable way that the malice of their persecutors could suggest. It is impossible here to mention a tithe of the saints who make their appearance in art and are recorded in legend.

It was speedily felt by all who were interested in maintaining the pagan rites that the new sect of the followers of the despised Nazarene could not be bent, and must therefore be broken. It claimed an exclusive allegiance, and its progress meant the downfall of all other systems of faith. Politically too it was regarded with disfavour; not only therefore did the bloodthirsty Nero fulminate against its followers, and strive to crush the rising Church, but even the just and generous Trajan saw in it a danger to the State that must be promptly dissipated. Against the new creed were arrayed the mighty material force of the empire of Rome; the intellectual power of the keenest minds, who brought their solid learning and acute argument to bear against it; the social influence of the old rites, that had been the stay and guide of their followers in times of trouble, and no less associated with them in the days of national and individual rejoicing; the conservative force that resented the intrusion of a new cult; the æsthetic force of all that was grandest in architecture and sculpture; the spiritual power wielded over the minds of men by the older beliefs; and, less reputable than these six great opposing influences, but as potent as any, the bitter, selfish opposition of such men as the makers of the silver shrines of Diana, who saw their gains diminished. Against these seven potent influences the infant Church, strong in a mightier power, prevailed and triumphed, esteeming the reproach of Christ greater riches than all the fading treasures of earth.

Fantastic legends have grown around the names of some, and many have had their glory dimmed by the mistaken zeal of those who strove to honour them, and yet imputed to them, in all good faith, actions far removed from the Christ-like

spirit, while not a few are wholly mythical; but above and
beyond all the great fact remains—the noble army of martyrs: and it is meet and right that the fearless saints of
the living God, the Church triumphant, should ever be held
in highest honour in the Church still militant on earth.

CHAPTER VIII.

Symbols of Sovereignty—The Crown—The Tiara—The Wreath—The Mitre—Cardinal's Hat — Sword — Coronation Swords — Resurrection Banner—Sceptre—Virge or Rod—The Budding Staff of Aaron —Glastonbury Thorn—Pastoral Staff—Crozier—Flabellum—Orb or Globe—The Umbrella—The Ring—Signet—Fisherman's Ring of the Pope—Posy-rings—Gold—The Gifts of the Magi—The Breastplate of Aaron—Precious Stones—Initial Rings—Onyx—Diamond —Amethyst—Agate—Emerald—Chrysolite—Coral—Sapphire.

WE pass now to a consideration of the various symbols of sovereignty and authority, spiritual and temporal. Of these the crown is naturally the first that occurs to us. It is sometimes introduced as an attribute of earthly sovereignty; at others, as a celestial reward and proof of victory won. In the arms of the see of St. Alban's, for instance, we find, see fig. 76, a sword surmounted by a crown : the first, a

Fig. 76.

symbol of the death of the great British proto-martyr; the second, the reward of his constancy to the faith. In Crivelli's picture in the National Gallery of " the Madonna in Ecstasy," two angels are seen supporting a crown over her

head, and many other such-like renderings may be met
with.[1]

The first mention of a royal crown is where the Amalekites
bring Saul's golden diadem to David. Tarquin, B.C. 616, was
the first Roman sovereign who assumed it, and the earliest
English crown was that of king Alfred, A.D. 872. The
tiara or triple crown of the popes was originally a plain high
cap, much like those in which the Doges of Venice are so
often represented in old pictures and medals. It was first
introduced by Pope Damasus II. in 1048. It is doubtful
when the first coronet was added, but the second was placed
by Pope Boniface VIII. in 1295, and the third by Pope
Benedict XII., about 1334. It has been held that the three
crowns refer to the Trinity, though that could evidently not
have been the original idea, or they would not have been
added one after the other with an intervening interval in
each case of many years. Others affirm that they denoted
the threefold royalty of the pope : one being the symbol of
the temporal power over the Roman states, another the
spiritual over the souls of men, and the third assumed as
ruler over all the kings and potentates of Christendom. A
third explanation is, that the three crowns are the lordship claimed by the papacy over heaven and earth and
purgatory.

The arms of St. Edmund were three golden crowns on a
shield of azure ; thus referred to by Lydgate,—

> " In which of gold ben notable crownys thre
> The first tokne in cronycle men may fynde
> Granted unto him for royal dignité
> And the second for his virginyté
> For martyrdom the thridde in his suffring."

While the crown is an emblem ordinarily of power, the
wreath is a symbol of victory.

> " Now are our brows bound with victorious wreaths."
> —*King Richard II.*

It is ordinarily of the bay or sweet laurel, as in fig. 2,
though the myrtle, olive, and other plants also appear.

---

[1] Another very good example in the same gallery is the " Virgin and
Child " of Botticelli, where two angels hold a crown over the head of the
Virgin mother. See also Guido's " Coronation of the Virgin."

On the magnificent gold medallion of Constantius II., Constantine I. is represented standing between his two sons, while a hand from heaven crowns him with a wreath ; and on many coins of ancient, mediæval, and modern date the laureated head of the victorious ruler is a marked feature.

Fig. 77.

The wreath expressive of triumph won is one of the commonest of symbols in the catacombs.

The mitre, the symbol of authority of the Jewish high priest, is also the attribute of bishops and archbishops. Cardinals anciently wore them ; but at the Council of Lyons,

Fig. 78.

in the year 1245, they were appointed the scarlet hats that are so familiar to us all. As an ecclesiastical emblem we find the mitre introduced in the arms of the sees of Carlisle (fig. 77), Norwich (fig. 78), etc. In Il Moretto's picture of St. Bernardino, at the feet of the saint are three mitres, inscribed with the names Urbino, Siena, and Ferrara, the bishoprics of which he is said to have refused.

The sword as the symbol of authority and power, or, in an evil sense, of bloodshed and wrong, is freely introduced. Four symbolic swords are used at the coronation of a British sovereign. (1) The sword of state, a large, two-handed weapon, having a gorgeous scabbard of crimson velvet, decorated in gold with the portcullis, harp, rose, thistle, and other heraldic symbols. (2) The curtana, or pointless sword of mercy. (3) The sword of spiritual justice. (4) The sword of justice of the temporality. In the very interesting series of figures of the prince-bishops of Würzburg, in the cathedral church of that city, the crozier, the symbol of their spiritual office, is held in one hand, while in the other is the sword of their temporal power.

The resurrection banner of triumph over death is freely met with in old pictures representing the risen Lord. It is of pure white, very long in proportion to its width, and having a red cross upon it. It may be seen very well in Fra Angelico's beautiful picture in the National Gallery of the Christ surrounded in glory by saints and angels. A banner is also borne as an attribute, often in conjunction with other symbols, by various saints. Thus St. Victorinus bears a banner and globe; St. Julian a banner and palm; St. Ursus, a banner and sword. Every one is familiar too with the importance of the flag in a secular sense as the emblem of the country, and of the deeds of heroism that its folds waving amidst the battle smoke have inspired.

The sceptre is a more ancient emblem of royal dignity than the crown itself. Homer makes it the only cognisance of the Greek kings, and the historian Justin declares that the ancient kings of Rome used no other ensign of royalty.[1] The Greek poets describe the gods as having sceptres to indicate their empire, and declare that an oath taken on the sceptre was the most solemn that could be sworn. In Jacob's prediction of the Messiah we find the sceptre specifically mentioned as the emblem of regal power: "The sceptre shall not depart from Judah, nor a lawgiver from between his feet, until Shiloh come." Justin tells us that

[1] Tarquin the Elder was the first who assumed the sceptre amongst the Romans. about 468 B.C.

among the Romans the sceptre was originally a spear; but the sceptres described by Homer were simply big walking-staves, designed to show that the monarchs ruled by acknowledged right, and not by force. Le Gendre tells us that in the earlier days of the French kings the sceptre was a golden rod, crooked at one end, and of the height of the king himself. At the coronation of an English sovereign the sceptre is placed in the king's right hand; and in his left, during the

Fig. 79.

ceremony of investiture, he takes the virge or rod, which is carried before him in the concluding procession. The distinction between the sceptre and the rod is that the former is surmounted by a cross and the latter by a dome. This distinction is of very ancient date, as we find that it was observed in the ceremonial of the coronation of Richard I. A very good illustration of a sceptre may be seen in fig. 79, the seal of Margaret, queen of Edward I. The lions embroidered upon her dress are the heraldic symbols of her

consort's kingdom ; the fleur-de-lys, those of her father's.
realm.

The rod, or staff, or wand of office is one of the most
familiar of symbols ; and its use stretches in an unbroken line
from the Pharaohs of Egypt in the childhood of the world,
to the baton of the field marshal and the signs of office of
the parish beadle, the cathedral verger, or Gold-stick in
Waiting of the present day. The Israelites were familiar,
during their residence in Egypt, with the notion that the rod
was the emblem or cognisance of dignity. Hence we find
Moses striking the rock at Meribah with his rod ; and when
the revolt of Korah rendered it necessary to affirm beyond
doubt the high priesthood of Aaron, the signal miracle per-
formed was the blossoming of this symbol of his authority.
The memory of this was perpetuated amongst the Jews, not
only by the preservation of the rod, but by the introduction
of a device of budding almond flowers upon the shekels of
Jerusalem.

"The Lord spake unto Moses, saying, Speak unto the
children of Israel, and take of every one of them a rod
according to the house of their fathers, of all their princes
according to the house of their fathers twelve rods : write
thou every man's name upon his rod. And thou shalt write
Aaron's name upon the rod of Levi : for one rod shall be for
the head of the house of their fathers. And thou shalt lay
them up in the tabernacle of the congregation before the
testimony, where I will meet with you. And it shall come to
pass, that the man's rod, whom I shall choose, shall blossom :
and I will make to cease from Me the murmurings of the
children of Israel, whereby they murmur against you. And
Moses spake unto the children of Israel, and every one of
their princes gave him a rod apiece, for each prince one,
according to their fathers' houses, even twelve rods : and the
rod of Aaron was among their rods. And Moses laid up the
rods before the Lord in the tabernacle of witness. And it
came to pass, that on the morrow Moses went into the tabernacle of witness ; and, behold, the rod of Aaron for the house
of Levi was budded, and brought forth buds, and bloomed
blossoms, and yielded almonds. And Moses brought out all
the rods from before the Lord unto all the children of
Israel : and they looked, and took every man his rod."

In fig. 80 we have an illustration of the Jewish shekel

In the centre is the budding rod of Aaron, and the inscription, Jerusalem the Holy. In fig. 81 we have the reverse, having in the centre the pot of manna, and around it the words, Shekel of Israel. The date of this coin is about 450 B.C.

In Christian art the bearer of a budding staff may be, not Aaron, but St. Joseph of Arimathæa or St. Ethelreda.

Near Glastonbury Abbey stands an old hawthorn that has been the subject of many legends, the current belief however being that it sprang from the staff of St. Joseph, who, it is asserted, was the first preacher of Christianity to Britain, and who, to convince the benighted islanders of his mission, thrust his staff into the ground, when it at once budded and blossomed. The tree has ever since flowered,

FIG. 80.   FIG. 81.

not only at its proper season, but also at each Christmas, the anniversary of its miraculous origin.[1]

In the earliest examples of Christian art, as in the catacombs or in the Museum of the Lateran (see appendix D), our Saviour is often depicted as bearing a wand, and employing it in the working of various miracles, as in the turning of the water into wine, the raising of Lazarus, and other instances of the exertion of Divine authority.

The error of confusing the pastoral staff or crook with the crozier is one constantly made. The two things are per-

---

[1] A piece that came under our notice on December 16th had eight bunches of flowers upon it, and each of these was composed of from twenty to thirty blossoms and buds, about a dozen in each bunch being fully expanded. The blossoms were a little smaller than would ordinarily be looked for, but had all the beauty and regularity of form and the characteristic hawthorn scent of the normal plant. The only thing abnormal in the appearance of the spray was the entire absence of foliage.

fectly distinct, and should be carefully discriminated. The
pastoral staff belongs officially to all cardinals, archbishops,
and bishops, and was also in mediæval times assigned by
courtesy to certain abbots and abbesses. It is borne in the
left hand, thus leaving the right free to perform the necessary functions of ceremonial and worship. The crozier, a
cross or crucifix on a staff, is never carried by the higher
ecclesiastics, but is borne immediately before them, to indicate and emphasise their office and dignity. In England
the pastoral staff was in use from a very early period: the
pontifical of Dunstan (A.D. 957–988) gives the form of service
for its benediction; while the Venerable Bede, in his treatise
" De Vii Ordinibus," dwells on its symbolic significance. In
the form for the consecration of a bishop in the first Prayer-
book of Edward VI., the archbishop puts into his hand the
pastoral staff, saying, " Be to the flock of Christ a shepherd,
not a wolf; feed them, devour them not; hold up the weak,
heal the sick, bind together the broken, bring again the out-
casts, seek the lost."

The carving in the head of the crook is religious or
symbolic in character. Several of these pastoral staves may
be seen in the South Kensington Museum. In one of them
the subject within the volute is the crowning of the Virgin
by Christ, in another the Annunciation, in another St. Michael
and the dragon, and so forth. Numerous beautiful examples
may be seen in monumental effigies and ecclesiastical seals.
Scores of the actual crooks were destroyed at the Reformation, partly because they were held to be popish, but probably more especially because, being often richly gilt and
adorned with precious stones, the appeal to the cupidity of
the king's underlings proved altogether irresistible.

The orb, mound, or globe is a symbol of sovereignty, and
is borne in the left hand. It was assumed as a cognisance by
the emperor Augustus, and was sometimes termed the apple;
in all cases it was regarded as the symbol of far-reaching
dominion. The surmounting cross was added to the globe
by Constantine, the first Christian emperor. Suidas, describ-
ing the statue of the emperor Justinian, says: " In his left
hand he held a globe, in which a cross was fixed, which
showed that by faith in the cross he was emperor of the
earth. For the globe denotes the earth, which is of like
form, and the cross denotes faith, because God in the flesh

was nailed to it." The globe and cross were first introduced as ensigns of authority in Western Europe by Pope Benedict VIII. Almost all the English kings, from Edward the Confessor, have the globe in their left hand on their coinages or great seals, and it seems also to have been frequently so placed when sovereigns lay in state after their decease. In the picture by Rubens, "Henry IV. entrusting the Symbol of his Power to Mary de Medici," the symbol is the globe, which he places in her hands.

As the orb signifies far-reaching dominion, we naturally find it associated in early art with the Deity. In Giotto's "Christ adored by Angels," we see over all the eternal

Fig. 82.

Father, bearing the globe in His hand; and we may see the same treatment again in the "Adoration of the Magi" by Fra Angelico, and in many other instances of early work. We have examples of this in figs. 82 and 83. The first of these is a gem dating from the sixth century, the letters on either side of the head clearly indicating, apart from the cruciferous nimbus, that the second Person of the Trinity is represented; while in the second illustration (fig. 83) we see above the sitting Christ the eternal Father, and in each case bearing the orb. Fig. 26 is another example that may be referred to.

Many other symbols of authority will doubtless occur to our readers; the fasces carried by the Roman lictors, the caduceus of Mercury, the trident of Neptune, the thunder-

Fig. 83.

bolts of Jupiter.[1]   The Pharaohs of ancient history again,
and the popes of mediæval and modern days, had gorgeous
feather fans borne before and around them ; while not merely
the cooling fan, but the sheltering umbrella becomes in hot
countries a sign of distinction.   In the wall paintings of
Egypt and the carvings of Nineveh and Persepolis, the
monarch has the sunshade held over him ; and one of the
most honourable titles of the king of Siam is Lord of the
Twenty-four Umbrellas.   On the coinage of Herod Agrippa
I. we find as a device an umbrella.

FIG. 84.

The flabellum had its origin in the Eastern Church, and
was of distinctly practical use, cooling and refreshing the
celebrant, and driving away the flies and other insect plagues
of the sultry East from the eucharistic elements.   With
the spread of ritual came also the flabellum or muscarium,
though in the less sunny lands of the North and West it
ceased to be of any practical value.   As its original employment was one of the duties of the deacon, it became a symbol
of the diaconate, and in the early service books full directions
were given at the ordination of a deacon as to the fit use
of the muscarium then bestowed.   The flabellum, though
often of feathers, was also made of vellum, linen, and other
materials of the kind, and we may sometimes find it a richly
decorated disk of brass or silver.   In an ancient Greek
fresco we have a representation of the Saviour preaching,
while an angel holds a circular flabellum of metal over His
head, as a protection against the sun.   Several examples of

---

[1] As we see in fig. 84, a coin struck by Nero, A.D. 66.   The eagle
thereon is a symbol of imperial Rome, and the palm branch, of victory.

its use in the Western Church may readily be cited.   We
see an illustration of it, for example, in the " Book of Kells,"
an Irish MS. of the sixth century, and the " muscatorium de
pennis pavonium " figures in the inventories of York, Salisbury, and other cathedrals.   It has been held that the use of
the peacock feathers symbolised the countless eyes, not of
men only, but of good and evil spirits, watching the actions
of the pontiff or other ecclesiastical dignitary, and reminding
him thereby of the urgent need for holy watchfulness in
return; but we may well consider such an explanation a
laboured after-thought, and see in the splendour of the
feathers a sufficient reason for their use at a time when men
gave freely of their best for the service of the sanctuary.

The ring is another very characteristic emblem of power,
as investiture by its means was the most ancient form of
conferring dignity: it was by this ceremony that Pharaoh
created Joseph his viceroy over Egypt.   "Thou shalt be
over my house, and according unto thy word shall all my
people be ruled: only on the throne will I be greater than
thou.   And Pharaoh said unto Joseph, See, I have set thee
over all the land of Egypt.   And Pharaoh took off his ring
from his hand, and put it upon Joseph's hand, and arrayed
him in vestures of fine linen, and put a gold chain about his
neck."

The ring appears to have been employed originally as a
signet; as, for instance, when the prophet was cast into the
den of lions, and a big stone was rolled to the mouth of the
den, the king sealed it with his own signet and with the
signet of his lords.   Sir Gardner Wilkinson, in his " Manners
and Customs of the Ancient Egyptians," refers to one bearing
the name of a king who was reigning about 1,400 B.C.   The
device is a scorpion.   Many excellent examples may be seen
in the British Museum.

In mediæval days a jewelled ring was part of the necessary
adornment of the higher ecclesiastics, and it was ordinarily
buried with them.   In the old romance of "Sir Degrevant,"
we are told that at the marriage of the hero there were

> " Archbishops with rings,
> More than fifteen."

and in another fourteenth century tale, "King Athelstan,"
the king exclaims to an offending cleric,

> " Lay down thy cross and thy staff,
> Thy mitre, and thy ring, that I to thee gaff,
> Out of my land thou flee."

The prayer for the blessing of the ring ran as follows :
" O Creator and preserver of mankind, Author of Spiritual
grace and Giver of everlasting Salvation, send Thy blessing upon this ring, that whosoever shall walk distinguished
by this sacred sign of faith may by the protection of Thy
heavenly power attain everlasting life, through Jesus Christ
our Lord. Amen." The bishop wore a ring as representative of the heavenly Bridegroom, and guardian of the Church.

The grand ceremony of wedding the Adriatic by casting
therein a ring will be familiar to all who have studied
Venetian history. The next thing we need refer to is the
famous " fisherman's ring " of the pope. It is a signet of
steel used for the marking of the official documents issued
from the papal court. A new one is made for every pope,
though all are based on a very ancient original, representing
St. Peter in his boat drawing his net to the surface. The
classic form of the boat and oar shows a direct derivation
from an antique original.

Rings were used too for the purposes of divination, as
amulets to protect the wearer from all harm, and as symbols
of affection.[1] These latter, the posy rings as they were
termed by our ancestors, had ordinarily an inscription upon
their inner surface; such as, " United hearts death only
parts "; " A faithful wife preserveth life "; " As God
decreed so we agreed."

It is said that king Edward the Confessor was met by a
venerable old man, who asked alms of him; and the chari-
table monarch, being at the moment destitute of money,
gave the suppliant his ring. Soon afterwards two English
pilgrims, who had lost their way, were met, at the approach
of night, by this same old man, who led them into a magnificent city with golden streets, the New Jerusalem, the

---

[1] Those who care to pursue the subject further may advantageously
turn to the following works : Warne's essay " On Ancient Coins, Medals,
and Gems "; King's " Memoir on Amulets and Talismans "; King's
" The Gnostics and their Remains, Ancient and Mediæval "; Fortnum's
" Early Christian Engraved Gems"; or Ayzal's " Symbolique des Pierres
Précieuses, ou Tropologie des Gemmes."

M

visible existence of which was a popular article of faith in
the Middle Ages. The old man entertained them hospitably
and gave them lodgings for the night. In the morning he
informed them that he was St. John the Evangelist, of whom
it was believed by many of the ancient Fathers that he was
appointed to tarry on earth until the second coming of the
Lord Christ. St. John told the pilgrims that it was to him
in person that their king had given the ring, and he sent
it back by them to him, with a promise that Divine grace
should encircle every British sovereign who was invested
with this ring at his coronation. The sacred ring was long
preserved at the shrine of St. Edward, and only brought out
at the time of a coronation. It deserves to be remarked
that legends of the appearance from time to time of St. John
continued to be held so late as the reign of Henry VIII.

Should we see in Christian art a figure holding out a ring,
the statue or painting is probably meant for St. Edward
the king and confessor; while SS. Theodosius and Gregory
have as attribute a large iron ring round their bodies. St.
Pelagia, the penitent, has the ground before her strewn with
jewels and ornaments, the vanities of earth that she has cast
from her.

Gold, as one of the two noble metals, has always been
held in symbolic honour. It is a favourite emblem in Scripture of faith triumphant in adversity and suffering,[1] while
its brightness and value make it equally appropriate as a
symbol of majesty and honour.

Gold, frankincense, and myrrh were the three symbolic
gifts brought by the wise men of the east to the Babe of
Bethlehem.

> " Eastern sages at His cradle
> Made oblations rich and rare ;
> See them give, in deep devotion,
> Gold and frankincense and myrrh.
>
> Sacred gifts of mystic meaning :
> Incense doth their God disclose,

---

[1] " They shall be tried as the gold in the fire " (2 Esdras xvi. 73);
" When He hath tried me, I shall come forth as gold " (Job xxiii. 10);
" The trial of your faith, being much more precious than of gold which
perisheth " (1 Pet. i. 7) ; " I counsel thee to buy of Me gold tried in the
fire, that thou mayest be rich " (Rev. iii. 18).

> Gold the King of kings proclaimeth,
> Myrrh His sepulchre foreshows." [1]

According to an ancient legend, this choice of gifts was to ascertain whether the mysterious stranger that they were going to worship was a king or a prophet or God Himself. If he were a king, he would select the gold; if he were a poor man, he would choose the myrrh; but if God, He would take the incense. As both God and man, the King of kings veiled in humanity, He accepted from them all three of their gifts.

> " An Age shall bring about the Day
> When Lord of Lords shall lodge in clay;
> Three kings from east him to adore
> Shall come with incense, myrre, and ore."

Other ancient writers assigned the gold to the race of Shem, the myrrh for Ham, and the incense for Japhet.

> " Then entered in those Wise men three
> Full reverently upon their knee,
> And offered there, in His Presence,
> Their gold and myrrh and frankincense."

The various precious stones have been endued with symbolic meaning and application. A notable example of this was the breastplate of judgment borne by Aaron when he entered the holy place. This breastplate had twelve precious stones, one for each tribe of Israel. The first row was a sardius, topaz, and carbuncle; the second, an emerald, a sapphire, and a diamond; the third, a ligure, an agate, and an amethyst; the fourth, a beryl, an onyx, and a jasper; and on each stone was engraved the name of the tribe it symbolized.

The episcopal rings of mediæval days were jewelled; and the stones usually chosen for such rings were ruby, emerald, or crystal. The choice had significance, as indeed almost all else had that entered at all into the ritual of the Roman Catholic Church: ruby being indicative of burning zeal, emerald of tranquil peace, crystal of simplicity and purity.

---

[1] " Thus, aurum, myrrham, regique, hominique, Deoque,
Dona ferunt."

" Aurea nascenti fuderunt munera regi,
Thura dedere Deo, myrrham tribuere sepulchro."

In like manner the diamond indicated invulnerable constancy; the sapphire, hope; the amethyst, humility; the
onyx, sincerity.

A hundred years or so ago it was the custom in England
to use the stones in such a way in a ring that the initials of
their names might spell out some little love message, some
political catchword, or the name of the donor or the recipient.
Thus, if we place, one after another, round a ring or bracelet
a ruby, emerald, garnet, amethyst, ruby, and a diamond, we
get the word REGARD.

The onyx was held to be a sure talisman of victory over
one's enemies. Our word diamond is a corruption of adamant,
and this in turn is derived from the Greek word for invincible;
not, as has been generally supposed, on account of its exces-
sive hardness,[1] but from the ancient belief in the inability
of the gods to resist the prayer of any suppliant who carried
one with him. " He who carries the diamond upon him, it
gives him hardness and manhood, and it keeps the limbs of
his body whole. It gives him victory over his enemies in
court and in war, if his cause be just; and it keeps him that
bears it in good wit, and it keeps him from strife and riot,
from sorrows and from enchantments, and from fantasies
and illusions of evil spirits. And if any cursed witch or
enchanter would bewitch him that bears it, all that sorrow
and mischance shall turn to the offender, through virtue of
that stone; and also no wild beast dare assail the man who
bears it on him. It makes a man stronger and firmer against
his enemies: heals him that is lunatic, and those whom
the fiend pursues or torments. And if venom be brought in
presence of the diamond, anon it begins to grow moist."
Thus says Sir John Maundeville, writing in the year 1356; [2]
but as, even in those ages of faith, some people evidently

---

[1] " Hard-hearted adamant."
　　　　　　　　—" Midsummer Night's Dream."

" Strike as hard as you will with an hammer upon the point of a
diamant, you shall see how it scorneth all blowes, and rather than it
will seeme to relent first flieth the hammer that splitteth in pieces, and
the very anvil itself underneath cleaveth in twaine. Besides it has a
Nature to conquer the furie of fire, nay you shall never make it hote,
doe what you can."

[2] We have of course modernised the language. The original English
is excessively quaint, and almost unreadable in places.

raised doubts, he adds : " Nevertheless it happens often that
the good diamond loses its virtues by sin, and for inconti-
nence of him that bears it, and then it·is of little value."
Any critic therefore who cavilled might be delicately re-
minded that there were undoubtedly occasions when the
diamond refused to exercise its beneficent power, and that a
little self-amendment might well take the place of adverse
criticism.

The amethyst was held to possess the power of preserving
wine-drinkers from the natural result of their over-indul-
gence; while the agate made its wearer proof against deadly
serpents, and the emerald strengthened the sight and the
memory. The chrysolite could drive away evil spirits, while
the onyx dispelled grief. Coral was held to keep off storm
and thunder.

It is possible that the pagan belief in the efficacy of certain stones, such as the diamond, the jasper, the topaz, the
sapphire, and the opal, to win from the gods a favourable
answer to prayer, and, in the case of other stones, to ward
from threatening dangers, may have not been altogether
without influence when Christianity superseded the worship
of the gods of paganism. The great wealth of jewellery
expended on shrines, crucifixes, vestments, and pictures may
have been partly the result of belief in its efficacy as well
as a gift of faith and homage to the glory of God and the
enhanced honour of the saints. A decree of Pope Innocent
III., in the twelfth century, ordained that henceforth the sapphire should always be the stone used in the rings whereby
the bishops at their investiture were wedded to the Church.
When sacrifices were offered, and responses sought from
Phœbus, it was thought that he was better pleased, and
that it was easier to get one's request granted, if the
sapphire were exhibited, since it was a sign of concord, and
therefore in the Middle Ages it was held to keep a man
safe from fraud, fear, or envy.

The mediæval writers attributed to each gem a special
influence over each month, and also assigned a precious
stone to each of the twelve apostles.

Amongst the treasures prepared by David for the glorious
temple that he would fain have built for the worship of
Jehovah we find "onyx stones, and stones to be set,
glistering stones, and of divers colours, and all manner of

precious stones." These are repeatedly introduced in the picturesque eastern imagery of the Bible as the symbols of prosperity and magnificence: "O thou afflicted, tossed with tempest, and not comforted, behold, I will lay thy stones with fair colours, and lay thy foundations with sapphires. And I will make thy windows of agates, and thy gates of carbuncles, and all thy borders of pleasant stones." [1]

The Book of Job again gives us many interesting references; but the most beautiful Biblical use of these gems is the attempt, the hopeless but magnificent attempt, to picture to mortal eyes something of the grandeur of the Paradise of God, with its walls of jasper, founded in sapphire and emerald and chrysolite, its gates of pearl, and streets of pure gold like unto clear glass. The writer could but put together all that seemed to him most splendid and radiant. He failed where it was impossible to succeed, since no material imagery that the heart of man can conceive can picture to our yet blinded eyes the ineffable grandeur and glory of that heavenly city, or give even a suggestion of the dazzling splendour of the New Jerusalem.

---

[1] Isa. liv. 11, 12.

CHAPTER IX.

Animal Forms—The Lamb—Agnus Dei—Lamb of the Apocalypse—The
Lion: in good and in bad sense—The " Book of Beasts " of Philip de
Thaun—Strange Mediæval Beliefs—Symbol of St. Jerome—Stag—
Ox—Ass—Elephant—Horse—Unicorn—Bear—Dog — Pig — Satanic
Possession—Wolf—Satirical Representations in Middle Ages—Fox
—Monkey.

WE proceed now to a consideration of the various animal
forms that have been employed symbolically in art.   These
are not very numerous; but one of them, the lamb, as a symbol of Christ, the great Lamb of the sacrifice, is one of the
most freely met with of all symbolic representations.   Its
occurrence ranges from almost the earliest days of Christianity, throughout all the intervening centuries, down to
the present time.

The sacrificial lamb is repeatedly referred to in the Old
Testament; and the prophets, looking beyond the material
rites of the Mosaic law, saw clearly in that sacrifice the
future Messiah.   John too, the great forerunner, announced
the Christ to his followers as "the Lamb of God."   It is
therefore very natural that we should find it as one of the
earliest symbols.

> " An hevenly signe, a token off most vertu,
> To declare how that humylite
> Above alle vertues pleseth most Jesu.
> Off Adamys synne was wasshe away the rust
> Be vertu only off thys lambys blood."—LYDGATE.

It soon became so favourite a form that we presently find
some little danger of idolatry creeping in.   In the sixth
century it was placed with crown and nimbus on the cross;
and in the year 692 a council of the Church was forced to
decree that it should not henceforth be thus substituted for
the human form.   In the catacombs, on the sarcophagus of

Junius Bassus, a lamb is represented as changing water into wine, raising the dead Lazarus, and performing other acts that clearly indicate that the animal form is but a symbol of the Christ. The early examples have no nimbus; but later on this is frequently added, being generally cruciferous or inclosing the sacred monogram. In other instances the lamb has the palm branch of victory.

In the church of St. Bavon, Ghent, may be seen a picture by Van Eyck of the " Adoration of the Lamb," where an actual lamb stands upon an altar, and is surrounded by worshipping angels and saints. We give in fig. 85 an illustration of this work.

In some of the early mosaics we see a lamb, and on either side of it six sheep, a symbol of Christ and His apostles. This may be very well noticed in the great mosaic in the apsis of St. Cosmo Damian in Rome, executed about the year 526. At other times a variable number of sheep is introduced; in which case it is to be understood that they are symbols of the Church, the general body of believers.

In mediæval art the lamb is associated with St. John the Baptist and SS. Agnes, Regina, Genevieve, Catherine, and Joanna; and in the form of the Agnus Dei, the symbol of Christ appears in numberless examples on embroideries, painted on wall surfaces or in missals, or sculptured on the tympana, capitals, or fonts. It ordinarily bears a cross of very slender proportions, to which a banner is frequently attached.

On the door of the church of St. Pudentiana at Rome, for instance, is a medallion containing the Agnus Dei, together with the inscription : " Dead or living I am but one; I am at once the Shepherd and the Lamb." On the celebrated Syon cope at South Kensington, amongst other devices, we see the Agnus Dei embroidered. In the Westminster inventory of 1540, we find " A nother albe haveyng wrought a egle, a gryffen, a holly lambe, and a lyon, with dyvers other beasts."

Louis IX. of France (St. Louis), who reigned from 1226 to 1270, caused the " agnel d'or " to be struck. This coin bore on one side the Agnus Dei, with the inscription, " Agnus Dei, qui tollis peccata mundi, miserere nobis," and on the other, " XPC vincit XPC regnat XPC imperat." This coin was imitated by Edward III., and, when the sacred

FIG. 85.

significance of the symbol was forgotten, was popularly called the mouton d'or.

Countless myriads of people the wide world over, who in many cases know or care nothing of symbolism, or regard it as quite a feature of the past, Sunday after Sunday raise the prayer to heaven, "O Lamb of God, that takest away the sins of the world, have mercy upon us."

The Lamb of the Apocalypse, with the seven horns and seven eyes that indicate the seven gifts of the Holy Spirit, is occasionally met with in mediæval art; but the poetic imagery of the Book of the Revelation does not readily lend itself to material representation, and of this "the Lamb that is in the midst of the throne" is but one instance of many that might be referred to. No painter or sculptor can reduce these images to form; the mere effort results in grotesque impossibilities that are only preserved from irreverence by the honesty and good faith of those who attempted them. The title of the Lamb is applied to Christ twenty-nine times in the Revelation, and any one turning to these passages will at once realize how natural it is that the Agnus Dei should be one of the most cherished of symbols. Earthly sorrow finds consolation, and the great burden of humanity and the mystery of life is irradiated with Divine light, in the touching words, "For the Lamb which is in the midst of the throne shall feed them, and shall lead them unto living fountains of waters: and God shall wipe away all tears from their eyes"; while, the sorrows of earth over for evermore, we listen in another passage to the great triumph song of the redeemed, as the thrilling anthem rises from the innumerable host, "Worthy is the Lamb that was slain to receive power, and riches, and wisdom, and strength, and honour, and glory, and blessing!"

St. John the Baptist is often represented in art as bearing a lamb. He may be thus seen in a picture by Murillo in our own National Gallery, where he is painted as a child caressing a pet lamb, the type of the mediatorial and sacrificial work of Christ. The standard is lying on the ground beside them. On St. John's Day in Venice a little fellow is selected to impersonate the great forerunner of the Messiah by appearing with a sheep's skin tied round his otherwise naked body, and attended by a lamb. Such customs are survivals from the Middle Ages, when, as in the Passion plays, it was endeavoured to appeal to the senses, and to render the scenes and characters of the Bible or the traditions of the Church in as realistic a manner as possible.

We pass now to a consideration of the use of the lion in religious art. We find it under several modifications of meaning, and it often becomes necessary to study the surroundings before we are able to appreciate the motive that may have led to its introduction. It is, for instance, sometimes used as a symbol of Christ, the Lord of life; at other times as a symbol of the prince of darkness. In the former case it illustrates such texts as "the Lion of the tribe of Judah has conquered"; in the latter it fitly personifies the lost angel fallen from his high estate, who " walketh about as a roaring lion, seeking whom he may devour." It is often introduced too in a general way as an emblem of strength, majesty, courage, and fortitude; or as the attribute of some especial saint; or, again, from its connexion with some particular historic event recorded in the Bible.

In a quaint old MS. of the twelfth century, " The Book of Beasts," [1] written by Philip de Thaun, we find a curious literary exemplification of the association of the lion with the second Person of the Trinity. As the tone of thought of that period naturally influenced the missal painter, the stone-carver, and all who were in any way concerned in art, we may very legitimately quote the passage. " The

---

[1] Of the " Livre des Créatures " seven copies only are known. The author had as patron Adelaide of Louvain, queen of Henry I. His poems are the earliest examples extant of the Anglo-Norman language. The MS. was written in the first half of the twelfth century, and in it he deals with the Creation. We give a sample, followed by the translation, as rendered by Thomas Wright, F.S.A.

> " En un livre divin, que apelum Genesim,
> Hoc lisant truvum quæ Dés fist par raisun
> Le soleil e la lune, e esteile chescune.
> Pur cel me plaist à dire, d'ico est ma materie,
> Que demusterai e à clers e à loi,
> Chi grant busnin en unt, e pur mei perierunt."

> " In a Divine book which is called Genesis,
> There reading, we find that God made by reason
> The sun and the moon, and every star.
> On this account it pleases me to speak of this is my matter
> Which I will show both to clerks and to laics,
> Who have just need of it, and will perish without it."

lion," writes our old author, " in many ways rules over many beasts, therefore is the lion king. He has a frightful face, the neck great and hairy; he has the breast before square, hardy, and pugnacious; his shape behind is slender, his tail of large fashion, and he has flat legs, and haired down to the feet; he has the feet large and cloven, the claws long and curved. When he is hungry or ill-disposed he devours animals without discrimination, as he does the ass which resists and brays. Now hear, without doubt, the significance of this. The lion signifies the Son of Mary. He is king of all people without any gainsay. He is powerful by nature over every creature, and fierce in appearance, and with fierce look he will appear to the Jews when he shall judge them, because they made themselves guilty when they hanged him on the cross, and therefore they have merited to have no king over them. The square breast shows strength of the Deity. The shape which he has behind, of very slender make, shows humanity, which he had with the Deity. By the foot, which is cloven, is demonstrance of God, who will clasp the world and hold it in his fist." We need not follow our old authority any further in his laboured mysticism; the passage given will sufficiently indicate the association in the Middle Ages of the lion with Christ.

It was an ancient belief that the lion cubs were born dead, but were brought to life three days after their birth by the roaring of the lion; and it was very easy to transfer this belief into a natural symbol of the resurrection of Christ.[1]

The use of the lion as an emblem of strength, majesty, and fortitude naturally arises from many passages in the Scriptures. Samson asks, " What is stronger than a lion ? " Job speaks of " the voice of the fierce lion." Any good concordance will supply an ample number of illustrative texts for the use of the lion as an emblem of the qualities we have named.

---

[1] " N'oublions pas que les Pères de l'Église se préoccupèrent toujours beaucoup plus de la pureté des doctrines qu'ils avaient à développer, que de l'exactitude Scientifique des notions sur lesquelles ils les appuyaient." —HIPPEAU, on " Le Bestiare Divin " of Guillaume.

And elsewhere : " L'objet important pour nous est de considérer la signification d'un fait et non d'en discuter l'authenticité " !

The lion was believed by the mediæval writers on natural —or perhaps we should rather say unnatural history—to always sleep with its eyes open, an idea that they in turn borrowed from more ancient authors in lieu of investigating for themselves. Hence the idea of watchfulness was superadded to the other qualities ascribed to the lion. This idea probably had some influence in the selection of the twelve flanking lions of Solomon's throne. The lion is not unfrequently

FIG. 86.

found in early Christian churches, and especially those under Lombard influence, as a sentinel at the doors, as the base to pillars, or at the foot of the pulpits.

The lion, again, as the attribute of some particular person, may freely be met with. The most notable example of this is seen, as we have already noted, in its association with St. Mark. Fig. 86, from some ancient stained glass in the South Kensington Museum, is a good illustration of this special

application of the lion. In mediæval art it is also largely
associated with St. Jerome. In sculpture or painting the
animal is ordinarily represented at his side. A well known
example of this, fig. 87, familiar to most of our readers,
doubtless, from photographs and engravings, is the "Last
Communion of St. Jerome," by Domenichino. The aged saint
has been brought by loving hands to the altar, the ministering priest hands him the wafer, and attendant angels hover
near to convey his soul to heaven. At his side crouches
a full-grown lion.

In our own National Gallery many good examples may be
seen. The friendship between the saint and the lion began
by a little kindly surgery on the part of St. Jerome, and in
a picture by Cosimo Tura the lion is seen in the background
limping with a thorn in one of his paws towards the kneeling saint. In a picture by Cosimo Rosselli St. Jerome turns
to meet the lion and is taking him by the paw, while an
attendant monk runs away towards the monastery, at the
door of which are several wondering and admiring monks.
It is a delicate point of discrimination that the artist has
given St. Jerome a nimbus, while the weak brother who flees
faithlessly and abandons his companion has no such distinction. In the "St. Jerome in his Study," attributed to
Giovanni Bellini, the "St. Jerome in the Desert," by Bono
Ferrarese, and in "The Virgin, the Child, attended by St.
Jerome and St. Domenick," of Filippino Lippi, the lion is
in each case conspicuously introduced.

In mediæval art the lion is introduced also in representations of several other saints. It is placed by the sides or
at the feet of SS. Prisca, Euphemia, Natalia, Thecla, and
Adrian. With St. Gerasimus it is represented as carrying
a basket in its mouth. It fawns in the amphitheatre on St.
Germanicus. It is represented as devouring SS. Silvanus,
Agapetus, and Ignatius, as digging the grave of St. Mary
of Egypt, and in the den with St. Pontianus. The student
who desires full information on the various legends involved
will do well to refer either to Butler's "Lives of the Saints,"
Newman's "Lives of the English Saints," and to Faber's
"Lives of the Saints and Servants of God." The first runs
to twelve volumes, the second to fourteen, while the last
needs forty-two to do the subject justice.

On the tombs of ecclesiastics, the effigy has frequently a

Fig. 87.

lion at the feet, significative of trampling upon the evil one.
Sometimes it is a dragon instead. In either case it is suggested doubtless by the text, " Thou shalt tread upon the
lion and adder, the young lion and the dragon shalt thou
trample under foot." [1]

We may, in conclusion, find the lion represented in illuminations, stone-carving, etc., in a way that is not symbolic
at all, but historic. Several such examples will readily occur
to the mind of the reader. We need only instance representations of Daniel in the lions' den. Even here such
treatments may be considered as in part symbolic very often,
since the particular example we have instanced occurs frequently in the catacombs, and there can be no doubt that,
beyond the illustration of a Bible incident, there was the
recognition also of the general deliverance from evil of those
who trusted in the God of Daniel.

The stag in Christian art is the emblem of solitude and
purity of life. It is the attribute of SS. Hubert, Eustachius,
Aidan, Felix, Julian, and Ida. When associated with the
two former of these, it bears a cross between its antlers, in
allusion to legends that are generally well known, and
somewhat foreign to our present purpose to here detail. It
was also taken as an emblem of religious aspiration, probably
from the passage in the Psalms, commencing " Like as the
hart panteth after the waterbrooks." The form appears
very commonly in the sculptures and wall paintings in the
catacombs of Rome and elsewhere in early Christian art.
In the old belief that the stag was "a great enemy to all

[1] The figures at the feet of monumental effigies are in their intention
at times incomprehensible, though we may ordinarily interpret their
meaning. They will generally fall into one of three classes. The first
of these includes all spiritual enemies to be trodden under foot ; and
these are symbolized by dragons, serpents, basilisks, and all such creatures, mythical or real, as bear evil significance. The second great class
comprises all forms used with heraldic intent, or that are allusive in
character to the name or vocation of the person with whom they are
associated ; such as the two hares at the feet of Bishop Harewell, on
his tomb in Wells Cathedral. The third class comprises emblems of
courage, strength, fidelity, and attachment. Dogs are frequently thus
introduced : that they were often pets may be seen from the collars and
bells attached to them ; on the brass of Sir Bryan Stapleton the dog's
name " Jakke " is inscribed on the collar.

kinds of serpents, which he labours to destroy when he finds any, though he be afraid of almost all other creatures," it became in the days of exaggerated symbolism a still more popular emblem, its supposed ruthless antipathy to the serpent rendering it not inaptly a symbol of the Christian fighting against evil.

The ox was emblematic of patience and strength, and in the writings of some of the early Fathers it is accepted as a symbol of Christ the true sacrifice; secondarily of prophets, apostles, and saints slain for the sake of Christ; and in the third place, of all who patiently bear the yoke, and labour in silence for the good of others. It is the well known evangelistic symbol attributed to St. Luke, and is also associated with SS. Leonard, Sylvester, Medard, Julietta, and Blandina.

The ox is, together with the ass, almost invariably introduced in representations of the Nativity, partly as natural accessories when the scene is treated historically, and more ordinarily as representatives of the homage due to God from all the creatures of His hand.[1] St. Bernard dwells upon this idea, and apart from this there is a very ancient tradition that an ox and ass were actually present at the birth of our Saviour. Besides this, the two animals were regarded as being symbolic respectively of the Jews and of the Gentiles.

SS. Germanus and Philibert have the ass as an attribute, and it kneels before the consecrated wafer borne by St. Anthony of Padua. It is a firm belief with many ignorant people that the conspicuous lines that form a cross on the back of the animal are a memorial of our Saviour's ride on the creature into Jerusalem, and that in remembrance of that event the whole race have ever since borne this badge of honour.

---

[1] In the "Historia de Nativitate Mariæ et de Infantia Salvatoris," we are told that once when the Holy Child lay upon the lap of His mother in a cave in the wilderness, during the flight into Egypt, dragons and other noisome creatures of the place came forth from their hiding-places and worshipped at His feet; a poetic fiction that finds its warrant in the words of St. Dionysius Areopagitica : " Such representations are less likely to mislead than those which pretend to pourtray the actual, since the former do not profess to contain the truth in themselves, and are rejected at once by the mind, which then passes on at once to the ideal and spiritual. The mind dwells in and is satisfied with the latter."

N

> " The mother of the eternall Sonne
> A Mayd shall be : Salvation
> Shall bring the world : yet far from Pride,
> Though King He on an asse shall ride."

In an example of French glass of the sixteenth century
we see that the angel who is sounding the trumpet of the
last judgment, at whose dread summons the earth is yield-
ing up her dead, is represented as riding on an elephant that
tramples a man underfoot; while on a seal in private hands
we see the device of St. Peter bearing the usual keys, and
riding upon an elephant too.   The invincible might of the
creature may probably have in each instance led to its introduction.   In the latter case it may represent the Church
under the guidance of St. Peter going forth to conquer.
The elephant was long regarded as the emblem of the kingly
rank from a belief that he could not bow his knees, an idea
that is met with from time to time in the old writers.

In Christian art the horse appears as the symbol of three
saints, Anastasius, Hippolytus, and Quirinus.   In any representations of those saints that approach the pictorial, they
are depicted as being dragged and torn by wild horses.   The
horse is sometimes regarded as an emblem of courage and
generosity.   In the Roman catacombs it ordinarily denotes
the swiftness of life.   Sometimes the palm branch of victory
is placed over its head.

SS. Martin, Maurice, Victor, and George are generally
represented on horseback.   The latter, as our own patron
saint, will be familiar enough to all; for, to quote the Golden
Legend, " the blyssyd and holy martyr Saynt George is
patron of this Realme of Englande," and he is represented
freely on our coinage and elsewhere.

The mythical unicorn was regarded as a symbol of purity
and strength, and is figured in the catacombs.   From its
supposed love of solitude it was also a symbol of the monastic life.   It is associated too with St. Justina.   In our
book "Mythland" we have gone at very considerable length
into the legendary, heraldic, and religious references to the
creature ; and to this we would beg to refer those of our
readers who care to follow out an old belief through its
various phases.

While we in England naturally regard the bear as a
creature only to be seen in zoological gardens, it was in

earlier days, as it still is, on the continent a common animal enough, and the hermits in their caves and woodland solitudes had abundant opportunities of making its acquaintance. Hence in Christian art we find the bear associated with SS. Maximinus, Blandina, Florentius, Corbinian, and perhaps more especially with St. Gall. In this latter case the bear is generally represented as carrying a log of wood. On the seal of the monastery of St. Gall in Switzerland the saint is represented sitting on a throne, and offering a small loaf of bread to a bear, who stands on his hind legs and receives the gift in his two forepaws. The same device is found on the seal of the town of St. Gallen on a document dated 1300. According to the accepted legend it appears that, as St. Gall was praying in the wilderness on the spot where the famous monastery called after him was afterwards erected, he saw a bear come from the forest and devour the fragments that remained of his frugal supper. He at once called the beast before him, and commanded him as some little set off to the lost meal to fetch some wood for his fire. The bear retired to the forest, and shortly emerged with an enormous log, which he cast upon the embers, whereupon the saint in kindly good nature went to his small store, gave the bear a whole loaf from his scanty supply, and dismissed him in peace.

Probably one great reason why the dog, " the friend of man," as we call him, is so seldom introduced in religious art is that it is an animal that is but rarely mentioned in the Bible, and when referred to at all is seldom named in aught but an evil sense. The only indication of their possessing any value is in a passage in Job,[1] where the dogs of the flock are referred to, though even here the reference is somewhat contemptuous. Elsewhere the children of Israel are told not to bring the price of a dog into the house of the Lord for any vow. The thankless people of God are compared by Isaiah to dumb dogs, elsewhere to greedy dogs; and in the last chapter of the whole Bible we read that dogs, sorcerers, murderers, and idolaters shall be excluded

---

[1] In the apocryphal book of Tobit the dog figures fully as a companion. Ver. 16 of chap. v. is a pleasant picture: "And when his son had prepared all things for the journey, his father said, Go thou with this man, and God, which dwelleth in heaven, prosper your journey, and the angel of God keep you company. So they went forth both, and the young man's dog with them."

from the paradise of God. It will be naturally objected to this latter passage that it cannot be taken in any literal sense; but if the animal be introduced in a symbolic sense, it only strengthens our assertion that all the associations connected with the dog in the Bible are unfavourable to its introduction in any art under religious influence. If our readers will take the trouble to look up some of the passages, and there are over thirty of them where the animal is expressly named, they will find that our statement is fully borne out by the facts. The dog even to the present day throughout the East occupies a very inferior position. He is tolerated as a public scavenger, but he calls no man master, and, prowling as he does with his fellows in large packs, goes far to become a public nuisance. In mediæval art he is generally intended as a symbol of fidelity. He is placed at the feet of SS. Bernard, Wendelin, Sira, and Roch; while St. Parthenius is represented as slaying a mad dog by the sign of the cross.

The pig is intended in a good sense as the symbol of St. Anthony; in an evil sense, as one of the forms in which Satan has from time to time appeared. St. Anthony was said to have been originally a swineherd, and is therefore ordinarily represented as accompanied by a hog; and pigs were in some cases dedicated to him. In Pisano's picture in the National Gallery of "St. Anthony and St. George," the two saints confront each other, and at the feet of one is the pig, and of the other the vanquished dragon. Amongst the figures carved in Henry the Seventh's Chapel at Westminster will be found St. Anthony, a bearded figure in frock and scapular, and at his side a gaunt pig is standing.

The use of the pig in an evil sense has probably been a good deal influenced by the Biblical story of the possession of the herd of swine by the evil spirits cast out from the demoniacs,[1] and by its being included amongst the unclean beasts forbidden to the chosen people.[2] Such texts again as that in Proverbs, "As a jewel of gold in a swine's snout, so is a fair woman which is without discretion," or that in Matthew against casting pearls before swine, show a tendency towards depreciation of the animal.

---

[1] See Matt. viii. 28 *et seq.* ; Mark v. 2 *et seq.*; Luke viii. 27 *et seq.*
[2] See Lev. xi. 7 ; Isa. lxv. 4, lxvi. 3 and 17.

" Gregory relateth in a dialogue in his third book that when a certain church of the Arians having been restored to the Orthodox was being consecrated, and reliques of St. Sebastian and the blessed Agatha had been conveyed thither, the people there assembled of a sudden perceived a swine to be running to and fro among their feet: the which regaining the doors of the Church could be seen of none, and moved all to marvel. Which sign the Lord showed for this cause, that it might be manifest to all that the unclean inhabitant had gone forth from that place. But in the following night a great noise was made on the roof of the same church, as if some one were running confusedly about. The second night the uproar was much greater. On the third night also so vast a noise was heard as if the whole church had been overthrown from its foundations, but it immediately ceased, and no further inquietude of the old Enemy hath appeared in it." [1]

The goat, wolf, fox, and ape were ordinarily employed by the old writers and sculptors in an evil sense as symbols of lust, cruelty, and fraud. St. Anthony, for instance, is represented as tempted by Satan in the form of a goat.

" The Wolfe indeede signifieth craft, subtiltie, greedinesse of mind, inordinate desire of that which appertaineth to another, to some discord and sedition : for it is saide how that the Wolfe procureth all other beasts to fight and contend. He seeketh to devour the sheepe, that beast which of all other is the most hurtlesse and simple and void of guile, thirsting continually after their blood : yea, nature hath implanted so inveterate a hatred atweene the wolfe and the sheepe, that being dead, yet in the secret operation of Nature appeareth there a sufficient trial of their discording natures, so that the enmitie betweene them seemeth not to dye with their bodies : for if there be put vpon a harpe, or any such like instrument, strings made of the intrailles of a sheepe, and amongst them but only one made of the intrailles of a wolfe, be the musician never so cunning in his skil yet can he not reconcile them to an vnity and concord of sounds, so discording always is that string of the wolfe. It may well likewise denote the seditious persons, of which sort if there be but one in a whole commonwealth yet he is

---

[1] Durandus.

able to disturb the quiet concord and agreement of many thousands of good subjects, even as one string of that beast is able to confound the harmony of many other well tuned strings."

In Scandinavian mythology the wolf is the bringer of victory, and amongst the Romans, from its association with Romulus and Remus, it was held in honour; but the extract we have just given from Ferne, a mediæval writer on heraldry, very fairly reflects the feeling of the Middle Ages, and helps to account for its evil repute.

Though every allusion to the wolf in the Bible is of an unfavourable nature, the creature is often in the legendary history of the saints represented in a favourable light, doubtless with the idea of making the miracle still more miraculous. He is in the Bible the "grievous wolf," "the ravening wolf," the "fierce evening wolf"; while to St. Vedast he brings a goose in his mouth, and to St. Mark a ram's skin (in each case, we fear, making the saint a receiver of stolen goods). He guards the dead body of St. Carpophorus and that of our own St. Edmund until they receive fit interment and the last rites of the Church.

We often in the Middle Ages find bitter and satirical evidences of the feud between the various orders of clergy and the itinerant friars, leading to such representations as a fox preaching to geese, an ass's head beneath the cowl, a monkey at prayers, a fox with the mitre and staff of the bishop. These illustrations, whatever may be lacking of grace, or frequently even of decorum, are often pungent and graphic in the extreme, and remain as curious records in our old churches of this strong antagonism. The following title from a book written by one of our bishops, but secretly printed under an assumed name at Zürich in 1543, is a good literary illustration of the opprobrious use of the fox in theological controversy : " Yet a Course at the Romyshe Foxe, a Dysclosynge or Opening of the Manne of Synne, Contayned in the late Declaratyon of the Popes old Faythe, made by Edmonde Bonner, Byshopp of London. Whereby Wyllyam Tolwyn was than newlye professed at Paules Crosse openlye into Antichristes Romyshe Relygyon agayne by a newe Solempne Othe of obedyence, notwythstadnge the Othe made to hys Prynce afore to the contrarye."

While the predatory disposition and crafty policy of the

fox rendered the creature an apt emblem where such features
had, with more or less of charity, to be satirised, the monkey
and ape were rather the symbols of indecorum and of unseemly
levity; though in a fourteenth century window in the north
aisle of the nave of York Minster we find them (very excep-
tionally) introduced in an entirely different spirit, playing
on musical instruments as a part of the great choir of creation: "Praise the Lord from the earth, ye dragons and all
deeps: . . . beasts, and all cattle; creeping things, and flying
fowl." "Praise Him with the sound of the trumpet: praise
Him with the psaltery and harp. . . . Let everything that
hath breath praise the Lord."

CHAPTER X.

The Dove—The Sevenfold Gifts of the Spirit—The Pelican—" Armorie of Honour "—Extracts from Skelton and Guillim—Phœnix—Eagle—Peacock—Cock—" Mystical Mirror of the Church "—Swan—Owl—Raven—Magpie—Hen and Chickens—Vine—Palm—White Lily—Passion Flower—Amaranth—Rose—Olive—Tree of Jesse—Yew.

AMONGST bird forms the dove, the symbol of the Holy Spirit, is most freely met with in art. Such distinct Bible references as that in Matthew iii. 16, where upon the baptism of Christ "the Spirit of God descending like a dove," or in the words of St. Luke, " the Holy Ghost descended in bodily shape like a dove," are an ample warrant and justification of the symbol. See figs. 26, 56, 69, 85, 88, 89. Doves of carved wood are frequently found on font covers in our old English parish churches, and probably in former days no font would have been considered duly complete without such a symbol of the sacramental rite, and of the presence of the Holy Spirit in it. The symbol is one of the few that have fully retained their place and meaning throughout the centuries down to the present day, and it is as intelligible to us now as to the Christians in the earliest ages of the Church. The three scenes in which the figure most freely occurs are in representations of the baptism of Christ, of the annunciation of the Virgin, and of the creation of the world, though we also see it introduced hovering over the heads of the saints of God as the inspirer of noble thoughts, or at times resting on their shoulders. In the picture by Borgognone of the " Coronation of the Virgin " all the persons of the Trinity are present; and here, as elsewhere, when any event which concerns all the Persons of the Godhead is represented, the Holy Spirit, with but few exceptions, is in the form of a dove.

Examples are so numerous that it seems scarcely worth while to particularize at any length. As three typical ex-

amples however we may mention the " Baptism of Christ,"
by Francesca, in the National Gallery; the " Annunciation,"
in the same collection, by Crivelli; and the " St. Peter of
Alcantara," by Zurbaran (fig. 89). In the last example
the dove is hovering over the saint, while in a statue at
Chartres Cathedral of Pope Gregory the Great the dove is

FIG. 88.

on his shoulder, holding commune with him, and inspiring
holy thoughts.

Sometimes in old work (as in fig. 90) we find a ring of
seven doves surrounding a figure; but the significance is the
same, the reference is still to the Holy Spirit, though in this
case the sevenfold gifts of the Spirit are more especially
emphasised.[1]

---

[1] At other times the symbol for these gifts is a group of seven lamps,
in illustration of the passage: " There were seven lamps of fire burning
before the throne, which are the seven spirits of God."

FIG. 89.

In Isaiah xi. 2 we have in the Authorized Version but six of these Divine gifts mentioned : " The spirit of wisdom and understanding, the spirit of counsel and might, the spirit of knowledge and of the fear of the Lord " ; but in the Vulgate rendering of this passage we have " Sapientia, Intellectus, Consilium, Fortitudo, Scientia, Pietas, Timor."

Authority is the attribute of God the Father ; and as ruler of all things He bears the orb, the symbol of universal sway. Love is the attribute of God the Son ; hence as Redeemer of the children of men He bears the cross of Calvary.   Knowledge is the special attribute of God the Holy Spirit ; hence He bears the book, the symbol of intelligence and reason. He is the instructor of the ignorant, the illuminator of the blind, the Spirit of truth to abide with man for ever.   The

Fig. 90.

Spirit of wisdom reveals God to man ; the spirit of understanding teaches us about Him ; the Spirit of counsel teaches us to distinguish good from evil ; the Spirit of strength enables us fearlessly to struggle for the right ; the Spirit of knowledge guides into the way of peace ; the Spirit of godliness gives us love ; the Spirit of fear teaches us humility, and the reverence due to the great King.

In a more general sense, the dove becomes the symbol of all believers.   Such a text as " be ye harmless as doves " would naturally suggest the idea.   Doves are generally employed in the Bible as the symbols of guilelessness, gentleness, innocence, and faithfulness.   David, in the midst of his troubles, dreams of a haven of peace, and sighs for the wings of a dove, that he might flee away from earthly turmoil to celestial rest.   Other passages will be found in the Canticles, Isaiah, Jeremiah, Ezekiel, Hosea, Nahum, and elsewhere. Doves as emblems of believers figure largely in the cata-

combs of Rome, and throughout early Christian art. As
emblems of conjugal affection sometimes two are placed
together.

On the martyrdom of St. Polycarp the legend tells us that
his blood extinguished the flames that surrounded him, and
that from the ashes arose a white dove which flew heavenward out of sight. In representations of St. Celestin and St.
Cunibert the dove is whispering in their ear the heavenly
message; to St. Albert it brings the eucharistic elements; to
St. Agnes, virgin bride of heaven, a ring; to St. Remigius, a
cruse of oil.

The dove with the olive branch in its mouth points to its
association with the receding waters of the Deluge, and is
thus an emblem of restoration to prosperity and peace.

The pelican, though without Biblical authority, and only
having its symbolic meaning based upon an error in natural
history, is perhaps, next to the dove, the most familiar of
bird symbols.

The pelican is in an especial manner a Christian symbol,
an emblem of the Redeemer of mankind; and we know of no
instance of its use with any symbolic meaning in pre-Christian times. The bird has at the tip of its long bill a crimson
spot, and this gave rise to the belief amongst the older
naturalists that the pelican, while really pruning its
feathers, was feeding its young with its own blood. It is
the symbol therefore of loving sacrifice. Hence Dante
calls the Saviour "nostro pelicano."[1] In the black-letter
" Bibliotheca Biblia " we read that " the Pelicane, whose
sons are nursed with bloude, stabbeth deep her breast, self-
murtheresse through fondnesse to hir broode." Shake-
sperian students again will recall the lines in " Hamlet " :

> " To his good friends thus wide I'll ope my arms,
> And, like the kind, life-rend'ring pelican,
> Refresh them with my blood."

While in the " Giaour" of Byron we find allusion to

> " The desert bird whose beak unlocks her bosom's stream,
> To still her famished nestlings' scream."

---

[1] In the inventory of the goods of Westminster Abbey of the year 1540
we find mention of a " Crosse Staff of Syluer Gylt withe the Salutacon
thereon and a Pelycan," the latter the symbol and type of the coming
Messiah (Luke i. 42).

In the " Account of the Antient Rites and Monuments of the Monastic Church of Durham," as they existed before the suppression, written in 1593, we read : " At the north end of the high altar there was a goodly fine letteron of brass, with a great pelican on the height of it, finely gilt, billing her blood out of her breast to feed her young ones, and her wings spread abroad, whereon lay the book.   Also there was, lower down in the choir, another letteron of brass, with an eagle on the height of it, and her wings spread abroad, whereupon the monks laid their books."   The first of these was for the epistle and gospel, the second for the lessons.

In the year 1649 an enthusiastic admirer of Charles. I., and an evident believer in the idea that he shed his blood for his people, wrote a book on that king, entitling him " The Princely Pelican."

A variation in the mediæval pelican legend may occasionally be met with, where, instead of the young being nourished by the blood of the bird, their dead bodies are restored by it to life.   Whichever reading we accept has equally valuable symbolic meaning, though the generally accepted version is the more pleasing.   The alternative reading—we quote from Bossewell's " Armorie of Honour "—is as follows : " The pellicane feruently loueth her young byrdes.   Yet when thei ben haughtie, and beginne to waxe hote, they smite her in the face and wounde her, and she smiteth them and slaeth them.   And after three daies she mourneth for them, and then striking herself in the side till the bloode runne out, she sparpleth it upon their bodyes, and by vertue therof they quicken againe." [1]

We find the same idea again in the " Armorie of Birds " of Skelton :

> " Then sayd the Pellycane :
> When my Byrdts be slayne,
> With my Bloude I them revyve.
> Scripture doth record,
> The same dyd our Lord,
> And rose from deth to lyve."

---

[1] " Le pélican est un oiseau merveilleux qui habite les bords du Nil. Quand les petits du pélican sont devenus grands ils frappent leur père à coups de bec, et celuici dans sa colère les tue.   Mais trois jours après il revient vers eux, se déchire le flanc avec son bec, et son sang répandu sur ses petits les rappelle à la vie."—GUILLIM.

Though all belief in the phœnix has been for some centuries exploded, that mythic fowl was firmly believed in by
the ancients; Pliny, Ovid, and many other writers giving full
details of its mysterious existence. As we have in our
"Mythland" fully gone into the whole subject, we forbear to
do so afresh, contenting ourselves here with just explaining
that the ancient belief was that the phœnix, after living a
thousand years or so, committed itself to the flames that
burst at the fanning of its wings from the funeral pyre of
costly spices that it had itself constructed, and that from its
ashes a new phœnix arose to life. Tertullian, one of the

Fig. 91.

early writers of the Christian Church, in all good faith
accepts it as a most marked and evident symbol of the
resurrection and of eternity. The phœnix is represented
in some of the earliest Christian mosaics in the churches
of Rome, and often has a star-shaped nimbus.

The powerful heavenward flight of the eagle, fixing its
gaze upon the sun, has made it a very natural symbol in
Christian art of the Ascension, while it is still more widely
employed and far more commonly recognised as the symbol
of St. John. SS. Medard and Bertulph are represented in
art as sheltering beneath an eagle with outstretched wings;
and St. Servatius, sleeping in the hot sunlight, is shaded

and fanned by the pinions of an eagle that hovers over him.

The peacock, like the dove, is a very favourite form in Byzantine art; though now-a-days thought of rather as an emblem of vanity or pride, it was in earlier days regarded as a symbol of the Resurrection. Hence it is generally represented as standing upon a small ball or globe, the glorified spirit rising above all mundane cares. Many good examples of it may be seen in the mosaics of Ravenna and Venice.[1] (Fig. 91 is from an early Christian monument at Athens.)

The peacock was regarded as an emblem of the resurrection, from the yearly changing and renewal of its brilliant feathers, and from an old belief in the incorruptibility of its flesh.

The cock is another very ancient symbol. If associated with any representation of the denial of Christ by St. Peter, it signifies repentance, since the crowing of this bird awoke the time-serving apostle to a sense of the depth to which he had fallen. At other times it is employed as a symbol of vigilance. In the "Mystical Mirrour of the Church," by Hugo de Sancto Victore, we learn that "the cock representeth the preacher. For the cock in the deep watches of the night divideth the hours thereof with his song, and arouseth the sleepers. He foretelleth the approach of day, but first he stirreth up himself to crow by the striking of his wings. Behold ye these things mystically, for not one of them is there without meaning. The sleepers be the children of this world, lying in sins. The cock is the company of preachers, which do preach sharply, do stir up the sleepers to cast away the works of darkness, which also do foretell the coming of the light, when they preach of the Day of Judgment and of future glory. But wisely before they preach unto others do they rouse themselves by virtue from the sleep of sin and do chasten their bodies."

The swan figures but rarely in Christian art. It is represented by the side of St. Hugh, St. Ludger, and St. Cuthbert. We find a curious passage in Foxe's "Book of Martyrs,"

---

[1] Even to mediæval days examples of its use are not uncommon. Thus for instance in an inventory of the property of Westminster Abbey, made in the year 1388, we find an alb " cum pavonibus rotulas in rostris tenentibus," and another vestment embroidered " cum floribus et avibus viridibus pavonibus et bestijs aureis."

wherein, speaking of the martyrdom of Huss, he tells us
that he said, "You are now going to burn a goose (the name
of Huss signifying a goose in the Bohemian language), but
in a century you will have a swan, whom you can neither
roast nor boil." Foxe goes on to say that "if this were
spoken in prophecy he must have meant Martin Luther, who
shone about one hundred years after, and who had a swan
for his arms, whether suggested by this circumstance or of
family descent and heraldry is not known."

A mediæval moralist says that "swans are looked upon as
symbols of hypocrites, because they have fine wings, and yet
can scarce raise themselves from the earth, so that they are
of no use to them; besides the feathers of a swan are white
to perfection, but their flesh is very black, as are the hypocrites, appearing outwardly virtuous, and being inwardly
very wicked."

In religious art the owl is associated with the idea of
mourning and desolation. "The owle betokeneth alwaies
some heavie newes, and is most execrable and accursed. He
keepeth ever in the deserts, and is the verie monster of the
night, neither crying nor singing out cleare, but uttering a
certaine heavie grone of dolefull moning. Therefore if he be
seene within citties or otherwise abroad in any place it is
not good, but prognosticateth some fearfull misfortune." We
see the same idea again in Shakespeare : "Out on ye owls !
Nothing but songs of death!" and another well-known
passage in Macbeth will readily occur to our readers.

In some cases no doubt the Christian symbolism was a
deliberate reaction from the pagan. Thus the owl, as the
bird of Athene, was held in especial esteem by the Athenians,
who claimed that goddess as the patron and founder of their
city, and stamped her emblem on their coinage. Hence
therefore the early Christians would feel an objection to
the introduction of the bird. The raven again, the standard
of the Norsemen, and amongst the classic nations a bird
dedicated to the sun-god Apollo, was, like the magpie,
held in later days to be a symbol of ill fortune. When
these birds therefore are introduced in Christian art, they
ordinarily reflect the prevalent idea; thus in some MSS.
they are represented as perching in the tree from whence
Eve gathers the forbidden fruit. The association of the
raven with the story of the subsiding Deluge has also made

it an emblem of wandering and unrest. It is connected with the legendary history of some few saints ; it is placed at the feet of St. Benedict, it bears a ring in its mouth to St. Ida, brings a letter to St. Oswald, and guards the body of the sainted martyr Vincent.

Fig. 92.

The hen and chickens, as an emblem of God's providence, are sometimes met with in old sculptures on ecclesiastical buildings. Their introduction evidently springs from that passage in the Bible that shows us the infinitely tender Redeemer mourning over the guilty city of Jerusalem, and declaring that, had its inhabitants so willed it, God's good providence would have been to them a shield and sure defence, an effectual succour, even as the hen gathers her young beneath her wings, and guards them from every harm.

Many other animal forms might have been referred to, the spotless ermine and the stork, the emblem of filial piety, until in descending scale we reached the ant, the emblem of industry, and the bee, the symbol of busy forethought; but it is scarcely desirable, in pity to our readers, to make an exhaustive catalogue, so we pass now to a consideration of some few of the plants that have had symbolic meaning attached to them in Christian art.

The vine as a symbol of Christ, based upon His own words, "I am the Vine," has at all times been freely employed. Often, as on the tomb of the empress Constantia, the sister of Constantine, it is the sole symbol of the Christian faith. In the early Christian mosaics (as in fig. 92) the vine plays a conspicuous part; and we see in

FIG. 93.

these early works how persistently, in the well nigh exclusive use of such symbols as the vine and the Good Shepherd, the mind of the Church then dwelt almost solely on the risen Lord.

The vine is several times employed in the Old Testament as a symbol of the chosen people: "A vine Thou didst bring out of Egypt. Thou castedst out the nations, and plantedst it. Thou preparedst the ground for it; and it spreads its roots and filled the land. The mountains were covered with its shade, and with its tendrils the lofty cedars."

Sometimes it is used in a general sense as expressive of temporal blessing, as in the benediction of Jacob by Isaac. "God give thee of the dew of heaven, the fatness of the earth, and plenty of corn and wine"; or later on as an emblem of the joyous, festive innocence of the Christian life. It is also often found as one of the symbols of the Eucharist.

The palm, the symbol of victory, is one of the earliest of Christian symbols, and commemorates, times without number, in the catacombs the triumph of the martyrs for the faith.[1] In the darkness of these subterranean vaults, to the survivors it bore testimony of conflict past and death vanquished, as in fig. 94, while in the light of heaven we see it recognised and honoured as a testimony for evermore of

FL. IOVINA. QVAE. VIXIT. ANNIS. TRIBVS. D. XXXII. DEPOS NEOFITA. IN PACE. XI. KAL. OCTOB

Fɪɢ. 94.

victory won, where the great army of the faithful unto death, out of every nation and kindred and people, stand before the eternal throne, clothed in spotless white and bearing the palms of victory in their hands.

In the " Peter Martyr " of Titian, the saint looks up to heaven in expectation of speedy death, while hovering over-

---

[1] In fig. 93, a gem of about 380 A.D., we have an interesting representation of the martyrdom of a follower of Christ. The sacred monogram indicates her Lord's presence in her time of need, the dove and olive branch point to the rest and peace into which she is soon to enter, and at her feet is the victor's palm.

head a cherub bears a palm branch; and in the "Massacre of the Innocents," by Guido Reni, in the clouds above the scene of violence and bloodshed two cherubs bear large bundles of the palm branches in their arms.

Fig. 95.

Fig. 96.

It was an ancient belief that the palm tree would always grow erect, no matter how it might be weighted or pulled aside, hence it was a favourite emblem in the Middle Ages of triumph over adversity. Mary Queen of Scots adopted it

Fig. 97.

Fig. 98.

for instance, in this sense; and on the frontispiece of the "Eikon Basilike" we see, amongst many other emblems, a palm tree standing erect, with two heavy weights attached to it, and the legend, "Crescit sub pondere virtus," and the "Explanation of the Embleme":

Fig. 99.

> " Though clogged with weights of miseries,
> Palm-like depressed I higher rise." [1]

The palm is also associated with the triumphant entry of
Christ into Jerusalem, commemorated thereafter as Palm
Sunday. It was the special emblem of Judæa.[2]

The white lily, or annunciation lily, from its association in
art with the Virgin Mary, is one of the commonest of floral
symbols. The fragrance, purity of colour, and beauty of
the flower render it a most appropriate emblem. Abundant
examples of the association of this flower with the Virgin
mother may be found in the National Gallery and elsewhere, so that it is almost needless to particularize special
instances.[3] In Roman Catholic countries the snowdrop is,
from a similar motive, dedicated to the Virgin Mary; and on
the festival of the Annunciation in March, when white lilies
are not procurable, her altars are decked with it.

The passion flower is freely used in modern work to
symbolise, as its name implies, the passion of our Lord. It
is a good illustration of that exaggerated symbolism that one
so often encounters, in that straining after analogy that sees
a wealth of meaning in the most natural and ordinary of
arrangements. The ten members composing the perianth
of the flower, we are told, represent the apostles, Peter being
absent because he deceived his Master, and Judas because he
betrayed Him. The rays within the flowers are the nimbus

---

[1] For many curious illustrations of such like old fancies the reader
may advantageously turn to the " Symbolorum et Emblematum ex Re
Herbaria, Animalibus Volatilibus Aquatilibus et Insectus de Sumtorum "
of Camerarius, or to the " Symbola divina et humana," the first being
issued in the year 1654, and the second in 1666.

[2] We may see this very well illustrated in figs. 95, 96, 97, representing coins struck by the Romans on the defeat of the Jews and the
destruction of Jerusalem.

"Beneath her palm, here sad Judæa weeps."—POPE.

In fig. 95 we see two captives at the foot of the symbolic palm; and
fig. 96 is very similar, except that the place of one of the captives is
taken by a Roman soldier. In fig. 97 a winged figure of Victory in-
scribes the SPQR on the shield, in token of the subjugation of Judæa
by the armies of Rome. Fig. 98 gives the obverse of this coin, and
shows us the laurel-crowned head of the conqueror, the emperor
Vespasian.

[3] Fig. 99 will suffice as an illustration; it is taken from a bas-relief
by Andrea della Robbia.

or glory. The ovary is supposed to resemble a hammer, while the three styles with their rounded heads are the nails, the five stamens being the five wounds. Though the passion flower is now not uncommon, our readers will remember that it was introduced from abroad ; hence it does not occur in early English art in our cathedrals, illuminations, or elsewhere.

The immortal amaranth has a literary [1] rather than an artistic existence. Clement of Alexandria refers to it as the "amaranthus flos, symbolum immortalitatis." The name is derived from two Greek words, signifying not withering. The passage in our New Testament, "a crown of glory that fadeth not away" is in the original Greek "the amaranthine crown of glory."

The rose is only twice referred to in the Bible, and the commentators are generally agreed that the plant so called has been wrongly named. One reference will be found in the Song of Solomon, "I am the rose of Sharon, and the lily of the valleys"; while the second is in Isaiah, where we read that when the kingdom of righteousness shall be established on earth, the desert shall rejoice and blossom as the rose.

Though the rose was known in Syria, and one species, the damask, takes its name from Damascus, the word translated rose in the Bible indicates a bulbous-rooted plant. The plant intended was probably the narcissus, a flower that is abundant throughout Syria.

Amongst the various flowers consecrated to the Virgin

---

[1] Milton introduces it several times in the "Paradise Lost," as for example :

> "The multitude of Angels, with a shout
> Loud as from numbers without number, sweet
> As from blest voices, uttering joy—Heaven rung
> With jubilee, and loud hosannas filled
> The eternal regions. Lowly reverent
> Towards either throne they bow, and to the ground
> With solemn adoration down they cast
> Their crowns, inwove with amaranth and gold,—
> Immortal amaranth, a flower which once
> In Paradise, fast by the Tree of Life
> Began to bloom, but, soon for Man's offence
> To Heaven removed where first it grew, there grows
> And flowers aloft, shading the Fount of Life."

by our forefathers, the rose occupies a conspicuous position, and amongst the numerous titles bestowed upon her we find that of Santa Maria della Rosa.   This title therefore is given to several pictures in various continental collections, in which a rose is placed either in her hand or in that of her Divine Son.   We may see a good example of the introduction of this flower, together with the white lily, in one of the pictures of the Virgin and Child, by Benozzo Gozzoli, in our own National Gallery.   The Virgin is hailed in some books of devotion the Rosa Cœli, the Rose of Heaven, or the Mystic Rose.

The rose figures again in the legendary history of St. Dorothea, who suffered martyrdom under the government of Fabricius, and who converted afterwards one Theophilus to the Christian faith by sending him some roses from Paradise.   It is also associated with SS. Casilda, Elizabeth of Portugal, Rose of Viterbo, Rose of Lima, Rosalia, Victoria, Angelus, Francis, and several others.[1]

The olive has been celebrated from the earliest ages.   It must have been known before the flood, as the dove returned to Noah in the ark with a leaf of it in her mouth.   There can be little doubt of this incident having been the origin of the recognition of the plant as the emblem of peace and good-will.   It is frequently mentioned in the Scriptures. Jacob, for instance, poured the oil of the olive on the memorial pillar that he set up in Bethel, and the Promised Land was to be "a land of wheat, and barley, and vines, and fig trees, and pomegranates; a land of oil olive, and honey."   The holy anointing oil of the Temple was olive oil, scented with myrrh, cinnamon, sweet calamus, and cassia.

As sacred history made the olive emblematic of peace, so from its great value to man has it been also considered the

---

[1] " For als moche as a fayre Mayden was blamed with wrong and sclaundered sche was demed to the dethe, and to be brent in that place to the whiche sche was ledde.   And as the Fyre began to burne about hire sche made hire Preyers to our Lord, that als wisely as sche was not gylty of that Synne, the he wold helpe hire and make it to be knownen to alle men of his mercifulle Grace.   And whan sche hadde thus sayde sche entered into the Fuyre, and anon was the Fuyr quenched and oute ; and the Branddes that were brennynge becomen rede Roses, and they that were not kyndled becomen white Roses.   And these were the first roses, both white and rede that ever ony man saughe."

sign and expression of plenty. As a symbol in one or other of these senses we thus find it on the coins of those countries where the plant is not a native. Our own Britannia, for instance, holds in her hand the olive branch of peace and good-will on some of the coinage of previous reigns.

In Christian art the old illuminators and glass-painters often represented the genealogy of Christ under the form of a tree, the tree of Jesse, in allusion to that text in Isaiah where it states that " there shall come forth a rod out of the stem of Jesse, and a branch shall grow out of his roots." Jesse is represented as recumbent, and the tree springs from his loins, spreading into luxuriant foliage and bearing on its numerous branches the various royal and other personages who are mentioned in the first chapter of St. Matthew's Gospel. The name of each is usually inscribed on a label in close proximity to the figure, and crowning all, at the summit of the tree is the Virgin Mary in an aureole, bearing in her arms the Divine Son. Sometimes, though more rarely, the tree terminates in a cross bearing the dying Christ. The tree of Jesse first appears as a device in the twelfth century, and in the thirteenth and fourteenth centuries becomes exceedingly popular, occurring in stained glass, mural paintings, illuminated manuscripts, sculpture, wood carving, and embroidery.[1] The foliage is often that of the vine, the symbol of spiritual fruitfulness, and allusive to Him who said, " I am the Vine, ye are the branches."

The Celtic priesthood regarded the yew as an emblem of immortality, and therefore planted it in their sacred groves. It has been conjectured that the early Christian churches were of set purpose erected on the sites of the old heathen shrines as a more distinctive token of the supplanting of the old creed by the new, and that in that case some of the magnificent old yew trees seen in many country churchyards may be relics of a yet older faith. In Brady's " Clavis Calendaria." we read that " amongst our superstitious forefathers the palm tree or its substitutes, box or yew, were

---

[1] " A cope of blewe velvett rychely embrothered with a Jesse, the ymages of the Jesse beyng garnysshed with perle."—Inventory, Westminster Abbey, A.D. 1540. In inventory of St. Paul's, A.D. 1245, we find a "Jesse quam dedit Rex," and a red cope " bene breudata Jesse."

solemnly blessed on Palm Sunday and some of their branches burnt to ashes and used on Ash Wednesday in the following year, while others were gathered and distributed amongst the pious, who bore them in procession." Caxton in 1483 also shows that the yew was a substitute in these northern regions for the palm; for he says in his book on the Church festivals, "but for that we have none olyve, therefore we take yew instead of palm olyve."

Many of the ancient and mediæval beliefs in various branches of natural history affected theologians and artists, and gave rise to symbols that lived for awhile; but when the false ideas upon which they were based were corrected (though the myth of the pelican is a marked instance to the contrary), the symbols in most cases lost their force, and were discarded.

It is manifest that we have but referred to some few of the more common vegetable forms. In some cases, as in the apples presented to a king for the restoration of his sight by St. Malachy, a plant may only once appear in Christian symbolism. It is impossible to extend our remarks to such a length as would include all these exceptional cases. In other legends "flowers" alone are mentioned, without any attempt at distinction of species, while many well-known references, such as the withering grass, the fading flower, the purging hyssop, the parable of the wheat and the tares, and the illustration of the grain sown in the earth as a symbol of the resurrection of the dead, are very familiar to us, but scarcely appear in art representation, and are therefore somewhat outside the limits of our work.

CHAPTER XI.

The fish—Jonah as a type of the Resurrection—Escallop Shell—Pilgrimages—The Crocodile—Water—Exorcism—Salt—The Rock—The Ship—The Ark of Noah—Anchor—The Sun—The Moon—The abodes of the Archangels—Crescent of Byzantium—The Stars—The Star as symbol of Christ—Star of the East—Representations of the Seasons and Months—Signs of the Zodiac—Geometrical Forms—The Equilateral Triangle—Octagon—The Pantalpha—Interlacing Circles—Fylfot—Stauracin—Patterns based on the Gamma—The Y of Pythagoras—Triquetra—Conclusion.

THE multitudinous forms of the earth have supplied us with numerous illustrations of their symbolic use. We turn now to the great water depths, and find in sea and river further examples of emblematic forms, and to the firmament of heaven in search of the lessons taught by the revolving seasons and the starry host.

Men have naturally, in the earlier days, given the greater attention to the more distinctive and prominent forms. Thus while the lamb, the lion, wolf, horse, fox, eagle, and many other animal forms are introduced, the list of symbolic plants is a much shorter one. This is still more marked when we pass to marine creatures, where one or two conventional types do duty for all the finny denizens of the deep, while the eschallop shell sums up its conchology.

It is as an emblem of our Lord that the fish is most abundantly met with in Christian art. St. Augustine and Tertullian both refer to the fish as an emblem of Christ, and Clement of Alexandria enumerates the fish, the anchor, the ship, dove, lyre, and fisherman, as fitting objects to be employed by the Christians on their seals and lamps. When it was discovered that the letters in the Greek word for a fish are the initials of " Jesus Christ, the Son of God, the Saviour," the symbol at once sprang into use. Though the fish symbol arose from the Greek word, the Greek Church never adopted it. It is found in the Latin communion alone. In fig. 100 the Church, in the form of a ship, is borne by Christ amidst the storm and stress of life. It is somewhat curious that such a symbol should have held its ground so long, since it sprang merely from a verbal, or rather a literal coincidence, and that too of a somewhat forced nature. It had nothing of the poetical feeling of that beautiful symbol, the Lamb, nor did it express, like the lion, anything of the

FIG. 100.

royal majesty of the great King of kings. The form was based on no allusion in any text, and the difference and distance between the cold-blooded and apathetic creature of the waters and the Creator, the Lord of all, who suffered so freely for the sheep of His pasture, is something infinitely great, and would, we should have thought, have led men earlier to feel how unworthy the symbol was of One so infinitely tender, One so immeasurably exalted.

The fish was sometimes applied secondarily as a symbol of believers, and we find the early Fathers of the Church writing of their flocks as *pisciculi*, since they cast off the former life and became new creatures as they emerged from the waters of baptism.[1] Tertullian says, "We are born in water like the fish"; and Clement speaks of Christ as "drawing fish out of the waters of sin." It is one of the earliest symbols employed, being freely found on the sepulchral slabs in the catacombs of Rome, often alone, but sometimes with the wreath or crown, the emblem of triumph won through Christ, as in fig. 101; sometimes with the anchor, as in fig. 102, the emblem of a sure and certain hope of the resurrection. The name piscina, given to the baptismal font, is derived from the Latin word for a fish.

Jonah, as a type of the resurrection, is freely introduced in early art, and the big fish, his attribute, is always associated with him in these representations. Fig. 103, a gem

PR] MM M FECIT PR]ME
VENEMERENTI QVAE VIXIT
ANNIS LI MES IDVS V DIEBVS

FIG. 101.

of the fourth century, is a very quaint illustration of this. As is common in much archaic art, several independent incidents are grouped together into one composition, in defiance of the possibilities. Thus in the present example we get the prophet three times over : we see him sitting beneath his sheltering gourd, tossed to the great sea-monster, and, finally, preaching repentance to the men of Nineveh.

The fish is introduced in the legends of many saints, and may be seen duly figured in art. To St. Congall a fish is brought by an angel, and to St. Walter by a bird. Associated with St. Mauritius we have a fish with a key in its mouth. St. Zeno has one hanging from his crozier. The

---

[1] Another very favourite reference to baptism in the catacombs is the representation of the passage of the Israelites through the Red Sea, as the first step toward entrance to the promised land.

corpse of St. Chrysogomus is borne up in the water by their aid, and St. Anthony of Padua is represented as preaching to a congregation of fish.

TI·CL·MARCIANVS·ET·
CORNELIA·HILARITAS·
CORNELIAE·PAVLAE·PAR·
FECR·QVAE·VIX·ANN·X·DIEB·
VIIL·DEC·X·KAL·AVG·MAX·ET·
VRB·COS·

FIG. 102.

The dolphin is often introduced in art as a symbol of maritime power, but it finds no place in Christian symbolism.

The escallop shell (fig. 104) is more particularly associated in religious art with St. James the Greater. In represen-

FIG. 103.

tations of the saint the shell is either held in the hand or fastened on the hat, cloak, or wallet. St. Felix, a less widely known preacher of the faith, though, like St. James, one of the noble army of martyrs for that faith, is represented as laid upon a bed of shells.

Every pilgrimage had its special symbol, which sign the pilgrim on his return wore conspicuously, that all might know that he had accomplished that particular pilgrimage. That for the Holy Land was the cross; and it had this distinction above all others, that it was worn as a special sign directly the vow to visit the sacred land was made. Some even branded it with a hot iron upon their breasts in their enthusiasm, until a rubric was inserted in the "Officium Peregrinorum" forbidding the practice. When the pilgrim had fulfilled his vow and had visited the Holy Land, he was entitled to wear the palm, and was hence termed a palmer.[1]

FIG. 104.

The pilgrimage to Rome, the centre of the religion and civilization of the West, was held in next highest esteem. Many shrines were there visited, each indicated by a special sign; the chief of these were the figures of St. Peter and St. Paul, the cross-keys, and the vernicle or kerchief of St. Veronica. Hence we find that the pardoner in Chaucer, "a vernicle hadde he served in his cappe," for "he strait was comen from the court of Rome." The great Canterbury pilgrimage had as its sign the ampulla, or flask suspended round the neck, while that for Compostella was the escallop shell.[2]

---

[1] " A prest that a palmer was,
    A palme in his hand he had."—TUNDAL.

[2] The old Spanish writers affirm that while the body of St. James was being miraculously conveyed in a boat, without either oars or sails, from Joppa to Galicia, it passed a little village on the coast on the day that a marriage had taken place there. The bridegroom and his friends were riding on the sands, when the horse of the former became unmanageable and plunged with its rider into the sea. The miraculous

In the description of a pilgrim in "Piers Ploughman's Vision," we read that he had

> " An hundred of ampulles : on his hat seten
> Signes of Synay and shells of Galice,
> And many a crouche on his cloke, and keys of Rome,
> And the vernicle before, for men sholde knowe
> And se bi his signes whom he sought hadde.
> Then folk prayed hym first fro whence he came ?
> From Synay he seide, and from our Lordes Sepulcre :
> In Bethlem and in Babiloyne I have ben in bothe :
> In Armonye and Alesaundre, in many other places
> Ye may see by my signes, that sitten in my hat,
> That I have walked ful wide in weet and in drye,
> And sought good seintes for my soules helthe."

Another interesting reference to this custom of going on pilgrimage may be found in the " Canterbury Tales " of Chaucer :

> " And thries hadde sche ben to Jerusalem ;
> Sche hadde passed many a straunge streem ;
> At Rome sche hadde ben, and at Boloyne,
> In Galice at Seynt Jame, and at Coloyne."

The pilgrimage to the Holy Land naturally took the highest rank. Why Rome too was visited calls for no explanation. "At Boloyne " a notable image of the Virgin was preserved, while at Cologne were to be seen the bones, real or reputed, of Gaspar, Melchior, and Balthazar, the Wise Men of the East.

The city of Compostella became in the eighth century one of the great centres of attractive force to the pilgrims, from a legend that the body of St. James had been discovered there ; and in the ninth century the Galilæan fisherman was transformed into the patron saint of Spain, and led her chivalry, we are told, against the Moorish infidels. At the

---

ship stopped in its course, and horse and man rose from the sea beside it. The disciples on board, who were in charge of the remains, apprised him that he owed his rescue from death to the good offices of the saint; and on explaining the Christian religion to him he was baptized there and then. The ship then resumed her voyage, and the knight galloped back over the waves to his astonished party. On narrating to them all that had happened, they too were converted to the faith. When the knight rose from the sea his dress and the trappings of his horse were covered with the shells of the escallop, hence the shell was ever after-ward recognised as the cognisance of St. James.

battle of Clavigo, A.D. 844, in which sixty thousand Moors were slain, St. James was said to have appeared on a white horse, the housings charged with escallops, and led the Christian host to victory. Thenceforth enthusiasm for so potent a champion of the faith rapidly grew, and, as in the case of St. Thomas of Canterbury, national feeling and religious fervour combined to pay due honour to his shrine.

> " The poor with scrip, the rich with purse,
> They took their chance for better for worse,
> From many a foreign land;
> With a scallop-shell in the hat for badge,
> And a pilgrim staff in hand."

While the foregoing extract from Southey introduces the literal facts of the pilgrim's journey to the shrine of the saint, the following passage from Raleigh deals rather with the broader view of pilgrimage; though we still find the escallop selected as a notable symbol of the pilgrim's equipment.

> " Give me my scallop-shell of quiet,
> My staff of faith to walk upon,
> My scrip of joy, immortal diet,
> My bottle of salvation,
> My gown of glory, hope's time gage,
> And thus I'll make my pilgrimage."

The crocodile has been accepted as a symbol of dissimulation, from an old belief that this reptile sheds tears to attract the sympathy of the passers by, in order that it may bring them within reach of its formidable jaws and devour them. Though the crocodile has occasionally been introduced in art in this sense, the symbol has, on the whole, had a literary rather than artistic application. Thus in Shakespeare, 2 King Henry VI. iii. 1, we find the lines:

> " As the mournful crocodile
> With sorrow snares relenting passengers."

While Quarles writes:

> " Oh what a crocodilian world is this,
> Composed of treacheries and ensnaring wiles!
> She clothes destruction in a formal kiss,
> And lodges death in her deceitful smiles:
> She hugs the soul she hates; and there does prove
> The veriest tyrant, where she vows to love;
> And is a serpent most, when most she seems a dove."

P

Lelia, in "The Captain" of Beaumont and Fletcher, exclaims:

> "No, I would sooner trust a crocodile
> When he sheds tears, for he kills suddenly,
> And ends our cares at once."

Water, though sometimes associated in a bad sense with the idea of an overwhelming flood of evil and of swift destruction, is ordinarily a symbol of cleansing and regeneration or of refreshment. "I will take you from among the heathen, and gather you out of all countries, and will bring you into your own land. Then will I sprinkle clean water upon you, and ye shall be clean." "As cold waters to a thirsty soul, so is good news from a far country." Biblical examples could however be given in scores, and any one with but little search will readily see excellent illustrations of the symbolic use in both the good and evil sense.

In the Middle Ages, at the consecration of a church, evil spirits were exorcised by the use of water, wine, salt, and ashes. "These," to quote Durandus, "be four things which expel the Enemy. The first is the outpouring of tears, which is denoted by the water; the second is the exaltation of the soul, which is denoted by the wine; the third is natural discretion, which is the salt; the fourth a profound humility, which is signified by the ashes. Therefore not one of these ingredients ought to be wanting, because the Church is neither sanctified nor released from sins without the union of these qualities.

Salt, in the Divine language, is often a symbol of wisdom: "Let your speech be savoured with salt." Christ too said to His disciples, "Have salt in yourselves, and have peace one with another." And again, "Ye are the salt of the earth: but if the salt have lost its savour, wherewith shall it be salted?" In the second part of "King Henry IV.," Shakespeare writes: "Some smack of age in you, some relish of the saltness of time."

One of the most constantly recurring symbols in the catacombs, mosaics, etc., of the primitive Church, was a representation of a rock from which four rivers proceed. Some little doubt arises as to its significance. Ambrose, Bede, and other authorities tell us that these streams represent the writings of the four evangelists, flowing forth to fertilize and enrich the world; others see in them the four rivers of Eden, while others again think them the four great councils of the early Church.

The rock is primarily a symbol of Christ. "They drank of that spiritual Rock that followed them, and that Rock was Christ." It is often used in the Old Testament as a symbol of stability and of the Divine protection, the place of refuge in the day of trouble. "Unto Thee will I cry, O Lord, my rock." "Thou art my rock and my fortress." "In God is my salvation and my glory: the rock of my strength, and my refuge is in God." Our readers will readily recall the parable of the house that was established immovably upon the rock, and there is perhaps no more popular composition in the whole Christian hymnody than that of Toplady which commences, "Rock of ages, cleft for me." The rock is, secondarily, a symbol of the Church, an idea naturally flowing from the words of the Saviour : "Thou art Peter, and upon this rock I will build My Church." It is, finally, a general emblem of steadfastness. Thus in the frontispiece of the "Eikon Basilike," we see amongst other forms of symbolic meaning a raging sea having a rock rising from the midst, with the words added, "immota triumphans." The sky is black with rolling clouds, and on either side of the rock we see dark faces amidst the storm blowing vehemently against it. Beneath are the lines—

> " As the unmoved Rock outbraves
> The boistrous Winds and raging Waves :
> So triumph I and shine more bright
> In sad Affliction's Darksom night."

The ship riding in safety amidst the storms was a very frequent and favourite image of the Church in the earlier days of Christianity. The mast is generally in the form of a cross, and is surmounted by the dove or the monogram. St. Clement of Alexandria and other early writers dwell frequently upon this symbol, and Tertullian says that the church, using the word in its more restricted sense as a place of assembly for worship, must be oblong in form, and expressly declares that it thus better symbolises a ship. The Church of Christ, as a ship, is often found on early gems (as in fig. 100), lamps, and other objects, and is freely depicted (as in fig. 105), on the walls of the catacombs. Instead of a masted vessel, it is often (see fig. 106) the ark of Noah,[1] a form of perhaps additional significance, as it would appear to promise future protection and deliverance to the

REFRICERIVS   QVI VIXIT
ANNOS PL. M. VI. MENS VIIII
V. ·QVESCET. IN PACE

FIG. 105.

Church by a reminder of the past mercy of God to His faithful followers in the midst of a world of abounding

FIG. 106.

wickedness.   In many cases the ship is merely introduced in a lower symbolic sense, as an emblem of maritime power,

<hr />

[1] " Quemadmodum enim post aquas diluvii quibus iniquitas antiqua purgata est, post baptismum (ut ita dixerim) mundi pacem cælestis iræ præco columba terras annunciavit dimissa ex arca et cum olea reversa . . . eadem dispositione spiritalis effectus terræ, id est carni nostræ emergenti de lavacro post vetera delicta columba Sancti Spiritus advolat pacem Dei afferens emissa de cælis ubi ecclesia est arca figurata." —TERTULLIAN.

as in fig. 107, where we see the prow of an antique galley and the trident of Neptune.   St. Jude is represented with a ship, or sails, or an oar in his hand.   St. Raymond in a boat hoists his cloak for a sail.

Fig. 107.

The anchor, often, as in fig. 108, terminating in a cross, is primarily the symbol of steadfastness and hope : "a strong consolation, which hope we have as an anchor of the soul, both sure and steadfast."

Fig. 108.

It is, secondarily, associated with St. Clement as the instrument of his martyrdom, he being bound to an anchor and

Fig. 109.

cast in the sea.   The antique form of anchor may be very well seen in fig. 109.

In the legends of the saints we find St. Bertulph changing

water into wine; St. Gummarus drawing it from a rock;
SS. Rufina and Secundus, thrown into the sea, float miraculously on the surface; while SS. Nazarius, Celsus, Aldegondes,
and Birinus walk in safety over the waves.

The beneficent sun, the source of light and heat, has naturally been accepted as a symbol of the " Sun of righteousness," the Dayspring from on high, to give light to them
that sit in darkness.   The ancient Egyptians depicted the
providence of God as a radiant sun, with wide, outstretching
wings; while our English word Sunday remains as a reminder
of the sun-worship of our ancestors.[1]

The sun and the moon are often introduced together in
representations of the crucifixion, as symbolic of the great
powers of nature adoring the Lord of the universe; or
veiled and eclipsed in the darkness that was over all from
the sixth to the ninth hour, when the earth did quake
and the rocks were rent, and all nature shuddered at the
deed enacted.   Though the face often represented in sun
and moon is sufficiently, though involuntarily, grotesque, it
bears record to the belief, current in the Middle Ages, that
each was the home of an archangel, who was in turn the
leader of thousands of the angelic host.   Thus the sun was
the abode of Michael, and the moon of Gabriel.   Mercury,
in like manner, was the abode of Raphael, Venus of Anael,
Mars of Samael, Jupiter of Zadkiel, and Saturn of Cassiel.
Our illustration, fig. 110, is taken from the " Dialogus Creaturarum," A.D. 1480.

The crescent moon was the symbol of Byzantium.   When

---

[1] " Surely vain are all men by nature, who are ignorant of God, and
could not out of the good things that are seen know Him that is:
neither by considering the works did they acknowledge the work-master;
but deemed either fire, or wind, or the swift air, or the circle of the stars,
or the violent water, or the lights of heaven, to be the gods which
govern the world.   With whose beauty if they being delighted took
them to be gods; let them know how much better the Lord of them is:
for the first author of beauty hath created them.   But if they were
astonished at their power and virtue, let them understand by them, how
much mightier He is that made them.   For by the greatness and beauty
of the creatures proportionably the Maker of them is seen.   But yet
for this they are the less to be blamed: for they peradventure err, seeking God, and desirous to find Him.   For being conversant in His works,
they search Him diligently, and believe their sight: because the things
are beautiful that are seen."—Wisdom xiii. 1–7.

Philip, the father of Alexander, was besieging the city in the fourth century before the Christian era, the sudden appearance of the moon betrayed the details of the intended assault; and the citizens, grateful for their deliverance, erected a statue to Diana, and took the crescent moon, her symbol, as their device. When the Turks took the city in the fifteenth century, they found the device still in use, and in turn adopted it, and it remains to this day the symbol of the city and of the Turkish sway.

The starry host of heaven is often introduced as an emblem of the universe; and in times when men believed in

FIG. 110.

the stellar influences, the presence of the stars had a deeper meaning than now appears, as they would represent to them a watching, guarding, and guiding Providence. The Virgin Mary is often depicted with a number of stars around and above her, and SS. Dominic, Humbert, Athanasia, Bruno, and Swidbert have a star on head or breast. Richard I., on his great seal, placed a star over a crescent in token of his victories over the Saracens, and as a symbol of the triumph of Christianity over Muhammadanism.

The star is one of the less common symbols of Christ. It owes its origin to the text in the Apocalypse, "I am the root and offspring of David, and the bright and morning

Star"; which in turn is a fulfilment of the prophecy of Balaam, "There shall come a Star out of Jacob, and a Sceptre shall rise out of Israel."

The star is associated again with Christ at the Nativity and Epiphany (see figs. 1 and 65), the star of the East being always a feature in representations of that event.[1] A false Messiah, a century afterwards, in the reign of Hadrian, called himself Bar-Cocheba, the Son of a Star, and caused a star to be stamped upon the coinage that he issued.

During mediæval times we very frequently find representations of the seasons, or of the months, or of the signs of the zodiac. The introduction of the several employments of the months often had mystical significance, showing too that all labour is honourable, and teaching at the same time that the God of grace is God also of nature.

These representations are especially common in the early Norman doorways, though we have no examples in England that will at all compare with some of the examples met with on the continent. In the great west doorway of St. Mark's at Venice, for instance, we get the signs of the zodiac carved with great life and spirit; and then emblematic figures of the months,—an old man in fur coat and hood warming himself before a blazing fire, a man with a sheep on his shoulders, a mower amidst the long grass, a reaper in the harvest-field, and many others; and in the centre, hallowing all, a grand figure of Christ seated in a firmament of stars. At Modena, Verona, Lucca, Sens, Rheims, Amiens, Saint Denis, Chartres, other excellent illustrations may be found. We also find these figures on paving tiles, fonts, capitals, and stained glass.[2] Very good Renaissance examples may be seen in twelve large circular medallions of enamelled terra cotta, preserved in the South Kensington Museum, and attributed to Luca della Robbia. They are painted in blue, the subjects being representations of the agricultural operations symbolic of each month, and in each case the appropriate zodiacal sign is introduced.

In conclusion, we have to deal with some few geometrical

---

[1] "Frontal for the day of ye Epiphanye of whyte wyth starrys."— Inventory, Westminster Abbey, A.D. 1540.

[2] The whole subject will be found very fully and excellently worked out in a paper in vol. xliv. of *Archæologia*.

forms and arrangements that have defied classification and incorporation in any of the preceding chapters.

Conspicuous amongst these forms is the equilateral triangle, fig. 111, the simple yet most effective symbol of the Trinity in unity. It occurs very rarely in the early Church, but later it became commonly employed, and is still in use. St. Angilbert, contemporary with Charlemagne, had the abbey of St. Riquier built in the form of a triangle, and devoted three hundred monks to its service, expressly stating that this was so done in honour of the adorable Trinity. On the coins of Edward I., the monarch's head, full-faced, is placed within an equilateral triangle, in some cases the apex being upwards, above the crown, and in others below the beard. The idea of its use was no doubt symbolic, and expressive of the king enjoying the Divine protection and surrounded by Divine grace.

FIG. 111.

The octagon, as we have seen in our remarks upon numbers, was symbolic of regeneration, an old writer affirming that as the whole creation was complete in seven periods of time, the number next following may well be significative of the new creation. We give the theory for what it is worth, and the reader will doubtless concur with us in deciding that its value is not very great. However defective the theory, the use of the octagon in actual practice was very marked. We note that in the ancient examples given by the Cambridge Camden Society, in a pamphlet drawn up for church builders, the Norman fonts that are octagonal only number fifteen, while those of all other shapes amount together to forty-three. In the Early English period the octagonal examples are nineteen, while the others amount to thirty; but in the Decorated or fourteenth century period, the fonts of octagonal form that are given are twenty-four in number, and there is only one of any other form; while in the next period, the Perpendicular, the numbers are respectively fifty-seven and two.

The pentalpha, pentacle, or pentangle, is a five-pointed star. If we mark off on the circumference of a circle five equal divisions, and join each point in succession, we shall form a pentagon; but if we join instead every other point, the result will be a pentalpha. The crossing of the lines suggests five A's, hence the name. It was formerly considered the symbol of health, and within the five points we sometimes find the five letters SALVS. It is sometimes termed the pentacle of Solomon, and when it is delineated on the body of a man, it is pretended that it points out the five places wherein the Saviour was wounded, and that therefore all evil spirits flee from it. It was held to be a magic talisman against the powers of witchcraft, and in many ways a sign of great power.[1] The pentalpha may be seen in the eastern window of the south aisle at Westminster Abbey. It was at one time used by the Greek Christians in lieu of the cross at the beginnings of inscriptions, and the Jews also employed it. It is said to have had its origin in the secret rites and doctrines of the Pythagoreans. From its association with witchcraft and demonology it is also sometimes called the Fuga Dæmonorum.

The simple equilateral triangle is sometimes superseded by a symbol of like significance, composed of three equal and interlacing circles. This came into use first in the thirteenth century, and its appropriateness, no less than its greater beauty, soon gave it firm hold. The three equal circles symbolise the equality of the three Persons in the Trinity, the binding together into one figure the essential unity, while the circular form signifies a never-beginning, never-ending eternity.

The form known as the fylfot is frequently introduced on the vestments of the Greek Church, and is found also some-

[1] "It is always necessary," says an old author, "to have this Pentacle in readiness to bind with, in case the spirits should refuse to be obedient, as they can have no power over the exorcist while provided with and fortified by the Pentacle; the virtue of the holy names therein written presiding with wonderful influence over the Spirits. It should be made in the day and hour of Mercury upon parchment made of a kidskin, or on pure clean white paper, and the figures and letters wrote in pure gold, and ought to be consecrated and sprinkled with holy water."

what more sparingly in the West, both in ecclesiastical and heraldic work. It was most commonly employed amongst the Western peoples in the thirteenth and fourteenth centuries, and many examples of it may be seen on monuments, brasses, and so forth. Amongst the various mediæval textile fabrics we find one called stauracin, a material taking its name from the Greek word for a cross, and so called from its being figured over with the form of the cross, the design being sometimes of the simplest character, and in other examples of very elaborate enrichment of detail. This was also known as gammadion. In the Greek alphabet the capital letter Gamma consists of two lines at right angles to each other, like an English letter L, and many of the mystical writers of earlier days have seen in this form a symbol of Christ as the corner-stone. On this idea as a basis the mediæval designers combined these L-like forms into many more or less

Z ᙍ T I K ᙍ   Z O T I K H

Vitalis Vitalia

FIG. 112.

decorative arrangements. Four of them placed with their four angles towards each other create the form of the Greek cross; at other times they were so arranged as to form the letter H; or, placed with their angles outwards, a square is produced.

By far the most ancient and most common form, fashioned out of the repetition of the Gamma, is that known as the fylfot. This may be found even in the catacombs, as in the examples figs. 112 and 113; and from its resemblance to two rough S's or Z's crossing each other—S and Z in old work being often interchangeable—it has been conjectured that it was probably the cross represented as *signum*, the sign, *i.e.*, of faith in the Crucified.

In the use of the fylfot the early Christians merely adopted and diverted to their own purpose a symbol centuries older than the Christian era, a symbol of early Aryan origin, found abundantly in Indian and Chinese art, and spreading westward, long before the dawn of Christianity, to Greece and Asia.   The subject is beset with difficulties, and many theories have been propounded in attempted elucidation, one being that it represents a revolving wheel, and symbolises the great sun god ; while another is that it stands for the lightning wielded by the omnipotent Deity, whether this Deity be the Manu, Buddha, or Brahma of the East, or the Thor or Zeus of the West.   The fylfot is abundantly found on the terra-cotta objects dug up by Dr. Schliemann at Troy, and conjectured to date from 1000 to 1500 B.C. ; and the Greek fret or key pattern is frequently seen in combination with the fylfot, or is itself a fuller and more decorative development of the form.   The subject is one of immense interest, but its consideration lies entirely beyond the limits we have

DOMITIA. IVLIANETI FILIE IN PACE
QVE BIXIT. ANNIſ III. MEſIſ . X. ORAſ
XEX. NOTIſ DEFVNTA Eſ T IDVS
MAZAſ

Fig. 113.

imposed upon our work.   Any one caring to pursue the subject at greater length will find an excellent paper upon it in *Archæologia*, vol. xlviii., and it has also been dealt with by Dr. Schliemann, Max Müller, Fergusson, Ludwig Müller, Waring, and many other writers of authority and learning.

The letter Y is sometimes used symbolically.   It is sometimes called the Y of Pythagoras, because that philosopher called it the emblem of human life.   The foot of the letter represents infancy, but a time comes to all as their life goes on when two paths open out before them, one leading to good, the other to evil.   A very good example of this symbolic use may be seen in the frame of a mirror of Italian workmanship of the sixteenth century in the magnificent museum at South Kensington.   At the branching of the Y are placed two figures, one the recording angel, the other a human skeleton.   An acanthus scroll is interwoven through-

out, and within this are various animals, on the one side
those symbolic of the virtues, and on the other those representing the vices of human nature. Each animal is
accompanied by a golden letter, the one series spelling out
the word BONUM, the other MALUM.

The triquetra, made by the interlacing of three portions of
circles, is used in Christian art as a symbol of the Trinity
It may be frequently met with on Celtic crosses. On the
cross at Margam in Glamorganshire it is placed above the
figures of the saints that stand on either side of the shaft,
and at Llanfrynach it occurs in association with the figure
of a dove. On a cross at Calf of Man the triquetra appears
on the dress of the crucified Saviour, and on the breasts of
the evangelists in a sixth century manuscript in the library
of Trinity College, Dublin. Numerous examples may be
found figured in Stuart's " Sculptured Stones of Scotland,"
in Westwood's " Lapidarium Walliæ," and in Cumming's
" Runic Remains of the Isle of Man."

In conclusion, we venture to express the hope that these
pages, the writing of which has been so enjoyable a task to
ourselves, may not prove altogether destitute of interest and
profit to others. The study is one of the greatest value, and
the fault is that of the exponent and not of the subject if we
have failed to transfer some idea of this from our own con-
victions to the mind of the reader.

Therefore "now pray I," in the quaint and honest language
of Chaucer, " to hem that harkene thys tretyse or rede, that
yf ther be onything that liketh him, that thereof they thank
HIM of whom proceedeth al wit and goodnes, and yf ther
be onything that displease hem, I pray hem also that they
arrete it to the defaulte of myn unkonnyng and not to my
will, that would have seyde better yf I had knowing."

APPENDIX.

SOME few matters that are desirable to dwell on, and that yet form too long a break in the general flow of the subject, and are therefore somewhat out of place in the body of the text or in the limited space available for footnotes, may advantageously find a resting place in an appendix.

A.

The Magi in art and literature are ordinarily three. Gaspar an old man with a long gray beard and venerable aspect; Melchior, a man of the prime of life, and always given a short beard; and the third, Balthazar, a young, beardless man, often depicted as a negro, and having the thick lips and curly hair of that race. The scene of the Nativity is in the East always shown as a grotto or cave, while in the West it is a poor stable. The following extracts from old carols indicate this very clearly, art and popular belief reacting always upon each other.

> " In Bethlehem, in Jewry,
>   This blessed Babe was born,
> And laid within a manger,
>   Upon this blessed morn;
> The which His mother, Mary,
>   Did nothing take in scorn."

> " And when they came to Bethlehem,
>   Where our dear Saviour lay,
> They found Him in a manger,
>   Where oxen feed on hay;
> His mother Mary kneeling down,
>   Unto the Lord did pray."

> " Onward then the Angels sped, the shepherds onward went,
> God was in His manger bed, in worship low they bent.
> In the morning, see ye mind, my masters one and all,
> At the Altar Him to find who lay within the stall."

> " Then were they constrained in a stable to lie,
> Where horses and asses they used for to tie :
> Their lodgings so simple they took it no scorn,
> But against the next morning our Saviour was born."

> " Good Christian men, rejoice
> With heart and soul and voice ;
> Give ye heed to what we say :
> News! News!
> Jesus Christ is born to-day :
> Ox and ass before Him bow,
> And He is in the manger now.
> Christ is born to-day ! "

B.

St. Christopher was of heathen birth and parentage, and the old chronicles tell us that he was twelve cubits high, " a right grete " stature indeed. He was ambitious to dedicate his strength to the service of the mightiest monarch on earth, and after considerable quest he arrived at the court of a sovereign who seemed to meet the requirement, and he therefore entered his service, and was gladly accepted.

One day however a strolling minstrel arrived at the court and sang a lay in which the name of Satan was referred to, and the king, being a good Christian, crossed himself and muttered something at each repetition of the name. The puzzled and observant heathen asked the monarch for an explanation; but the prince evaded the question for some time, and finally confessed that it was to protect himself from the power of the evil spirit. Christopher exclaimed: " Then am I deceived in hope, for I had thought that I had found the greatest lord in the world; but this devil of whom you speak and whom you fear is mightier than yourself. I go then to seek him and to become his vassal."

Having left his first master, as he wandered over a great and savage wilderness he encountered one who demanded of him the cause of his travels, and, being told the object, the stranger assured him that he need seek no further, as the object of his quest stood before him; and he at once welcomed Christopher into his service. One day, as they were riding along together, Satan espied a road-side cross some little distance ahead, and at once turned out of the track into the thorny wilderness, and only returned to the high road when well past the cross. Christopher was much puzzled, and asked his lord why this curious wooden object had so affected him. The devil, like his former master, would have evaded the question, but at length admitted that Christ, an old enemy of his, had vanquished him by its means, and that whenever he saw a cross he fled. Then answered Christopher, "This Christ then is a mightier than thyself; I go to seek Him as my king."

After a lengthened search, "whan he had demanded where he shold fynd Crist, atte last he came to a grete desert to an hermyte that dwelled there, and this hermyte preched to hym of Jhesu Crist, and enformed hym in the fayth dylygently, and sayd to hym, 'Thys kyng whom thou desirest to serve requyres the seruyse that thou must faste oft.'" But Christopher replied, fasting not being at all to his taste, "Requyre of me somme other thynge, and I shall doo it, for that whiche thou askest I cannot." Whereupon the hermit replied, "Thenne must thou wake and make many prayers." Then answered Christopher, "I wot not what this is; I can doo no suche thynge." The indulgent friar, unwilling to lose the services of one so willing, yet so very unconventional, taking a glance at the brawny limbs of the giant, thought of yet another acceptable form of service, and replied, "Know you a certain river in whych manye perish?" On the disciple's affirmative reply, the hermit bad him, "by cause he was noble and hye of stature and strong in the membris," to dwell by the foaming torrent and carry all comers across. This being a kind of service very much more to Christopher's taste, he willingly accepted his instructions, and having built himself a hut on the bank, bore over all who came that way.

One night as he was sleeping he heard the cry of a little child, "Come out, good sir, and bear me over the stream"; so he at once ran out, but in the darkness saw no one, and concluded that it was a dream. A second time the same thing happened; but as he decided that the sounds were a device of his late master to annoy and frighten him, he composed himself to sleep again. Scarcely had he closed his eyes than he heard himself again called; so hurrying again to the water's edge he found a little child "whiche prayed hym goodly to bere him over the water." So Christopher lifted him on to his shoulder, and bore him into the stream. As he plunged into the foaming current the water rose ever higher and higher, and the child "heavyer and heavyer," until Christopher began to fear for his life. On at last reaching the opposite bank, he exclaimed, "Childe, thou hast put me in grete peryl; thou wayest alle most as I had had alle the world upon me, I myght bere no greater burden." The child answered, "Chrystofre, merueyle thee nothynge, for thou hast born Hym that created and made alle the world upon thy shoulders. I am Jhu Cryste, the king whom thou seruuest in thys werke,[1] and bycause that thou knowe that I saye to thee

---

[1] Hence called Christopher, the Christ-bearer, in the same way that Simeon is sometimes called Theodokos, the receiver of God (Luke ii. 28), and Ignatius, Theophoros, borne of God, from a tradition that he was one

truth, sette thy staf in the earthe by thy hous, and thou shalt
see to morne that it shalle bear flowres and fruyte, and anon he
vanysshed from his eyen." Christopher obeyed the command,
and on the morrow found that the promised miracle had been
fulfilled.

Full of joy at the Divine recognition, he hastened to the city
of Lycia to serve his new Master more fully; but on arrival
there he was met by the practical difficulty of being wholly
unable to speak the language of the people, so he fell on his
knees in the market and besought the gift of tongues, a petition
that was immediately answered. He then hurried to the place
where the martyrs for Christ were imprisoned, and brought
them much comfort. The pagan judge, greatly incensed at this,
struck him in the face, whereupon Christopher said, "If I were
not Chrysten I shold anon auenge me of myn injurye." Plung-
ing his staff anew into the earth, he prayed that the miracle
might be repeated, and on the rod bursting into blossom eight
thousand men of the city immediately became Christians.

The king of that country, greatly alarmed at this startling
event, sent a party of knights to arrest this disturber of the
ancient faith; but when they found him on his knees praying to
his God, and realized moreover what kind of reception so very
doughty a champion of the faith might have in store for them,
they thought discretion preferable to valour, and parleyed with
him as to their instructions from the king. Christopher, learning their business, "commanded them that they shold bynde
his hondes behynde his backe, and lede hym so bounden to theyr
kyng." The king when he beheld him fainted with fear, but
seems to have got over his apprehension when he saw that he
was tightly bound. Christopher replied, on being asked who he
was, that originally his name was Reprobus, but that he had been
baptized into the Christian faith, and was now named Christopher. The king told him that he was a great fool for bearing
the name of a crucified malefactor, and added: "Yf thou wilt
now doo sacrefyze to the goddes I shall geue to thee grete geftes
and grete honours, but yf not I shall destroye thee by grete paynes
and torments. But for alle thys he wold in no wyse do sacrefyse,
wherefoe he was sent into pryson."

The king commanded Christopher to be thrashed with red hot
rods and a ring of glowing iron to be placed upon his head. He
was bound too on an iron chair under which a fierce fire of pitch
and bitumen was kindled, so that his seat presently melted "like
waxe" in the intensity of the heat, the only result being that
when the chains by which he was bound melted from him the
saint "yssued out wythout ony hurte."

of the children whom Christ took in His arms and blessed (Mark x. 16).
Christopher was of course not the original and pagan name of the saint.

The monarch, full of rage and fury, then gave orders that he should be fastened to a tree and shot by the royal bodyguard of archers ; but all the arrows missed their aim, though one of them, on glancing from the tree, smote the king and blinded him. St. Christopher on seeing this exclaimed, with the Christian spirit that he had exhibited all through the proceedings, "I shal die thys mornynge, tempre a little clay withe my bloude and anoynt thy wounde, and strayhtwaye thou shalt be healed." Though the flame and the skill of his marksmen had alike failed, the king commanded that the saint should be beheaded ; and the saint, having made "hys oryson," died at the hands of the executioner. The king, impressed with the fulfilment of the first part of the saint's prophecy, was eager to put the rest to the proof ; and on following the instructions given, his sight was immediately restored. This softened his heart, so that he too became a convert to the faith, and with all the fervour of a new convert published a decree that whosoever should fail to worship the God of Saint Christopher should be put to death.

C.

No attempt at a description of the various symbols introduced in art could be at all complete without reference to that great storehouse of early examples, the catacombs of Rome, excavations which it is conjectured contain some seven million graves, and having a combined length altogether of some five hundred miles. These burial places were in use for some three centuries, the earliest dated inscription being A.D. 72, the latest A.D. 410. They were also places of refuge during the fierceness of persecution, and later on were used as places of worship when a deepening superstition led to adoration of the relics of the first martyrs of the faith. The passages are some seven or eight feet high and about three feet wide, and their sides are lined with the slabs that cover the resting places of the members of the early Church.

After their abandonment in the year 410, bodies were so often abstracted from them as relics that Pope Paul I. in 757 removed many to a church in Rome, and Pope Honorius III., about the year 1220, transferred many others. The catacombs after this date appear to have been absolutely forgotten, until a vine-dresser in 1478 accidentally dug into one of these subterranean passages.

The investigations of Padre Marchi and the two De Rossi, his pupils and companions, are full of interest, and their books on the subject may well be consulted : "I Monumenti delle arti Christiane primitive nella Metropoli del Christianesuno," the "Inscriptiones Christianæ," and the "Roma Sotteranea." The soil is a tufa that is readily worked, and yet of sufficient rocky solidity to bear excavation. It was at first thought when they were re-discovered that the catacombs had been the common burial places of both heathens and Christians, as many pagan inscriptions were discovered; but in by far the greater number of cases these slabs were found either sideways, upside down, or with their heathen inscriptions on the inner face, showing that the Christians often used old slabs without troubling to remove a former inscription. At the same time there are several examples that cannot be thus explained away. The letters D·M : or D·M·S· occur some forty times amongst the fifteen or twenty thousand inscriptions that have been recorded. On heathen monuments these letters occur abundantly, and they then signify *Dis manibus* or *Dis manibus sacrum*, and it has been very reasonably surmised that the Christians, finding useful slabs thus marked, were glad to employ them, and in doing so gave an altered significance to these letters, as for instance *Deo Maximo* or *Deo Maximo Salvatori.*

Nothing could often be ruder or less artistic than the Christian symbols on the early monuments; but they are most valuable as expressing contemporary beliefs, and what later forms gain in grace they may lose in sincerity.

The most favourite subject on these slabs after the various symbols or inscriptions is the raising of Lazarus, in itself a symbol of faith in Jesus and the resurrection of the dead. Other very common Bible subjects are the three children in the fiery furnace, Daniel in the den of lions, and the story of Jonah; but by far the commonest symbol is that of Christ as the Good Shepherd.

D.

The Christian Museum of the Lateran. One of the most interesting of the unrivalled collections of art treasures of the Eternal City. The objects are chiefly casts from the reliefs on ancient sarcophagi, paintings copied from the originals in the catacombs, and inscriptions. In the catacombs the originals have to be sought in far-reaching subterranean galleries, and examined as well as may be by the light of flickering lamps; but in this museum the choicest examples are collected together, and, thanks to the admirable descriptive catalogue, made much more instructive and intelligible. Nevertheless no collection of casts, however instructive, well arranged, or excellently lighted, can for a moment compare in interest with the study of the original slabs still in the position where these memorials of the saints of God were placed centuries ago by the loving hands of the brethren of the early Church.

INDEX.

"Order gave each thing view."—"King Henry VIII.," act i., sc. 1.

Abbreviations, use of, 47.
Action, symbolism of, 10.
Ages, seven, of man, 14.
Agnel d'or, 168.
Alexander, Dr., passages from, 40, 105.
Alhambra, inscriptions in, 9.
Allegorical personifications, 57.
Allegory, its nature, 2.
Alpha and Omega, 49.
Amaranth, 199.
Amethyst, 164, 165.
Ampulla, 207.
Anachronisms, apparent, 136.
Anchor, 3, 203, 213.
Ancient books of colour use, 19.
Ancient colour-names, 23.
Angels, 105, 132, 133, 178.
Animals at feet of effigies, 176.
Anthony cross, 76.
Anvil, 146.
Ape, 181.
Apocryphal authorities, 127.
Apostles, symbols of, 129, 130.
Archangels, 107.
Arch of Titus, 12.
Ark, 2, 124, 200, 212.
Arm of the Lord, 33.
"Armorie of Birds," 189.
Art traditions, 138.
Ascent of Elijah, 125.
Ash-colour, symbolic use, 27.
Ashes, 100, 210.
Ass, at Nativity, 127, 177, 224.
Assyrian animal forms, 133.
Attributes of Deity, 11.
Aureole, 68.

Axe, 146.

Bag of money, 145.
Banner of resurrection, 152.
Battle of Clavigo, 209.
Bayeux tapestry, 34.
Bear, 178.
Beaumont and Fletcher, extract from, 210.
Bee, 194.
Bell, Durandus thereon, 5.
"Biblia Pauperum," extract from, 125.
"Biblia Sacra," illustration from, 63.
"Bibliotheca Biblia," extract from, 188.
Bishop Clifford, pontifical of, 17, 22.
Bishop Grandisson, instructions of, 25.
Black, 28.
Blessing, symbolic, 9.
Blue, 26.
Book as symbol, 46, 144.
"Book of Beasts," 171.
Bossewell's "Armorie of Honour," 189.
Box of ointment, 145.
Brahma, priests of, 16; throne of, 14.
Breastplate of Aaron, 163.
Broken column, 99.
Budding rod of Aaron, 155.
Buddhist saints, nimbed, 52.
Burial of war hatchet, 10.
Butterfly, 104.
Byzantium, crescent moon of, 214.

Caldron, 147.
Calvin, extract from, 97.
Cambridge Camden Society, 217.
Carols, 223.
Carved crosses, symbols on, 3.
Catacombs of Rome, 22, 42, 50, 143, 167, 178, 195, 227.
Caxton, extract from, 202.
Celtic crosses, 7, 87, 221.
Chalcedon, Council of, 13.
Chalice, 39, 91.
Champions, seven, of Christendom, 13.
Charlemagne with nimbus, 54.
Charles I., coronation of, 17.
Charters prefaced with cross, 81.
Chaucer, passages from, 14, 25, 26, 208, 221.
Cherubs as aureole, 72.
Chinese mourning observances, 18.
Chinese symbolic colours, 23.
Chrisma, 48, 50.
Christian and Jewish Churches, 123.
Christian Museum of Lateran, 228.
Christmas Eve, custom on, 29.
"Christus Consummator," 6.
Chrysostom, extract from, 5.
Churches of Asia, 12.
Church inventories, 18.
Church symbolized, 121.
Claude Villette, extract from, 27.
Clavigo, battle of, 209.
"Clavis Calendaria," 201.
Clement of Alexandria, 3, 205.
Cloak, 143.
Cock, 191.
Colour, in good sense or bad, 20.
Colour, symbolism of, 16.
"Complaint of a Dying Lover," extract from, 26.
Consecration crosses, 82.
Constantinople, Council of, 13.
Corn, 9.
Corner stone, 219.
Coronation swords, 152.
Councils of early Church, 13.
"Court of Love," extract from, 26.
Cowley, extract from, 99.
Cowper, extract from, 94.
Creation of Eve, 38.

Crocodile, 209.
Cross, 44, 73, 167, 211, 218.
Crown, 36, 123, 149, 167; of thorns, 88, 91.
Crozier, 156, 205.
Cruciferous nimbus, 63.
Crucifix, 44, 86.
Cyprian, passage from, 16.

Dance of Death, 96.
Dante, extracts from, 25, 110, 188.
Deacons of early Church, 12.
Deaf adder, 117.
Death, representations of, 95.
Dedication of church to cross, 80.
Dedicatory cross, 81.
Deeds prefaced with cross, 81.
Definition of symbol, 1.
Deity, attributes of, 11.
Destruction of old work, 88, 93; of MSS., 135.
Deviation of chancel, 78.
Devil, representation of, 107.
"Dialogus Creaturarum," illustration from, 215.
Diamond, 164.
Diptych, ivory, inscription on, 81.
"Display of Heraldry," 7.
"Dissertatio de Colore Sacro," 19.
Divergence of colour use, 19.
Divine oval, 70.
"Divinity of our Lord," extract from, 40, 105.
Doctors of the Church, 31.
Dog, 179.
Dolphin, 206.
Dove, 3, 31, 32, 36, 44, 50, 60, 121, 184, 195, 203, 211.
Dragon, 111, 156.
Dream of Pharaoh, 12.
Durandus, writings of, 5, 25, 60, 82, 210.
Durham rites, extract from, 189.
Dust and ashes, 100.

Eagle, 132, 190.
Earl of Surrey, extracts from, 26.
Egyptian examples, 36, 102, 103, 133.
Eight, 14.
"Eikon Basilike," 93, 196, 211.

Elephant, 178.
"Enchologion" of Goar, 19.
Enrichment of nimbus, 62.
Ephesus, Council of, 13.
Episcopal rings, 163.
Equilateral triangle, 60, 217.
Ermine, 194.
Escallop shell, 206.
"Essay on Criticism," extract from, 20.
Eternity, symbol of, 49.
Evangelists, 11, 132.
Exeter Cathedral inventory, 28.
Exorcism, 210.
Eye of the Lord, 33.

Feast of tabernacles, 6.
Feast of the lance and nails, 90.
Ferne, extract from, 28.
Field of Cloth of Gold, 21.
Fish, 39, 203.
Flabellum, 159.
Flying serpent, 115.
Forced symbolism, 4.
Forces against Christianity, 147.
Forty, symbolic value, 15.
Four, symbolic number, 11.
Fox, 181, 183.
Frankincense, 162.
Frescoes, early examples, 3.
Fresco of Last Supper, 2.
Fruiterers' Company, arms of, 114.
Fuga Dæmonorum, 218.
Funeral palls, 98.
Fylfot, 218.

Gammadion, 219.
Gay, extract from, 16.
Gems, works on, 161.
Geometrical forms, 216.
Ghiberti, gates, 38.
Globe, 156, 191.
Gnostic influence, 33, 118.
Goar, "Enchologion" of, 19.
Goat, 181.
God's acre at Basel, 98, 104.
Golden candlestick of temple, 12.
Golden robes, 21.
Gold in heraldry, 21; symbolic use, 162.
Good Shepherd, 3, 4, 43, 122, 228.

Gray, extracts from, 98, 99.
Gray, symbolic use of, 27.
Greek cross, 77.
Greek form of benediction, 34.
Green as alternative with black, 26.
Green as symbolic colour, 24.
Gregory, St., extract from, 103.
Gridiron, 140.
Ground-plan a cross, 78.
Guillim, extracts from, 7, 19, 22, 28, 113, 189.
Gurgoyles, 108.

Hand of the Lord, 33, 57.
Hawthorn of Glastonbury, 155.
Hebrew name of Jehovah, 60.
Hell, 15, 110.
Hen and chickens, 193.
Heraldry, cross in, 80.
Herbert, extract from, 98.
Herrick, extract from, 94.
Hindu Trinity, 30.
Hippeau, extract from, 172.
"History of the Liturgical Colours," 23.
Holy days of Jewish Church, 12.
"Holy War," 2.
Horse, 178.

Iconoclasts, 135, 136.
I·H·S form of monogram, 51.
Illuminant power of nimbus, 66.
Illuminated books, 3, 135.
Incarnation of Christ, 41.
Innocent III. on colour symbolism, 19.
Interlaced circles, 218.
Invention of the cross, 84.
Inventory, St. Paul's, 145, 201; Westminster Abbey, 21, 24, 52, 188, 191, 201, 216.

Jehovah, representation of, 31, 32.
Jeremy Taylor, extract from, 97.
Jewish and Christian Churches, 123.
Jonah, as a type, 205.
Joseph, type of Christ, 125.
Joys, seven, of Virgin, 13.
Jubilee, year of, 12.

Keys of St. Peter, 145, 178, 207.
Knights Hospitallers, cross of, 77.
Krausen on colour symbolism, 19.
Krishna, 118.

Labarum, 48, 51.
Labourers in vineyard, parable of, 5.
Lamb, 4, 39, 122, 167, 204.
Lamp, 143, 185.
Lance, 147.
Language, symbolism of, 9.
Last Judgment, 39.
Latin cross, 77.
Latin form of benediction, 34.
Laurel wreath, 92, 150.
" La Vraye et Parfaite Science des Armoires," 19.
" Lays of Ancient Rome," 15.
Leaven, as symbol, 4, 5.
Le Deuil blanc, 18.
Lenten use of white, 17.
" Les Couleurs Liturgiques," 17, 20, 22, 25, 27, 106.
Levitical colours, 18.
" Liber Clericorum," 26.
" Liber Sacerdotalis," 26.
Lily, 198.
Lion, 4, 132, 133, 153, 171, 204.
" Liturgical Colours," Legg's, 23.
" Livre des Créatures," 171.
Lorraine, cross of, 77.
Lost sheep, parable of, 5.
Loving cup, 10.
Luther, memorial ring, 98.
Lydgate, extracts from, 150, 167.

Magi, or Wise Men, 10, 126, 223.
Magpie, 192.
Malais, "Les Couleurs Liturgiques," 17, 20, 22, 25, 27, 106.
Mandola, 70.
Man of sorrows, 40.
Mary, Queen of Scots, portraits of, 18.
Maundeville, writings of, 83, 88.
Mecca, sacred stone of, 14.
Mediæval spelling, 24.
Memorial rings, 98.
" Merchant of Venice," 25.
Merlin and the White King, 17.

Messenger of God, 107.
Michael, St., and the dragon, 112.
Millstone, 147.
Milton, extracts from, 28, 107, 111, 199.
Ministry of angels, 105.
Mitre, 151.
Monogram, 39, 47, 48, 168, 195, 211.
Moon, 214.
Moore, extract from, 115.
Mors janua vitæ, 100.
Mosaics, 3, 7, 42, 48, 54, 59, 124, 210.
Moses, nimbus of, 56.
Mouton d'or, 170.
" Much Ado about Nothing," 20.
Museum of Lateran, 155, 228.
Myrrh, 162.
Mystical almond, 70.
" Mystical Mirrour," extract from, 191.

Name inscribed in nimbus, 62.
Nativity, scene of, 127, 223.
Nicæa, Council of, 13.
Nimbus, 52, 167.
Nine, symbolic number, 15.
Number of perfection, 11.
Number, symbolism of, 10.

Oberammergau passion play, 43.
Octagon, 217.
Old Testament references, hand of God, 33.
Olive branch, 188, 200.
One side of truth only often given, 4.
Onyx, 164, 165.
Ophite sect, 117.
Orb or globe, 156.
Orders of angels, 106.
Orpheus, 3, 42.
" Othello," 25.
Owl, 192.
Ox, 127, 132, 133, 144, 177, 223, 224.

Palm branch, 3, 159, 195.
Palmer, 207.
Papal crown, 150.

·Parabolic teaching of our Lord, 5.
Parnell, extract from, 99.
'Passion cross, 77.
Passion flower, 15, 198.
Passion symbols, 39, 88.
Passover symbolism, 6.
Pastoral staff, 155.
Patriarchs, symbols of, 129.
Pavement, symbol on, 3, 78.
Peacock, 57, 160, 191.
Pearl of great price, 5.
Pelican, 4, 39, 188.
Penitential psalms, seven, 12.
Pentangle or pentalpha, 218.
Peterborough Cathedral, inventory, 22.
Phœnix, 51, 57, 190.
Picture worship, 135.
" Piers Ploughman's Vision," 208.
Pig, 180.
" Pilgrim's Progress," 2.
Pilgrims' signs, 207.
Pincers, 142.
Pipe of peace, 10.
Plant symbols, 202.
Political colours, 26, 27.
Pontifical of Bishop Clifford, 17, 22, 25.
Pope, extracts from, 20, 198.
Posy rings, 161.
Poverty, with nimbus, 57.
Prayer for blessing ring, 161.
Precious stones, 163.
" Princely Pelican," 189.
Prodigal son, 5.
Proverbs, a picture language, 9.
Purple, 27.
Pythagoras on the number three, 10.

Quarles, extract from, 209.

Raleigh, extract from, 209.
"Rationale Divinorum Officiorum," 5.
Raven, 192.
Red, 21.
Red-hot ploughshare, 147.
Red-letter day, 23.
Reformation zeal, 52, 88, 93, 135, 156.

Regeneration, number of, 14.
Ring, 160.
Rock, 124, 147, 210, 211.
Rod or staff, 154.
Roll, 46.
Rose, 199.
Ruby, 163.
Russian sacred pictures, 6.

Sacraments of Romish Church, 12.
Sacred dramas, 44.
Sacred stone of Mecca, 14.
Sacred writing of Egypt, 6.
Samson, type of Christ, 126.
Salt, 10, 210.
Sapphire, 164.
Sarcophagi in catacombs, 3
Satan with nimbus, 54.
Scapegoat, 6.
Scarlet, 24.
Scene of Nativity, 127, 223.
Sceptre, 152.
Serpent, 111, 113, 115, 177.
Serpent worship, 118.
Sevenfold gifts of Spirit, 12, 187.
Seven, symbolic number, 11.
Shakespeare, extracts from, 15, 20, 25, 94, 111, 117, 188, 209.
Sheep, 121, 168.
Shelley, extract from, 28.
Ship, 203, 204, 211.
Sibyls, 127.
Signet ring, 160.
Sir Thomas More, extract from, 145.
Six, 11.
Skelton, " Armorie of Birds," 189.
Skull, 97.
Song of Solomon, imagery of, 6.
Sorrows, seven, of Virgin, 13.
Soul of man, 101.
Southey, extract from, 209.
Spenser, extract from, 110.
Square nimbus, 58.
Stag, 176.
Stained glass, symbolism in, 3.
Star, 215.
Stauracin, 219.
Stigmata, 91.
Stork, 194.
Sudarium, 142.

R

Sun, 44, 214.
Sun-worship, 53, 214.
Sword, 146, 149, 152.

Talmud, 12.
Tau cross, 74.
Tertullian, 3, 205, 212.
Theophilus on Trinity, 30.
Three, 10.
Tiara, 150.
Time, 94.
Titus, Arch of, 12.
Tobit, extract from, 179.
Torch of life, 104, 143.
Tree of Jesse, 201.
Tree of life, 83, 114.
Trinità, the, in Italian art, 31.
Trinity, representations of, 30.
Triple cross, 78.
Triquetra, 221.
"True blue," a party colour, 26.
Tundal, 207.
"Twelfth Night," extract from, 20.
Twelve, 14.
Type, its nature, 2.
Tyrian purple, 27.

Umbrella, 159.
Unicorn, 178.
Unjust judge, parable of, 5.
Unknown God, altar to, 42.
Urn, 99.

Value of pictorial teaching, 2.
Veiling truth by symbol, 2.
Venerable Bede, extract from, 49.
Vernicle, 207.
Vesica piscis, 70.
Vestal Virgins, 16.
Vine, 39, 194.
Violet, 27.
Virge or rod, 153.

Vision of Ezekiel, 133; of St. Augustin, 31.

Wand or staff, 154.
Water, 210, 214.
Wedding the Adriatic, 161.
Westminster Abbey, inventories of, 21, 24, 52, 188, 191, 201, 216.
Westcott, "Christus Consummator," 6.
Wheat and Tares, 202.
Wheel, 141.
White, 16, 17.
Wickham Legg on liturgical colours, 23.
Wine, 9, 210, 214.
Winged serpent, 115, 116.
Wisdom, book of, 214.
Wise Men or Magi, 10, 208.
Wise men of Greece, 14.
Wolf, 181.
Wonders, seven, of ancient world, 13.
Wood of cross, 83.
Wordsworth, extract from, 25.
Wordsworth, Bishop, quoted, 134.
Works on gems, 161.
Wreath, 50, 150.
Wyckliffe on evangelistic symbols, 134.

Xmas for Christmas, 50.

Y, letter, as symbol, 220.
Year of jubilee, 12.
Year 1000, 39.
Yellow, 20.
Yew, 201.
Young, extract from, 25.

Zeus, priests of, 16.
Zodiac, sign of, 216.

DATE DUE			
DEC 1 9 1980			
MAR 7 1983			
MR 9 '87			
MR 3 0 '87			
MAR 0 5 1990			
JUN 0 4 1990			